GHOSTKEEPERS

Scott J. Casey

*Thank you for your generous support of ...
... brothers!*

TACT16AL™

GHOSTKEEPERS

First Edition

Because of the dynamic nature of the internet, any web address or links contained in this book may have changed since publication and may no longer be valid.

The views expressed in this work are solely those of the author and do not necessarily reflect the views of the publisher, and the publisher hereby disclaims any responsibility for them.

Published by Tactical 16, LLC
Colorado Springs, CO

eISBN: 978-1-943226-15-3
ISBN: (hc) 978-1-943226-16-0
ISBN: (sc) 978-1-943226-17-7

Printed in the United States of America

*There is no safety for honest men except by
believing all possible evil of evil men
~Edmund Burke*

For Clarity

Let me be clear, the experiences the men of November Company had, were not much different from mine. Some of them experienced worse. In no way did I single handedly save the Yugoslav people from their own wretchedness. We were in this thing together, relying on one another as brothers. The words I have written on the following pages are my story. This is how I saw the events of the Balkans War and the Canadian Peacekeepers who were caught in the middle of it. I have done my best to keep the events in chronological order. The men portrayed here have paid with their sanity and in many cases their lives. Their names have been changed except for those who are famous in Canadian history and world events. I am proud to have served with them, to say many of them are close personal friends is to speak lightly.

For my friend

Ranger

GHOSTKEEPERS
A SOLDIER'S PERSONAL ACCOUNT OF THE FIRST CANADIAN PEACEKEEPERS IN THE
BALKANS WAR

INTRODUCTION
BY, LEWIS MACKENZIE, CM, OONT, MSC AND BAR, CD
MAJOR-GENERAL (RET'D)

Thanks to successive Canadian governments perpetuation of the great Canadian Peacekeeping myth, born of Lester Pearson's Nobel Peace prize in 1957, a good portion of the Canadian population genuflect in the direction of UN Headquarters in Manhattan at least once a d ay.

In fact, Lester Pearson did not "invent" peacekeeping. There were a number of ideas suggesting that a lightly armed impartial force interposed between warring armies who AGREED to stop fighting might actually keep a fragile peace until a political solution could be found. Nevertheless, Pearson richly deserved the Prize because he actually stick-handled the concept through a reluctant United Nations Security Council by way of an impassioned plea to the General Assembly and as a result defused what became known as the Suez Crisis in 1956.

Over the following thirty-three years the UN found itself launching thirteen peacekeeping missions in locations ranging from the Middle East through Africa to the Far East and Central America. Canadians participated on every one of them thereby reinforcing the myth. The numbers were relatively small rarely involving more than 2000 Canadian personnel in total. Most of the missions were successful in keeping the warring national militaries apart but diplomacy failed miserably to resolve the underlying causes of the conflicts. A good example is the UN Force in Cyprus which deployed to the Island in 1964 and is still there 48 years later and has become an essential part of the Island's economy. Arriving on a tour boat to the South coast as a tourist you can sign up for a bus tour of the green line which runs through the capital Nicosia and delineates the de facto border between resident Cypriots, Greek and Turk. You can take pictures of the British and Argentine peacekeepers manning their check points or purchase postcards showing the peacekeepers where their fathers stood duty a generation earlier. Ridiculous? You bet.

For a country to qualify as a "peacekeeping nation," a term frequently used by both the public and the media, the activity would have to rank at or close to the top of its foreign policy priorities. Peacekeeping never did as it was ranked below Sovereignty, Defence of North America (NORAD) and Multinational Alliance obligations (NATO).

Peacekeeping was always a distant fourth or lower. However, it was relatively safe. Most deaths were the result of accidents and most importantly, it was a cheap way to earn some brownie points with our allies.

In spite of the fact that the UN failed to notice at the time, all that changed in 1989/90 with the end of the Cold War and the destruction of the Berlin Wall symbolically separating East and West Germany. During the Cold War most of the fighting threatening international peace and security was between countries. These countries had delegations at UN Headquarters and their flag flew in front of the building. Peacekeeping commanders in the field could alert the UN

Security Council to a problem and the UN could deal with the country's ambassador to the UN and bring pressure to bear to help resolve a problem if necessary.

The first conflict facing the UN following the Cold War was the 1991 US led, UN sanctioned, Gulf War resulting in the defeat of the Iraqi forces that had invaded Kuwait. President George Bush Sr. declared "A New World Order" and suggested coalitions of the willing would be the solution to taking on future threats.

The New World Order had a short shelf life. The Balkans exploded in late 1991 as Slovenia and Croatia declared their independence from Yugoslavia. The participants were not all countries. There were large ethnic factions involved starting with a large Serbian population trapped within Croatia's borders and they wanted a relationship with Serbia not Croatia. Serious fighting broke out and the UN, still thinking Cold War peacekeeping techniques, decided to send

2

a 12,000 man, lightly armed, impartial force into Croatia to protect the Serbian enclaves while a diplomatic solution was sought between President Milosevic of Serbia and President Tudjman of Croatia (both former generals in the Yugoslav national army).

Canada acted more quickly than the rest of the countries responding to the UNs call for peacekeeping troops. Canadians were amazed that their soldiers were among the first to arrive in Croatia in March of 1992. In many cases even the media failed to mention that they arrived by train from southern Germany where they were stationed with NATO forces. Subsequent contingents had to cross the Atlantic, but this first deployment arrived within hours.

Enter the author, Corporal (ret'd) Scott J. Casey, who was a front line soldier on the first train to head south into the unknown. They ventured into harm's way with Blue berets and helmets, white vehicles with black UN markings, and thanks to the wisdom of his commander's, a good deal more, bigger weapons and ammunition than authorized or permitted by the UN. Every deploying soldier had followed the Balkan carnage on television and was smarter than the UN, and knew this was going to be no "peacekeeping" mission.

Weeks earlier in New York I had unsuccessfully argued that as Chief of Staff of the United Nations Protection Force I should not be ordered to put our Headquarters in Sarajevo. Bosnia was still part of Yugoslavia but rumours were rampant that the republic would seek independence from Yugoslavia within a month. The UN naively believed the presence of our Headquarters would have a calming influence on the situation. Over a hundred officers on my staff knew better that we would become the lightening rod for each and every complaint from Bosnian Serbs, Croats and Muslims upset with the International community. We arrived in Sarajevo on Friday the 13th of March 1992 and the war started three weeks later. We were ordered by UNNY to withdraw our HQ to Belgrade in mid-May. Embarrassed to be seen abandoning the city we worked out a deal with Serbia's President Milosevic and the Bosnian Serb leader Radovan Karadzic to let the UN take over the Sarajevo airport to permit the delivery of humanitarian aid.

The UN would take at least a month to find a security force from volunteer countries and by that time the window of opportunity would have been lost. Much to its credit the Canadian government agreed that the Canadian Battle group located for over two months in Sector West in Croatia could be "loaned" for one month to secure the Sarajevo airport and escort the delivery of the incoming aid. The popular myth suggests the Canadian Battle group was chosen because I, as a Canadian was given command of the airport operation. Not so. The Canadians were chosen because they had wisely ignored the UN restrictions imposed on the number of armoured vehicles and heavy weapons they were supposed to bring with them to the UNPROFOR mission. As a result, they were the most heavily armed and combat ready contingent in the 12,000-man force.

On 2 July 1992 Corporal Scott Casey and his fellow soldiers arrived in Sarajevo. The Royal 22nd Battle Group commanded by Lieutenant Colonel Michael Jones was the reverse of the Canadian National Representative Group (NRG), 2/3 Francophone (R22eR) and 1/3 Anglophone(RCR) which created a real synergy as each group worked extra hard to outperform the other.

My memory is not that bad that I cannot remember what it was like to be a Corporal many decades ago and before I was sent to officer training. I frequently asked myself, "What dumb ass thought this task up!"

Corporal Casey gives a long overdue perspective on the UNPROFOR mission from someone who implemented orders, mostly good but not all, on the ground. Many books, including a couple of mine, describe what commanders saw and did but with the exception of another RCR soldier, Sergeant Jim Davis' in his book "Sharp End," there is a dearth of books written by those who were in the weeds actually implementing orders and taking the serious risks. Those readers who have a touchy-feely image of peacekeeping and peacekeepers should probably stop reading at this point. Those who want to have a better idea of why post-Cold War "peacekeeping" should be approached with scepticism and caution – read on!

Lewis Mackenzie, CM, OOnt, MSC and Bar, CD
Major-General (Ret'd)

AFTER SHOCKS

"War is eternity jammed into frantic minutes that will fill a lifetime with dreams and nightmares."
~JOHN CORY

The old woman was running toward me, down the incline, through the tall grass that was her front yard. She was clad in a dirty light blue floral dress and she had a mouthful of rotting teeth. Her hair was askew and oily. She used her free hand to smooth one side down in an attempt to restore her dignity. Her other arm cradled a bouquet of flowers. The emotion she was feeling overcame her and she lost composure. She ran full out towards me, the bundle of flowers in her arms floundering under the strain of the laboured run. Sweat beaded and rolled down my face stinging my eyes. My combat shirt was half soaked from sweat. Fuck it was hot. I thought to myself. It was 49c today according to my Canadian Tire thermometer. She was at the 100 metre mark and closing fast. I slowly lowered my rifle into the crook of my arm and slid the fire selector to auto. As was common practice amongst the Company, I already had a round up the spout. The woman, upon seeing the look in my eyes and the fact that she was looking down the business end of my rifle, slowed down. I cautiously waved her in as I took up the slack on the trigger. The haggard woman slowly proceeded, the scent of the flowers only temporarily masking the smell of her body odour caused from months of improper hygiene. She laid the flowers on my lap and took my arm in her hands and began kissing it. The months of war streaming down her face. She had been witness to a husband and son being executed in her front yard before her, and her daughter's, eyes. At gun point she was forced to watch her daughter being taken away screaming into a backroom and raped repeatedly and then shot because she was young enough to bare offspring. Sobbing she exclaimed,

"Dobra, Dobra."

"Please, Please."

I was fighting to maintain my cool. She was so close to eating a burst from my C- 7. The thought went through my head to give this wretched soul the comfort she was seeking, however, I could not seem to reach out to her. I could end her suffering either through a hug or by squeezing the trigger. I looked into her eyes and I allowed her pain to transfer to me. It was as though she could see into my soul and may have gained some consolation from that. My heart was pounding and I could not stop sweating.

"What the fuck is wrong with these people?" I ask rhetorically. My Platoon Commander, Lt. William (Bill) Burke, who is sitting in the passenger seat of our Iltis, shrugs and my question hangs in the air-met by silence. The woman stands back. As we are about to leave, I smile and empty the entire magazine of shells into her. Her body slumps to the ground leaking its life blood onto the dirt at the side of the road. As we pull away I looked in the mirror and watched a bloody tear roll down my cheek.

"NOOOOO,"

I woke screaming. I sat up immediately drenched in sweat my hand on my cheek. I fought for my bearings. I was in the sleeper of my Freightliner tractor-trailer. It was dark and I quickly opened the curtain to confirm I was really there. The lights of the rest area parking lot were casting an eerie glow through the fog. The vision of that day played over and over in my mind. The dream always concluded that way. I sat there lost. Not knowing what I was feeling. Perspiration was still rolling down my spine as I sat trying to shake the dream imagery off.

"What the Hell. What the Hell is wrong?"

FLEDGLING STARTS

"The most loving parents and relatives commit murder with smiles on their faces. They force us to destroy the person we really are: a subtle kind of murder."
~JIM MORRISON

I grew up on the outskirts of the rural town of 100 Mile House in central British Columbia, Canada. 100 Mile House was a stop along the Cariboo Wagon Trail from the booming North American gold rush era. The buckboards and wagons would stop and exchange horses or take on supplies for the remainder of the journey to find the riches in the northern gold fields. Like in the 1800s, the decades of the 1900s were not much different for 100 Mile House. It has always been a sleepy little cowboy town with few venues to entertain kids. Living twenty-six miles away from the town centre ensured even less youth oriented activities. The distance made it virtually impossible to go to town daily so we went once a week. This trip to town was to buy groceries and feed for the animals. The farmhouse was a bit of a shocker when we first moved from the city of Surrey BC in the early '70s. There were no windows or doors as they had all been broken out or torn off by vandals. The range cattle had been using it as a barn. With shovels in hand we immediately went to work dunging it out. Poly was stapled over the windows and plywood with leather strap hinges were used for the doors. I recall our second night in the farmhouse as my dad ran down the hall in his shorts screaming like a wild man. He was in fact chasing a black bear that came roaming in looking for the source of the new scents. The farm was small in comparison to many others, only fifty acres in size with another one hundred subleased from the Crown. I worked the farm doing what kids did back in the day, ploughing the garden, baling and throwing hay bales. Tending to cattle, horses, and pigs were just a few of my daily chores. There was a cow or two to milk and eggs to retrieve from the chicken coop. My father was a tough son of a gun and he made sure that if I did not do my chores my ass took a whooping for it. He was known to stretch his anger out and give me a few kicks to make sure I was learning the lessons. It was as though on many occasions I could do no right. My inability to perform to his high standards was what earned me a lifetime of striving to be better. Perhaps his methods were questionable but they made me try my damndest. When I was not tending to the farm I was off playing with one or two of the neighbour kids who would ride their bicycles the four or five miles to meet up. Those were the days when moms stayed at home and dads worked hard. You kept your mouth shut or it would get shut for you. My parents were no exception to the rule. My schooling was done at a one room modular style schoolhouse. It was a one point eight mile walk from the house to the flagpole that stood by the schoolhouse. All seven grades were represented in one classroom and all taught by one teacher. When I turned eleven I became interested in the Army Cadet program in town. My uncle was a cadet and I thought it would be fun to join. I pleaded with my parents to let me enroll. After many days of badgering them both they relinquished and I was permitted to join, sneaking in the back door at eleven as enrolment age was thirteen. With my uncle already immersed in the program I warded off any attempt by my parents to say there was no transportation. I was awarded Best First Year Cadet for my efforts. Soon after, I received my promotion to Corporal. One evening at the cadet hall, which was located in the basement of the junior high school, I stopped to look at a recruiting poster for the Canadian Armed Forces. It showed an infantry soldier standing alone, with a group of support-personnel behind him in the distance. The caption read, "You stand alone, but you're never alone." I instantly conjured up dreams of being that infantry soldier. I could see myself standing on the battlefield with the support of a thousand men conquering a terrible foe. From there my future was set. I was going to join the Canadian Armed Forces (CAF) when I was of age. For now, though I would have to learn as much as possible about the cadets.

It was not long before my desire to shine took control of my future in the Rocky Mountain Rangers Army Cadets Corp. Each year I received a new promotion until I had eventually become the Regimental Sergeant-Major. With that position I was running the show. I could show my dad that I was succeeding. Unfortunately, my promotion did not have any effect on him. He was too caught up in his own life of hard work. His life was spiraling out of control and he had no time for me. His over indulgence in alcohol had forced his wife of eighteen years to move on to other pastures. I am not trying to paint my father as a bad person. He was rather a man of the times. Brought up in hard times of his own he did what he could with the tools he had been given. To this day he still has a heart of gold. My mother was the typical woman as well. Cooking, cleaning, and running the household wearing the matriarchal apron, she was living in a world of denial. It was the '70s. The '80s would prove to be difficult on the home front and I ran away a couple times. I was not finding the family unit to be strong enough to match my desire to belong. This desire would fuel my quest for approval, a sense of belonging, and lead me to join the CAF even before graduating from high school.

Through the summer of 1985 I enlisted in an infantry reserve unit, the Rocky Mountain Rangers located in Kamloops, BC. As much as I enjoyed working with them it was not fulfilling my desire to belong. In October of that same year, after aptitude and physical fitness tests, I enrolled in Canada's regular standing army. I officially entered the CAF in January of 1986. Before departing I spent two months in Vancouver at my dad's house trying to get myself into better physical condition. Every morning I would exit their home and run down the sidewalk, simultaneously another runner would come out of his home and run down the opposite side of the street. Without speaking a single word, we spurred each other along, unknowingly at first, to work harder and run faster. As the weeks went by we were practically sprinting down opposite sidewalks as if we were trying to win some sort of race. As my departure was only a day away I turned and crossed the asphalt that had divided our parallel paths for the last 60 days. My running partner and I shared the same concrete sidewalk for the last kilometre to his driveway.

"Hey, I just wanted to say thanks." I said extending my right arm.

"My name is Scott Casey, I'm shipping out for basic training tomorrow and this has been great," His sturdy black hand grasped mine firmly and we shook hands.

"My names Freddie, Freddie Sims." His smiled beamed back at me in the early morning light.

"Freddie Sims? As in the BC Lions, Freddie Sims?" I asked with astonishment.

"Yup that'd be me. Thanks to you too, training camp is coming and I want to be stylin for it," he said patting his belly with a chuckle.

"Well it's been fun, take care and good luck. I'm a big fan of the team."

"Good luck in boot camp, soldier," he encouraged as we both turned and went our separate ways. I jogged back to my dad's with a smile.

The following day I boarded the bus which would take me to the Vancouver International Airport and the beginning of my military career. Along with a few other BC natives, I flew from Vancouver to Halifax, Nova Scotia. Our flight was a milk run style, picking up new recruits along the way in each province. We landed in Regina and picked up one of my soon-to-be best buddies, Ranger. We continued making ascents and descents until we landed in Halifax. After our arrival in Halifax we climbed aboard dark green Blue Bird school buses and drove to the Canadian Forces Recruit School in Cornwallis, NS. Once there, the world as many of my new colleagues knew it, was about to change.

As we stepped off the bus we were met, at an alarming rate, by screaming Drill Instructors. Their verbal and physical tirade was so overwhelming that it virtually ripped us out of the buses. We were divided up alphabetically and ordered into our respective quarters for the continued well organized abusive tongue lashing. Standing in line the Staff of CFRS Cornwallis went up one side of us and down the other with a vocal onslaught that would have made many pee their pants. I was already somewhat versed in this performance from my cadet experiences. So I listened to the important parts and trash canned the abuse. It was not long after our induction that we made our first visit to the barber shop. It was entertaining to watch the transformations of some of the guys who had had hair long enough to make Farrah Fawcett envious. Some of the guys were unrecognizable to me after the barbers shaved off their locks. With the scalping we all looked the same, which I believe was the desired effect. Weeks of basic army skills went by with a few of us joking about how we ever dared to imagine that we knew how to walk before this. Weeks turned to months and Basic Training was coming to a close. After my training I was awarded the Commandant's Shield for best recruit. Aside from my buddies' back patting I enjoyed my accolades alone as my parents did not show up for my graduation from boot camp. With grad completed we were now considered men. With our government issued manhood we went to celebrate at the base pub, The Green and Gold, with a few beers. The celebration did not last long as the following day we were shipping out for infantry training in Petawawa, Ontario. After two months with no alcohol consumption we were polluted after only a half dozen. The following morning, we were escorted to our buses, with the respect afforded to graduates. There was no ranting and raving. Only calm congratulations and an eye-to-eye with the men who had destroyed us. The DIs shook our hands and wished us the best in our careers as professional soldiers. We mounted up and were off for the next leg of our journey. Many hours and stiff muscles later we arrived at our destination.

The bus lurched to a halt at CFB Petawawa in front of the Royal Canadian Regiment (RCR) Battle School building. Apprehensively we all looked out the bus windows knowing that our new found home also contained our new found Hell. The air assisted door swung open with a swooshing of air that sucked the stale air from the coach. For the first time since loading the bus the stocky lone Sergeant who had made the journey with us stood up and spoke.

"Welcome to CFB Petawawa, ladies. Now get off my fucking bus!" With that we made haste to exit. We were met on the ground by Battle School Staff. I did not think it was possible, but these instructors had found a new level of verbal and physical abuse that made that delivered by the boot camp staff of CFRS Cornwallis pale in comparison. For the next four months our platoon, Korea Platoon, named after a hard fought Regimental Battle Honour in Korea, was put through infantry combat training. We already knew the basics of tying our boots and walking. Now it was the duty of the RCR Battle School to teach us how to kill with all the weapons in the Canadian infantry arsenal without killing ourselves. The four-month course was some of the toughest training I had ever endured. It was designed not only to teach infantry skills but also to weed out the weak. The end result confirmed this. Our course started with seventy-eight recruits and ended with only forty-one. During this time, we were instructed in the use of the Belgian made C1A1 FN assault rifle. It would be our primary rifle for some years. The C1 was to be treated with the utmost respect and it was to become an extension of our arms. If you lost control of your rifle you better damn well hit the ground before it did to save it from injury or the Staff would be all over you for a month of Sundays.

We learned all about how an infantry unit conducts its business of warfare. Learning everything from using full out advance to contact, where the unit seeks out the bad guys in a direct attack, to how it lived in a defensive position and how to respond when attacked. We learned how to conduct reconnaissance (recce) patrols and ambush patrols too. Each of the training phases was a week or more in length and required us to perform with minimal sleep and rations. All of this helped to prove how we would react under actual combat conditions. When we were not doing combat drills in formation, we were learning about the various weapons at an infantry sections disposal. We had instruction on how to lay anti-personnel and anti-tank mines and also how to prod for and disarm them. We were shown how to use the C2 light machine gun the brawnier brother of the C1. We learned how to use heavy machine guns, to fire the 60mm mortar, and how to throw grenades. We had to stand in a bullet proof shack and observe our buddies throwing grenades from a trench position outside the shack. None of us had ever witnessed an actual grenade going off. The detonations were astonishingly anticlimactic. Grenades for the record do not blow up entire buildings in a fury of fire. There is a small concussion wave and a cloud of dust and smoke the size of a Mini-Austin. Even without the building shattering fireball, grenades still have a considerable kill zone of 5 metres and a casualty zone of 15 metres.

During our four months of training we were also subjected to the gas hut. Because our Cold War enemy at the time was the Soviets, who housed tons of weapons of mass destruction, gas training is done to teach soldiers to deal with a Nuclear Biological Chemical Warfare battlefield. This training was conducted using CS gas or what is commonly known as Tear Gas. On the day of gas training we shuffled into the gas hut with our gas masks on. They worked well and sealed out the CS fumes. However, part of gas training involves able to remove your mask and take a drink of water or eat. Well let me tell you there was not a dry eye in the room and some of the guys were doubled over vomiting. I managed not to puke but my eyes were burning and my nasal passages flowed like I had had the flu for a month. With a degree of dark enjoyment, we watched subsequent junior infantrymen doing gas training come out with faces drizzling with snot and mucus.

After four months of instruction and abuse we graduated as qualified tradesmen, 031 Infantry. I was very disheartened when at the end I was called into the Course Commander's office. He took the time to inform me that I was the top soldier in the platoon. Inwardly my chest puffed up with pride, only to have it quickly deflated when he told me that I was too much of a leader and would be winning the second place position because of it. Another candidate was given the first place award because he was a good follower. I silently stewed about the injustice. I thought to myself, that training was completed and that I had excelled was going to have to be good enough. We would soon be leaving the RCR Battle School for our posting to Battalions within the Regiment.

I would be going to 1 RCR at CFB London, Ontario. London, Ontario was a beautiful city in the lower southern tip of Ontario. It housed the University of Western Ontario and many nursing colleges. Prime ground for young soldiers who had been locked up for six months and were now full of piss and vinegar. I made a few new friends in my new home and we frequented the local watering holes, sowing our wild oats with abandon as the beer and girls seemed endless. Fighting was the norm amongst us young warriors vying for female attention. The local pubs felt our wrath every weekend as did the young men from the University of Western Ontario. Our Sergeant-Major at the time gave us a speech that only reinforced our immature animalistic behaviour.

"If you get into a fight and win, nothing will be said. If you get in a fight and lose, you will be doing shit duties until I retire."

So we did whatever it took to stay off his list. I was positioned in Alpha Company (A Coy). A. Coy was a rifle company which carried the nickname, The Duke of Edinburgh's Company. The Duke's, as we were called, are the protectors of His Royal Highness Prince Phillip whenever he comes to Canada. Having attained the Gold award in the Duke of Edinburgh's Awards Program in cadet's years earlier it took on an added meaning for me. During my time in London, The Duke's Company went on exercise quite a bit, doing field level tactics continuously. Because 1RCR was also a member of the Ace Mobile Force I spent a month in Denmark training with the Danish forces. During that month I fell in love with the idea of living in Europe. So in the fall of 87' I volunteered for a posting to Winnipeg, Manitoba and the 3rd Battalion (Bn) RCR. Had I really understood how cold a Winnipeg winter could be I may never have volunteered. However, I spent the winter in Winnipeg knowing that the prize was to come in the spring. The 3rd would be going to Germany for four years. Kapyong

Barracks in Winnipeg was the rotation base for troops rotating between Canada and Germany. While I was in Winnipeg I met my first wife. The winter was a brutally cold winter for everyone in Winnipeg as temperatures dipped to -60c, which may have been a foreshadowing of how my marriage would turn out to be.

In the summer of '88 the 3rd Bn rotated to Germany. Europe was all that I had envisioned. Standing on guard during the Cold War was relatively easy, especially with German beer and all kinds of festivals to be entertained with. My first week in Europe and I was treated to Tiger Meet '88. Tiger Meet was an air force festival built around jets from the surrounding nations that had been painted in tiger stripe style camouflage. The beer tent was overwhelming with all the 70¢ beer and scantily clad fräuleins. My buddy Ranger and I drank ourselves to oblivion. All was well until one of the repatriating Princess Patricia's Canadian Light Infantry (PPCLI) soldiers clambered on stage in a drunken stupor and started dancing with the Umm-pa-pa band. He was quickly hauled down off the stage by an American Military Police officer. The ensuing brawl spoke for Canadian loyalty to brother soldiers regardless of which unit they were from. American MPs and airmen's bodies flowed as freely as the blood. The fight only stopped when the Canadian MPs showed up. We Canadians raised our hands to show respect for our own Red-caps, as MPs are also called, by virtue of their red berets. The fight was over and a bunch of us went downtown to Hugelsheim, a neighbouring village, to continue our party. Tomorrow we would be back to work at our new job of defending the North Atlantic Treaty Organization (NATO).

Our Bn. was constantly training and was involved in multi-national exercises. The largest, being Fall-Ex which was conducted in and around the Hohenfels training area of Germany. This was all part of Canada's obligation to NATO. Hohenfels had a bush training area and a town style training area called a FIBUA site. Fighting-In-A-Built-Up-Area (FIBUA) is a skill that can be learned most effectively by having a complete town at your disposal. Canada offers this type of training to its soldiers at home in Canada but without the most critical aspect of the FIBUA concept. The premium FIBUA training towns provide many places to hide and defend from. When attacking a built up area it is preferable to have at least double the force size as the defending force. This disparity is required because of the casualties that an attacking force will sustain.

Urban warfare is brutal. This urban style training is invaluable and would be a skill to draw from in my near future.

In 1990 Iraq invaded Kuwait, and Operation Desert Shield, followed by Desert Storm, lasted into mid 1991, with continued media coverage long after. Members of Mike Company 3 RCR went to nearby Qatar to provide security to the military hospital there. The rest of us were detailed with base security and anti-terrorist team duties at CFB Baden in Germany. The end of the war brought Mike Company home and we continued with our regular NATO contributions including training for war. Many of us were let down by missing out on the war. Those that went were equally as let down by the meager contribution Canada provided.

Another valuable and enjoyable part of our training was the Escape and Evasion exercises. These exercises challenged the soldiers in their abilities to evade detection should they be trapped behind enemy lines. The exercise would start with a platoon's worth of soldiers being dressed in coveralls, much the same way as convicts are. They would then be driven a considerable distance from the base to a location in Germany and dropped off. The local civilian population would be notified by AM/FM radio. The German police or Polizei would also be notified that these men were on the loose and to inform Canadian military authorities immediately upon discovery of a soldier. The Canadian soldiers would be given a specific amount of time to make it back to base without being caught. It was a great exercise and forced us to be quick witted. Escape and Evasion, and all other training, was something that was offered to us because we were stationed in Europe. These fantastic opportunities did not happen in Canada. We would not want to scare the civilian population now would we?

The training was great, even under the circumstances, and I loved touring Europe. On one occasion our unit was afforded a border tour of the Wall. The Wall was the concrete separation that divided West from East Germany. The people of the Eastern Block desired change and it was not long before the Iron Curtain and the famed Berlin Wall came crumbling down. Other than that tour to the Wall I had not left the western part of Europe. That fact would change in 1992 with the violent uprisings in Yugoslavia. In the shadow of the Gulf War, Slovenia, Croatia and then Bosnia followed suit with the winds of change as the

Eastern Block began tearing itself apart. It would not be long before the world would be crying for United Nations involvement in the crumbling Yugoslavia. Canadians had a stellar reputation as peacekeepers and would be the first to volunteer for active duty in the region. In fact, the Conservative Government implored us to step in. The closest units capable of this task to deploy were those already in Europe. The Royal 22nd Regiment, R22ᵉR, Canada's French speaking infantry unit, in Lahr, Germany was selected. They would be accompanied by a wartime strength infantry company from 3rd Bn, RCR. November Company (N. Coy) would be used to bolster the R22ᵉR. I volunteered immediately for the duty. I did not know it then but my life was going to change forever.

NEW HOME

"No citizen has a right to be an amateur in the matter of physical training...what a disgrace it is for a man to grow old without ever seeing the beauty and strength of which his body is capable."
~SOCRATES.

The morning run was, as usual, boring. I was running along quietly at the front of the pack, listening to the griping and whining, or the laboured conversations of some of the guys. The March air was crisp and a haze of breath and sweat drifted over the platoon. The typical rain had let up momentarily. Occasionally I would turn my head to see how far back the guys who could not run were. I peeled off from the platoon and ran back to pick them up. Slowly increasing the pace and talking them up till we had caught up with the platoon.

"Come on, man, you can do this. You can't let that sack of shit up there kick you down." I was referring to our Platoon Warrant Officer. With my negative banter about our platoon's Second-in-Command (2IC) we gained a few more laboured steps. Thankfully it was just the right type of motivation this time. Each guy was a bit different with respect to what motivated him. It did not take me long to differentiate one from another.

"Get mad at him, whatever it takes. But don't quit."

Gradually we were closing the distance with the rest of the platoon. Once we had closed up, I would hold them there for awhile and then return to my position up towards the front. This procedure was one I would repeat several times during our morning runs. I would add an extra kilometre or two to our regular 10 to 12 km from following this practice. I was okay with this as it kept me in a little better shape. A type of physical and psychological advantage for me, or so I believed anyway. To add to my physical conditioning, I participated in as many special teams as possible. Teams such as Military Skills, March and Shoot and the Biathlon team, anything that would give me an edge in peacetime or in combat. I was a soldier and I loved being one. Having any kind of advantage was my way of believing I could someday cheat death in combat. I maintained a high standard of physical fitness as well as a high standard of mental preparedness. I studied everything that I was taught and more. Going out of my way to learn about other countries, weapons, armoured vehicles and the way their soldiers practiced their drills. Some of the guys thought it was excessive and others thought I was trying to score brownie points. But to me it was more than that. I believed the adage, 'knowledge is power', was not completely accurate. For me, it was deeper. I believed that the 'use of knowledge was power'. To be un-educated in soldiering was to be a hindrance to myself and to the team. So I tried, everyday, to perform to the highest standard. There was no way I was going to be responsible for letting the platoon down or, worse yet, come home in a rubber bag because of something I could have prevented through training. If I got capped otherwise, well then 'c'est la vie'.

When the run concluded back on CFB Baden-Solingen in Germany that early morning, we received word, that, what many of us had already speculated about was coming. Many of us were being handpicked from across the battalion to bolster up November Company. As indicated in my preface November Company was a rifle company in our unit, the 3rd BN RCR and they were known as The Men in Black. The distinction derived from the colour of t-shirt worn during battalion events. Each company had its own distinctive colour. We would be gearing up for a United Nations peacekeeping mission in what is now the Former Yugoslavia. Some of our daily activities would be changing gears soon.

Day to day we spent almost all of our time on effective training related to warfare. Doing 'dry' training, as it was called, meant we had no ammunition. 'Live' training was the exact opposite. Sitting in a classroom doing Armoured Fighting Vehicle Recognition, AFV, first aid, orientation, or patrolling around the army/air base with weapons going over contact drills were just a few things dry training encompassed. When we were not training for war we were doing equipment maintenance. By virtue of being in Europe our unit was a part of the rapid reaction force for NATO. With that designation we had to be ready to deploy at a moment's notice. Globally, Canadian soldiers have always been considered a very well trained group. Even with that global distinction we appreciated learning new things as well as going over old drills just to keep up on them. With the impending mission came the breakup of the usual monotony. So this was a welcome treat that helped to alleviate a day of fastidiously cleaning shovels and axes, and all the other mundane activities that a rifle company may employ in operations.

The rain was pouring down today as it did much of the time every spring in Germany. It reminded me so much of Vancouver, British Columbia with its winter drizzle dampening even the highest spirits.

"Man, is this shit ever going to stop" asked Sven Bauer. Sven hailed from Ontario. He was a good sport and liked to stir the pot with the rest of the guys. He was always good for morale, cracking jokes and laughing at most everything.

"Forty days and forty nights, brother" I retorted.

"Quack, quack, my feet are getting webs" he groaned.

"Look at it this way: we could be outside doing some shit job like butt – parade," I said trying to cheer him up.

"I hate that shit, I don't even smoke," Sven said emphatically. "I agree its BS that we have to clean up after those drug addicts." My comment elicited Sven's laughter.

"Ya you bunch of druggies should have to pick up all my beer bottles and pizza bones after a Friday night shack party."

"Shut up asshole. We already do." someone hollered.

A small bag of rags tied in a knot playfully bounced off the side of Sven's head.

"Well guys I've gotta get goin over to November Company," I said squarely, trying not to let my emotions get through.

"Okay, Casey, catch up with you buddy."

"See you over there soon, Sven," I said.

I stepped out the door and down the two steps. Turning left I walked the twenty paces to the end of the building. Stopping, I looked back. I had been with Anti-Armour Platoon for four years. Since before we rotated to Germany, since we had been in Winnipeg. I had built some good friendships in that time. Now I was heading back to a rifle company filled with what I believed would be eighteen and nineteen-year-old kids full of piss and vinegar.

"See ya, guys," I said quietly.

I turned and trotted along the paving stones that dotted the ground on the Marg. The Marg was a parking lot for jet fighters that had been converted into our daily working area. The Marg from an overview was one of four large three quarter circles adjacent to the runway. Two taxiways led into the centre of the three quarter circle from the runway. On the outside of the large circle were thirteen smaller circles where jetfighters, waiting to fly sorties, would park. These too were connected by short roads to the larger circle. In the centre of the circle were a number of buildings that housed our equipment and weapons.

The buildings also used as office space for our company and platoon headquarters. Each HQ had a platoon room designated for the soldiers to do indoor training. It was used more as a flop room during the day when training was not in session outside. I got to my new platoon building and met up with a couple of the guys from my old platoon, who transferred in earlier in the week. We already had a camaraderie established and were comfortable together so we gravitated to one another. With the increase in operational training it would not take long to gel with the guys from November Company. The young privates looked up to us, older corporals, in some ways. It is kind of funny when I think about it:

I am twenty-five years old, an old dog. I chuckled to myself.

I looked around the room. There actually were not many privates. Most of the guys in the Company were from other platoons. They too had rotated from their in-house units to November Company. In actuality we had been handpicked from across the battalion: the men with the most amount of time in service, combined with good tactical values. And that meant mostly corporal ranks. I spent the rest of the afternoon signing in to the Company office and CQ stores. I was then assigned to 5 Platoon, call sign Two-One or 21. I was informed at that time I would be the Platoon Commander's driver. I was somewhat unhappy to be slated as a driver. I was looking forward to being just one of the guys. By the end of the day I found out who the Platoon Commander would be. He was my Pl. Comm. from Anti Armour Platoon, Lieutenant Bill Burke. It was a relief as I already knew what would be expected of me. Maybe the driving job would not be too bad after all.

ROUTINE POUTINE

"We, the unwilling, led by the unknowing, are doing the impossible for the ungrateful. We have done so much, for so long, with so little, we are now qualified to do anything with nothing."
~KONSTANTIN JIREEK

The OC of November Company, Major Peter Devlin, stood, I estimated five foot six. We would learn in time, however, that he had a personality and heart that in contrast were monumental. Poking out from under his officer's style green-beret was short cropped blond hair. His eyes were narrow and piercing. He spoke to the reorganized 'wartime strength' November Company, The Men in Black. A wartime strength company was comprised of four 40 man platoons versus only three 40 man platoons in peacetime. "This is truly an amazing thing for me to be standing here in front of some of Canada's best soldiers. We, gentlemen," he paused and said with conviction, "The Men in Black, have been selected to undertake probably one of the most difficult and dangerous peacekeeping missions on the planet. The UN Security Council has asked if Canada would lead the UN mission into Croatia. This mission will be called UNPROFOR, short for United Nations Protection Force in Yugoslavia. Unfortunately, the Royal 22nd Regiment has been given the lead in this role. We will be bolstering up The Vandoos Battle Group."

"Well that oughta make it dangerous all on its own," sounded an anonymous comment from within our ranks. We all chuckled.

Silence returned and we stood shifting back and forth and wiggling our toes to keep the blood from pooling in our feet.

"As I'm sure many of you have been following on the news, Croatia has been fighting for its independence. Ethnic cleansing has reportedly been taking place. The United Nations has put together many peace deals and now feels that the one they have will last."

I looked at Sven and rolled my eyes thinking of the number of times the treaties had been broken.

"Ya right," I whispered. The OC continued.

"We will be going in shortly. The logistics in getting there are going to be difficult. We will have to cross through a few other 'Pink' states to get there. So I'm asking each of you to give your best to get us in to Yugoslavia as quickly as we

21

can. I know most of you and I'm aware of your professionalism, so with that being said, I'm confident that it will happen."

There were nods all around, confirming his comments.

"I will try and get together with you like this at least once more before we embark. I would like to welcome the fellows coming in from other platoons. I'm sure you will enjoy your time here in November Company. To everyone, work hard and pay close attention to details in your training. Vehicles need to be painted and equipment has to be selected. There is a lot of work to be done," he paused, "Sergeant-Major."

The CSM called out,

"Company, Atten-shun!" We all straightened up in perfect unison as Major Devlin handed the Company back to the CSM. The Major marched off. "All right lads, you heard the OC, there's lots of work to be done. Platoon Warrant's you know what to do. When I dismiss you, go to your respective platoon rooms and get to it. Orders at 15:00hours. November company, DIS-MISSED!"

Each morning the company would form up in line and go for morning physical training. Not as a complete company but by platoons. Morning P.T. consisted of a run and callisthenics. The format in my old platoon, basically, was the same implemented throughout the entire Battalion. We would start at 07:00 hours and be back just after 08:00hrs. After showering and putting our uniforms on the platoon would reassemble at the November Company buildings on

the Marg. At this time, we would be inspected and receive orders for the daily activities. Any paperwork that needed to be done could generally be done straight off.

Typically, many mornings were spent doing track maintenance. This was done to ensure that we were not only getting ready for our UN mission, but also to confirm that we were ready to assist NATO at a moment's notice. The afternoon was spent cleaning tools and weapons. Selecting the prime tools and setting the lesser tools to the side. A kit list for the personal equipment each soldier would have in his care was drafted and handed out. We had two days to get everything on the list together. Most of it was standard stuff. It was just a matter of packing it the way they wanted it packed. This was done so that if you had to use someone else's gear, the piece you were looking for would be in the same place as everyone else's.

Under normal circumstances these kit inspections were stressful and considered by most as chicken-shit. They were so ridiculous that at times, depending on who the CO was, you could be charged with a military offence for something as silly as not having lip chap in your butt pack. These charges could carry sentences of days confined to barracks or of hourly kit inspections where the layout would have to be changed for each inspection. If you got it wrong, they would make your life even more difficult. Some sentences included marching in double quick time with ALL your equipment on your back for hours at a time. This was called pack drill. Some of the higher ups in the past put more energy into kit inspections than they did in actual battlefield drills. Whether your socks were rolled up to three-inch thickness or not was more important than whether you could field strip and assemble your rifle under combat type stress. This particular inspection, however, would be different. It would be the final one.

Over the next couple of weeks all the vehicles were stripped down to their skeletons and painted. The Iltis, a German designed version of a jeep, assembled by Bombardier in Quebec, was our light vehicle. It was used by Recce platoon and by officers. The 5/4 ton pick-ups known to us by the name Five-quad were made by Chevrolet and came in different variants, like secure radio vehicles, ambulances and light troop transport. The medium troop transport truck MLVW, called the ML had replaced the Deuce-and-a-half of the Vietnam War era. The American made M-113 Armoured Personnel Carrier had come directly from Vietnam War technology and was known to us by a few different names, such as APC, carrier, and track.

The M-113 was slow, noisy and just slightly bullet resistant. It was made from an Aluminium-magnesium alloy. If it caught fire the magnesium would burn extremely hot. Once the vehicles were stripped of all the Company's equipment they were taken to the air force side of the base to the paint shop. Men from N. Coy were selected to assist in the painting. Here fresh coats of white paint would cover the green, brown, and black NATO camouflage paint schemes. After the vehicles returned from the paint booth we would carefully apply the big black UN letters to the sides, front, and rear. The upper hatch of the carrier when swung open would lay flat on the top. In theatre, it would almost always be open to allow the C-6 gunner to engage. So it too received a UN decal. This would make it visible as United Nations from the air or from high rises. The idea was to make all the vehicles as neutral and visible as possible. As United Nations pawns we could not appear aggressive.

However, because the Balkans was in such anarchy our officer staff was preparing for battle as best they could. The decision to take some of our artillery was ordered.

Unfortunately, one afternoon while the guys were in the process of painting three 105mm howitzers, the word came down to stop. We would not be taking anything this heavy to the Balkans. It was disappointing to our senior staff as well as to us. NDHQ and the United Nations clearly said NO.

Working concurrently with vehicle painting and equipment check lists, we were going to be doing a lot of peacekeeping style training. This would be our biggest challenge. As infantry soldiers we had only practiced full out, Kill, Kill, Kill. Like it or not, as infantrymen, that was our job. The role of the infantry is defined as follows:

To close with and destroy the enemy, by day or by night, regardless of weather, season, or terrain.

With the upcoming peacekeeping mission, we had to switch gears and practice restraint while still maintaining combat vigilance. It was a very difficult transition at best. We only had a few weeks to be UN operational. So the training began immediately. I knew that as a soldier I could at some point be-called upon to kill. I certainly did not want or desire that. My enthusiasm for the profession of soldiering was extremely high. My way of thinking was to preserve life and to secure Canada's borders from tyranny. I certainly did not have dreams or fantasize of killing people. The idea of killing, although an ancient global reality, to me, would be a last resort.

The training we had received in the army was strictly built around killing. Now we were going to have to learn how to deal with belligerents without killing them, a complete reversal from our training. It would prove, to say the least, interesting and in reality quite difficult.

PREP FOR BATTLE

"It is the job of thinking people not to be on the side of the executioners."
~ALBERT CAMUS

"What you are going to learn today is how to effectively search a vehicle," said Sgt Tugman, looking out at the forty of us.

We were formed in a loose semi-circle at the west end of the Marg.

"You will need to know this for operations in Yugoslavia. Doing these checks thoroughly can and will save your life and the lives of those around you." He paused as an F-18 Hornet went full after-burner for take-off only 700 metres away. The roar was deafening. Once the jet had gone, he continued.

"When a vehicle is navigating the checkpoint obstacles you will all have your weapons at the ready. Whichever one of you stops the vehicle, you will be responsible for controlling the search. It will usually be a Master Corporal or Sergeant. However, in the event that you, as junior NCMs, are running a checkpoint you will need to know this. One of you will order the vehicle to stop. The other will do the actual physical checking."

"Well if she's good lookin enough, there'll be some physical checkin goin on," we heard an anonymous comment. Everyone chuckled. Sgt Tugman rolled with the interruption, "If you haven't learned anything about women by being married or from watching married couples, it's the women you gotta watch for," joked the Sergeant. This evoked more laughter. When the classroom portion was completed, we moved to another area 100 metres away and got to the practical part. A checkpoint had already been laid out. A volunteer from the platoon drove his personal vehicle into the mock check point for inspection; Ray Gondole even rode his Harley Davidson in. Mirrors were used to check underneath the vehicles. Many explosive devices and other contraband had been transported in this fashion. The vehicle-if packed with explosives-could be driven into the check point and detonated, even before the inspection could take place. It was critical to make sure all occupants exited the vehicle immediately with their hands up, palms open as a remote detonator could be concealed, however, that still may not prevent a detonation. We were fully aware of the chances we had to take. We practiced vehicle searches through the day, until it became second

25

nature. In connection with vehicle searches were the lessons on how to detain the occupants should something be found. Particular rules that had to be followed. The United Nations and its participants all follow the rules set out in the Geneva Convention. An example of one of these rules in layman's terms is: 'Every person, regardless of race or action is entitled to water, food, shelter, and medical attention'. Much of this information had already been passed on to us during infantry battle school. As with any training though we learned and re-learned.

We learned how to properly remove bad guys from vehicles. There was the nice way:

"Sir, would you please exit the vehicle?"

"Thank you, please stand here."

"Thank you."

For the person in question, this was the approach that was preferred. Then of course there was the other way:

"Get out of the fucking vehicle, NOW!"

"Get on the ground!"

"If you so much as flinch or fart you are going to cry. A lot!"

I am sure for the person in question, this was not the preferred approach. This was usually said while the person was forced to lie face down on the ground with a knee wedged up between his legs resting comfortably on his reproductive, organs accompanied by a C-7 pointed at his head. Aggressive women would receive equal treatment. Once the person or persons were removed from the vehicle they would have to be contained. We learned methods regarding how to restrain without being malicious. Each checkpoint would have plastic tie straps on hand for field expedient handcuffs. Procedures for notifying local police services was also discussed.

"In the event that we detain bad guys, the local police have to be brought in to take responsibility for them." He continued,

"This can be done by notifying HQ, call sign '2' or your platoon Sunray, or Sunray Minor." He paused and allowed us to digest the info. "Okay, lads, that concludes training for today. We are back out here for P.T. tomorrow at 07:00. Dress will be combat pants, boots, and Company T-shirt. We will be conducting unarmed combat training so bring your nasty attitudes. Dis-missed!"

Unarmed combat training was a good way to relieve stress while learning an important skill. Unfortunately, it was not something that the Canadian military did much of because it was considered to be too aggressive. 'We want an Army but do not necessarily want to know about it, or pay for it'. Although the Conservatives under Brian Mulroney were in power, the Trudeau Liberals had taken great liberties to reduce the military to its sad state of poor equipment and low morale during their tenure. As an example, when I was in the Special Service Force we were not allowed to wear our camouflage smocks off base because it was considered to be too aggressive for the general public to view. The people of Canada were comfortable with the current state of affairs with the military. That was how many of us viewed the Conservative status quo.

"Wow I can't believe we are doing this," I said to Randy Dempster.

Randy hailed from Sarnia, Ontario. He was an athletic guy who played on the battalion hockey team. His face carried a permanent smile and he was happy most of the time. We had a good friendship with the background coming from serving in Anti Armour Platoon together.

"No kidding eh?!"

"If Trudeau knew this was going on, he'd freak," I said flatly. I continued sarcastically with a French accent,

"Impossible, we can't actually teach them to kill, they might actually do it. And how would that look to my constituents?" Randy and a couple others laughed in agreement. We learned and practiced many methods regarding how to fight the enemy. Should the enemy have a weapon, we learned to strip him of it and kill him either with it or anything at our disposal. Every one of us paid close attention to these lessons. We performed the moves repeatedly. When the hand-to-hand portion of training concluded we donned hockey cups slid over our pants for groin protection, hockey gloves, and football helmets. We formed a loose circle approximately twenty feet in diameter.

Once inside the circle we would arm ourselves with Pugil Sticks. These were an eight-foot-long staff with token padding on each end. They resembled huge Q-tips. With these in hand and our protection on we would commence beating the crap out of each other. It was like going to some sleazy back alley and being the roosters in a vicious cock fight. It was great! We absolutely let loose and fought. If you won, you got to remain in the circle. If you lost, you would pass your gear to the next combatant. The biggest lesson I derived from pugil fighting was that speed and conditioning went a long way compared to size and brute force.

The following day was designated for first aid training. First aid training was usually conducted once or twice a year, with basic revues done periodically during exercises. It was completely normal for training or umpire staff to walk up to a soldier and tell him, 'You have just been shot. You have a sucking chest wound, lie down.' Of course the soldier would oblige and flop down and revel in the coffee break. He would lie there until the next soldier passing by stopped to administer first aid. With the upcoming peacekeeping mission into the very hostile Balkans, first aid training was ramped up. We covered everything from typical fractures and how to stabilize them, to how to deal with a complete dismemberment. The training continued with a good portion being given to dealing with gunshot and shrapnel wounds. With any gunshot or shrapnel wound there is likely a good chance for loss of blood. So in this case we did not just get

needles, we were now going to learn how to give them. These needles would be in the form of IVs. Should one of our soldiers be wounded, he could now count on his brother to administer plasma through an IV. An entire afternoon was put aside for practising. One could only hope for a quick learner as a partner. The alternative was looking like a pin cushion.

During a break in training four of us, Randy Dempster, Tyler Campbell, Tommy Martin, and I sat at one of the booths in the Foxhole. The Foxhole was our canteen. It was a place that served coffee and minor meals, and poutine was the crowd favourite. A good portion of the money raised in this manner went to the Regimental Kit Shop. This money was used to purchase door prizes and other niceties for the troops. We were mulling over the impending tour.

"Any idea when we leave Tyler?" I asked.

Tyler was a very intelligent well spoken soldier with slightly reddish hair and standard military moustache. Physically you would not have expected to hear he was a soldier. He was a little bigger around the middle than some. His intelligence and overall mental toughness was what kept him in the ranks with the rest of the soldiers. I wondered sometimes why he was in the military. He should have been doing presentations on global demographics somewhere.

"No it's hush-hush till we get closer for obvious security reasons."

"Oh for sure I was just wondering if you heard anything from Rumour Control."

"Surprisingly, it's pretty quiet, Delanco normally picks up lots while working here." Danny Delanco was an ol' dog in the true sense of the expression. He had been in the army for years and was due for retirement. We joked that it must have been cool going through basic training with Napoleon. Danny worked the Foxhole and learned about the 'scuttle-butt' in the Regiment through his position there and because of that the Foxhole was nicknamed Rumour Control.

"Where the heck is Stone today?" I quizzed.

"Lil' Bobby is Toastmeister today," said Tommy smiling.

At 19, Bobby Stone was a 6'4" lanky kid from BC. He had a shoot from the hip way of telling you how he felt. Bobby never had issue with laying his cards out for you to help you make your decisions. He was not afraid to drop the gloves to defend what he believed in. I was impressed by how confident he was. It was not a cocky attitude, just a confidence that belied his boyish rosy red cheeked look.

Tommy on the other hand was the exact opposite of Bob. Tommy hailed from the other side of Canada. He was from Cape Breton. He was a mere 5'5" and was made from solid ripped muscle. His temperament was quite reserved. Tommy kept his opinion to himself when around others. Fortunately, because he and I had worked so closely together in AAP, he would open up to me without hesitation.

"That's funny, gotta love the privates for something," chuckled Tyler.

"Oh ya, better him than us," I added.

Toastmeister was a shit job that we did. It involved making toast and coffee for the officers in the unit. They would go to the officer's version of the Foxhole and have coffee and toast for coffee break. God forbid if you were an officer that the troops did not like. You could never tell what might end up on your slice of toast.

The next day of training included briefings by our Intelligence Section. We learned that Yugoslavia was broken up into states now. Slovenia to the extreme north had broken away first with no bloodshed. Republika Hrvatska or Croatia, was second to seek independence and the state we would be deploying in. Zagreb, the capital of Croatia was located a few hundred kilometres away from the fighting in the struggling breakaway state.

"You won't be going anywhere near there," explained one of the Int. gurus.

Croatia, unlike Slovenia, had not been so lucky to escape without violence. Bosnia and Herzegovina, with their capital being Sarajevo, were to the south. We would not be deploying there either. Or at least so we thought at this point anyway. Serbia was to the extreme south with Belgrade being its capital. Serbia was almost completely untouched by the war. The Yugoslavian National Army (JNA) had more or less been pushed out of 'Hrvatska vojna Krajina', which translated means 'Croatian Military Frontier'. It would be known to us as, The Krajina. We had intelligence on the type of vehicles they used, like their older Main Battle Tanks, (MBTs), were T-54/55s. Which we were very familiar with from all the Soviet information we had. There was little information on their newer MBTs and APCs. It would be a learning curve when we got there.

D.A.G., like many phrases in 'army-lingo' is the acronym for Departure Assistance Group. Before any military personnel can be employed in any obscure region, they must D.A.G. Green. D.A.G. Red and you are going nowhere. Every element on base gets to poke and prod everyone who is slated to go. We had to visit the dentist, doctor, military police, clothing stores, the Padre, pay office, and so on. You must be cleared in all these areas before you can proceed. Of course all of these, during regular transfers, require you to stand in line up after line up. For major moves like going on a peacekeeping mission, where a large portion of a unit is being deployed, the D.A.G. is brought together into one building. Even though everyone was under one roof, we still had to line up. And line ups in the Army are done alphabetically A-Z. We were in one of these line ups only this time it was reverse alphabet, Z-A. Ron Pendleton was scared to death about getting needles. And we were getting a few of them. Typhoid, Hepatitis, and Tetanus were some of the shots to name a few. The line gradually became shorter and shorter. Ron was up next.

"Where do you think Pendleton should fit in? The nurse who was administering the needle asked, "In between Allan and Anderson or Anderson and Ainsley?"

Ron could not answer. The nurse had showed him the needle and he passed out. There was harmless laughter. We had covered all the bases. All the necessary paperwork was done. Wills, next of kin notification addresses, payroll and the like were complete. Our vehicles were white with the UN letters emblazoned all around. Our weapons and equipment were as ready as they had ever been. The company was entitled to a few days' embarkation leave. Many of the

troops took the time to be with family. No one could predict how many of us would or would not be coming home.

My wife and I were not happily married so I spent much of my time with my daughter. We went on a spring Volksmarch in the town of Weitenung. Volksmarchs were organised walks where participants would receive a pin denoting their participation. There was a huge walking movement in Germany. It was a great way to get out and be involved in the community. I enjoyed the walks pushing my daughter's stroller as I went. The German people I met were very friendly and I loved my posting to such a wonderful country. The memories from school books I had read as a teenager depicting a different Germany of the '40s were now replaced by the new Germany I was living in. However, I would be leaving the beauty of Germany soon for war torn Yugoslavia.

MOUNT UP!
"Go to Heaven for the climate, Hell for the company."
~MARK TWAIN

We marshalled the vehicles in line at the inside perimeter side gate. We typically used this procedure for going on major NATO exercises. The Military Police (MP) opened the gate once we were all lined up and accounted for. The MPs were referred to in slang as Meatheads. It was a perception that the Meatheads were not the brightest lads in the service, and that they could withstand physical abuse, and hence had earned the name Meathead. We drove out along the golf course road to the outside perimeter back gate. Here again the Meatheads opened the gate. They were in place directing us out onto Hwy 22. They had blocked the highway to allow us to enter the roadway, unaffected by civilian traffic-an annoyance to the local German population, I was sure.

Highway 22 would lead us to the rail head in Solingen, where we were going to load the flat railcars for Croatia. After a couple of turns our convoy of shiny white combat vehicles was motoring down the highway. The trek to Solingen was a short 8kms. The next step was loading the vehicles which went quickly and without event. We had done this numerous times before. The whole procedure took an hour. The first carrier would line up on the ramp. A ground guide would then walk ahead of the carrier and inch him along. The railcars were very narrow. Every precaution was taken to avoid a catastrophe. Once each vehicle had been loaded and put in its place they were then tied down with chains. Steel chocks were placed in front and back of tires or tracks to stop the vehicle from rolling. Sentries were left to guard the rail convoy. The sentries would go with the rail to Lahr, Germany where they would marshal with the Vandoos vehicle train. From Solingen we returned to base in the back of a couple of MLs.

This was it. Everything had been taken care of. The final evening was spent with family. The next morning, we assembled, as the 'Advance Party' for departure. We were few at this point: only fourteen of us, each platoon commander and his driver, the OC, his driver and a couple liason officers. The main body of the Coy would follow in two to three weeks.

Families were present for the send off. There were tearful goodbyes and

33

wishes for safe returns. I hugged my little girl and told her I loved her repeatedly, in the event that I did not make it back. I hugged my wife and quickly turned and got on the bus. The 65km trip to Lahr was a solemn one. Everyone was dealing with the immediate separation anxieties. Some of the pressure was relieved when Donny Bralorne bit into a mayo and plastic wrap sandwich. For long road trips, travellers were provided with a box lunch. These lunches were assembled in the mess hall by soldiers who were doing 'extra duties' generally for bad behaviour. Soldiers making these sandwiches would slather both pieces of bread with mayonnaise, and instead of providing a meat filling, a large folded piece of plastic sandwich wrap was substituted. There was nothing quite as amusing as watching the reaction on someone's face, as they tried to chew their way through a sabotaged sandwich. This was a common practical joke amongst members in the unit, and we all laughed and chipped in to make sure he got fed.

The bus stopped at the front gate of CFB Lahr. The security detail boarded and made a quick check then waved us in. We were given a place to park our kit and our butts. After sitting in the sun for about seven hours we were given the loading instructions for our journey. The whole procedure was routine. I noticed, however, that there was a nervous energy to it although we had made many moves similar to this for exercises all over Europe. But this trip had a dangerously different destination, and it was realized in our every breath. With cheers and waves the train rolled out onto the mainline and we were whisked away.

I sat quietly in our train's cabin gazing out the window. A couple of the guys were sleeping to foil the boredom. Others were in their cabins playing cards. I was listening to the metal wheels of the train clatter and squeal on the steel rails. The sound was almost hypnotic. I stood and opened our cabin window. The breeze felt refreshing. The branches of trees rustled wildly as the train sped along. I wondered how we would be received in Daruvar. Daruvar was to be our first destination in Croatia. I wondered if we would be fighting our way in or whether it would be peaceful like the United Nations wanted us to believe. I really did not want to kill anyone. Soldier or not, killing was not something I longed for. Dying was something I also was in no haste for either. It was stressful to ponder what the future held for us. This time on the rail was driving me crazy.

I had no choice but to sit in my railcar and wait it out. I lazily gazed at my watch. Lunch was being served. I stumbled my way through the cars to the front where the kitchen car was located. Hanging on to the sides I held my melmac plate out and smiled at the slice of ham that hit my plate. The cook took the time to drizzle some honey glaze on my slice, potatoes and peas and I was set. I was especially happy to be a Canadian soldier at mealtime. One of the most fantastic cooks I had ever had the pleasure of being fed by was in our platoon. Slim Skeritt had served us countless premiere meals while I was in Anti Armour in Germany.

We were by far one of the better fed armies in the world. It was common while we were on multi-national firing ranges or training exercises that other nations armies would attempt to get in on our chow lines. None of us blamed them. For example, the French army had a mixed dry cracker and pâté ration for the whole day. The British soldiers were appropriately named 'Shit-eaters' for their, 'boiled in a vat of oil' meals. Another example is to imagine asking for two eggs over-easy, bacon and toast, and then watch them all being dropped into a pot of boiling oil. When the items float to the top, they are cooked, and placed on your plate.

I carefully made my way to one of the corners of the car and ate standing. Everyone around me was speaking French and I felt out of place. I ate quickly and went back to my cabin. They could have spoken English to me. But that would not have been within their normal behaviour. The rivalry between the English-speaking soldiers and the French-speaking was very real. Our inter-regimental hockey games confirmed that. Bloodshed would often make its way from the ice up into the stands. I put my minimal dinner scraps into the garbage can and held the wall for guidance back to my cabin. I looked at a couple of the guys who were sleeping on their bunks. We did not bother waking each other for meals, unless it was pre-arranged. The move kept the appetite down. So we ate only when we were hungry.

Later in the day I did my best to keep in shape. I stepped into the narrow hallway and did my usual round of push-ups and sit-ups. I then stripped my rifle and wiped it down with oil. I reassembled it. I stripped and assembled it another dozen times. It helped to quell the listlessness.

The 'Vance Peace Plan' was organized to have the former Yugoslavia broken into three UNPAs. The UNPA we would be patrolling was divided into four sectors. Sector West was to be our designated Sector for the tour. The bulk of the UNPA was in The Krajina. The other three, Sectors East, North and South, would be maintained by the Nepalese, Jordanians, and the Ukrainians, however, until those countries rallied enough money and support from their home nations we would patrol the whole block. Canadian taxpayers had provided us with enough funds to head to the Balkans right away and assume our increasingly high profile role as peacekeepers.

It was almost 7pm when the train came to a stop. Somewhat disoriented I sat up on my bunk. I leaned my head out the window. There was a commotion up at the lead car. There were men in blue uniforms outside having what appeared to be a heated discussion about something. I could not help but feel tense. I was not sure exactly where we were. I was certain that it was a Communist-style border. Word rustled back through the cars like leaves on the wind. We were entering Slovenia. Our train sat motionless for twenty minutes while the CO and the border guards chatted about our progression into Slovenia. The card games had ceased and everyone milled about in the train car hallways and rooms. We were all a bit uneasy. Up to this point none of us had been issued any ammunition. Within no time the train sounded its whistle and it lurched under the strain of our heavy payload.

As we rolled down the tracks through Slovenia and into Croatia, I looked over my National Geographic map of Yugoslavia, and tried to continuously to mark our location in case we were ambushed. We were never issued any topographical maps of the region. For whatever reason, maps and Intel were very limited. I am sure the fact that Yugoslavia was a 'Pink state' of the former Soviet Union had a part in the lack of information we had. I was gazing out the window at the countryside. A lot like the geography back home in British Columbia, the scene would change from mountainous to heavily wooded to arid in some areas. It was quite beautiful. I am not sure why, but I was somewhat expecting it to look completely foreign. The further we went into the former Yugoslavia, the more apparent, the signs of war became. The first sign of battle was a blown up church. It was riddled with bullet holes and the roof had completely collapsed. The surrounding buildings also carried the marks of battle.

The train ride in general was boring. We were cramped into cubicles with six bunk style fold down beds in each cabin. The air in these cabins was stale with the smell of soldiers sweating and only spit-bathing for days. Some of the guys played cards and others read books. There was always some form of music being played. Jokes and bullshit stories flew with reckless abandon. Nobody ever brought up their fears or openly contemplated the impending landing. Although it was on everyone's mind. The subject of death never arose.

One thing I noticed, outside of the fact that most everything was shot up, was that we had travelled through some type of a time warp. By entering Croatia, we had gone back in time by what appeared to be about fifty years. The automobiles that I observed here were lacking in Western options. They appeared to be poorly made. The cars I did see, although few, were parked. I assumed no one could afford fuel even if it could be transported in. No doubt fuel would be going towards keeping their war machine rolling. I noticed that people were moving mainly on foot or by bicycles and many chores were being done with the horse and cart. Of the dozen working train engines I saw, all but the one we were on, were steam driven. These facts made me think that many of the people were living on the borderline of poverty even before the war. As I sat there looking out the window, daydreaming about my days of racing my motorcycle, a Vandoo corporal came to the sliding cabin door. He slid it open using the green metal ammo box in his right hand.

"Fill your mags, boys," he said with enthusiasm.

With a breath of relief escaping from my lips, I dove in and filled my mags with fervour. Our ridiculously long train, and noticeably white UN vehicles, made for an easy target for fast air or infantry ambush. Paranoid thoughts for some, perhaps, but normal for many of us soldiers. I just could not help feeling vulnerable. And I guess the feeling was warranted: we really were vulnerable. The train began to decelerate and I thought that we must be getting close to the unload point. Then something made my stomach twist like a bowl full of snakes. My mind raced to formulate a personal plan. We had not been given any semblance of instruction should we be engaged by hostiles. There was no quick reaction plan in place should someone attack us. This was totally against everything we had been trained to do.

The breeze through our window slowed as the train decelerated, and my faced flushed with disappointment. Our fabulous French CO had dropped the ball already. Or was I just over-reacting? I leaned toward the window and watched the surroundings for any sign of trouble.

We clattered into Daruvar, Croatia just short of the train terminal. The others in the railcar, were shocked somewhat by my chambering of a round into the breach of my rifle, but followed suit. I wondered if our stopping short was planned or just a fluke. Pulling right in to the platform could have been deadly. Stopping short may have thrown off an ambush attempt. I mused that it was probably the latter.

As we exited the train there was a bit of a scuffle with a handful of Croatian soldiers. The mandate given to us from the UN was already being enforced. No one but UN soldiers would be allowed to possess weapons within Sector West. The Croatian soldiers were having difficulty understanding that we were now in-charge. One of these hapless Croatian morons raised his AK-74 and loosed off a magazine of 7.62mm bullets into the air. With some heated words and bitch slapping they were disarmed. These poorly disciplined lads became well versed in our introductory course:

Canadians Don't Take any Bullshit-101.

Ah yes, the perfect entrance into a country not belonging to us, I thought. A country ravaged by civil war. There should not be any retribution for this public display of foreign belligerence. I was not scared. I was however, feeling a great deal of anxiety. Like when it is your first day of school in a new town. Only my training helped me overcome the jitters. I started looking for something to do. Our sentries were placed all around the train. Orders were 'Shoot to kill' should anyone think of hindering our deployment. After a few basic orders the Advance Party began unloading vehicles. The APCs had to be driven off the railcars onto a rail platform and then down to the ground. This was a dangerous procedure as the Croatian rail yard was not accustomed to this sort of cargo. Only inches of platform could be seen on either side of our 12-Ton carriers. It was a tighter job than the ramps back in Germany. A slip of the tiller bar steering mechanisms and the APC could slide off the platform and crash on its side injuring or killing the driver and possibly others. MLs and Iltis' were unchained and also driven off. A small crowd had drawn close to watch the parade of starch white military vehicles clatter off the rusty metal rail cars.

I looked at the crowd and thought of the past. Canadians took Vimy Ridge in the First World War when no others could. Canadian soldiers, including my grandfathers, had stormed the beaches of Normandy and Sicily in WWII. Now, here I was standing with my blue helmet and rifle in the middle of a crumbling Yugoslavia. We were a handful of Canadians, alone in the Balkans War. No other country had stepped up to the plate. It was juvenile of me to think that the locals,

who had chosen to venture out of the safety of their homes, were rewarded with a look at their foreign saviours. They stood mesmerized by our methodically quick unloading process. We had unloaded over sixty trucks, Iltis', and a multitude of trailer configurations. The trailers included portable kitchens, water tankers, and a portable post office to name a few. Amongst the Iltis', trucks and trailers we unloaded, were a few APCs that would accompany Battle Group HQ. The whole affair took about an hour and a half. Not bad considering the amount of work to be accomplished. Once it was complete we spent little time farting around and we headed off to our Area of Operations.

HOUSE FULL OF HOLES

"Do not take life too seriously. You will never get out of it alive."
~ELBERT HUBBARD

Dismounting the train was the first step toward heading for a former Yugoslav military base. Camp Polom was an abandoned JNA base before the war. We would spend the night there, then move to our new home in the village of Sirač. Sirač, we would learn, was a small village thirty kilometres to the south. Like most villages in The Krajina it too had seen its share of battles. This was evident in the less than cosmetic appearance of its buildings. We had no APCs at this point so the members from November Company jumped into our Iltis'. My Iltis was assigned the call sign Two-One Whiskey (2-1 W). The 2-1 represented the platoon radio call sign for the platoon. The whiskey stood for 'wheeled' because the jeep had wheels. It was simple military logic. In eloquent words, of one of my Sergeants had said,

"K.I.S.S. is the acronym here lads, Keep-It-Fucking-Simple-Stupid."

"But Sergeant there is no F in KISS," commented a young private. To which he replied,

"The F is silent, now sit down and shut your pie-hole stupid."

So with four platoons came four Iltis'. The others followed suit with call signs 22-W, 23-W, and 24-W. The cool breeze made me shudder a bit. The flimsy plastic doors for the jeep were tucked in their protective bag and fastened down on the hood. The weather was cool and we had not bundled up for the trip. Arriving at Camp Polom just before the sun went down we quickly set up camp. The accommodations were nothing fancy. We pulled out our air mattresses and bivi-bags, spread them out and lay down in the open air in all around defense.

'All-around-defense' is the term we use to indicate getting in a circle so we could fire in any direction in the event of an attack. There were only twelve of us in the group. We playfully nicknamed ourselves the Dirty Dozen from the famous Lee Marvin war flick. Sentry duties were divied up amongst us with the officers pulling shift too. We were too few to think that rank had its privileges. The officers gained some respect from us that night. Even though we had our sentries posted, no one slept well. Battles could be heard all hours of the night in the distance. Thankfully for us, the night passed without incident.

In the morning, before coffee, each man worked with a purpose and packed up his gear so we were ready to move at a moment's notice. We had been professional soldiers for quite some time so we did most things without direction. Once our weapons had been given a going over, we shared a brew over a mountain stove that one of the lads had fired up. A mountain stove is a small single burner stove that creates high heat quickly. The temperature was -2c and our breath showed every time we exhaled. Still processing our surroundings, no one spoke much through coffee. My eyes, along with those of the others, constantly scanned the tree line around us. There was a light frost on everything. With coffee and packing complete, we mounted up. Our small UN task force headed for the village of Sirač. After a few kilometres I spoke to the Lieutenant.

"You noticing what I'm noticing, Sir?"

"If it's the fact every building is destroyed, yes," Lt. Burke replied.

"Yes, sir, that's it, every house. It's bizarre."

"Hey check that out, Casey." He pointed out the right side of the jeep. "What the fuck is that?"

"Hell if I know but they don't look healthy." I responded as I surveyed the brown lumps he was referring to. Upon closer inspection in the field to our right, a dozen cows lay dead and were now bloated to the size of elephant calves.

"Steak, anyone?" I jeered.

Lt. Burke just pointed to the road in front.

"Drive," he curled his lip in fake disgust.

"City boy," I laughed out loud.

The building November Company would occupy was the community hall for the village of Sirač. Sirač was a typical Croatian town, containing a corner store, small bank, a number of residential homes, and an industrial complex which housed the gravel pit and cement plant. The village also had a pub, named IKO's, which was frequented regularly by the Croatian soldiers. After a few days in country it was easy to tell when they were in for R&R, because the sky would be alive with bullets fired at random. I often wondered how many innocent civilians died from out of trajectory gunshot wounds. We regarded this as undisciplined conduct.

The community hall from the outside was a typical cinder block building with a red tile roof and the walls were riddled with bullet holes. The inside was a bit of a shock. As we entered the smell of death was too close to mistake for anything else. It permeated the air with the smell of iron. It was a scene right out of a horror film. The walls and floor appeared to be painted with blood. There were a few folding tables stretched out and a couple that had toppled over. These, we observed, had been used as operating tables. All the windows but two were smashed out.

This was a triage for the Hrvatska Vojska (HV) Croatian Army troops being brought back from the front line. As I walked carefully through this lifeline for an enemy I had not become acquainted with yet, I could visualize and audibly imagine the screams of pain and prayers for forgiveness from devastated men defending their homes and families. I could only imagine the hatred that coursed through some of their veins. We spent the rest of the day and well into the night cleaning. All the blood had to be mopped up. The cleaning supplies we had were very limited. They did not include rubber gloves or masks or any means of protection from becoming contaminated by the blood we were cleaning up. Tables were washed off and stacked. Windows were cleared of all broken glass and covered with plastic and black hessian. The plastic was to keep out the weather out. The hessian, a material like burlap, was to keep prying eyes out and to cover our movements so we would not be clear targets for would be aggressors. By 01:00hours we were bushed and ready for some rack time. Sentry duty was posted and everyone else turned in.

Donny Bralorne and I tagged the 0300-0400 shift. We always did sentry in pairs. Good for back-up in a pinch and insurance against falling asleep on shift. Our shift was kept to one hour from the usual two-hour shift. This was done to keep everyone as fresh as possible due to our low numbers. Once again the night sky was full of tracers and the sounds of battle drifted in on the wind. Our shift ended and I gladly woke Earl Bledsoe and Glenn Downton. I drifted off and slept till 0530hrs.

Today was day three and we were going back to check out the former JNA base, Camp Polom. We had spent the night there but had not seen it in its entirety. This dismantled base would be the main base for our battle group.

Alpha Company, R22ᵉR, known as The Vandoos, would live here while we were in Croatia. Burke and I drove through the make shift front gate security post. I noticed HV soldiers using mine sweepers being accompanied by Canadian Engineers. The Croats were digging up most of the mines that the JNA regulars had planted before leaving the base. However, there were a few Canadians on their bellies prodding the ground with bayonets. There was a pile of PMA-3 land mines. They looked like cans of tuna, only the cans were plastic and green.

The base was in tatters. Buildings had been destroyed in what looked like a battle of some duration. Bullet holes peppered the white stucco showing the red cinder block innards. In the upper left corner of what would have been some of the housing for the soldiers, were the sprayed out marks of where an RPG round had exploded. There were the odd blackened blood pools dotting the pavement signalling someone's demise. We drove around for a bit inside the compound. I stopped when we got to a large clearing. We dismounted to have a look around, being mindful not to step off the hard pack. There would always be the threat of landmines. The clearing we were standing in was man-made, or should I say explosives-made. There had been a building on this spot until just recently. It had been destroyed in an explosion so fierce that the surrounding trees had been sheared off at the butt. Some of these stumps measured seven feet across. What was left of them was scattered like toothpicks amongst what was left of the cinder blocks the building had been constructed of. I stood there for quite some time mesmerised by the amount of C-4 or DM-12 it would have taken to do this. C-4 and DM-12 were the explosives that Canadians used for demolitions. Lt. Burke and I walked to the building next to where this one once existed. It had extensive damage on the side next to the former shack. The remainder was still intact and surprisingly enough it still had quite a bit of equipment in it. We were just about to enter when Bill said,

"Stop, this isn't right. Why would they leave all this stuff behind?"

"Booby-traps," I stated, more as a warning.

We carefully examined the room from the doorway. It was loaded with MRUDs, the Yugoslavian version of the US Claymore mine, a directional anti-personnel mine, each filled with one pound of high explosive, which is curved and covered with several hundred steel ball bearings. When detonated the ball bearings shred everything within fifty metres in its arc. This room had hundreds of these mines. Right under our noses at the doorway was a trip wire. This wire was accompanied by more trip wires at each entry point to the building. Had either of us stepped through the door we would have been blown to kingdom come. My mind reeled with the thoughts of explosions and our being vaporised in a concrete powder and bloody mist.

We walked back to the Iltis, radioed it in and informed them that we would be putting minefield tape up immediately. HQ agreed and called for Holdfast. Holdfast is the radio nickname for the Engineers. They would have to come and dismantle the trip wires and defuse the mines, a very dangerous job to say the least. I had tons of respect for the Engineers. We spent an hour walking around and found another half dozen booby traps. One booby trap consisted simply of an M-31 81mm mortar bomb all shiny and new, placed on a stump, just calling out to some trophy hunter. We had grabbed a roll of mine tape and marked all the spots so they could be dismantled.

Camp Polom would house almost everything we would have on a regular base: the hospital, dental clinic, the pay office, and of course the post office just to name a few. After about three hours at Camp Polom we mounted up and headed back to Sirač. Just as well, as it was getting dark. All of our early trips to and from Sirač were made through a maze of uncharted roads so travelling them in the dark was even more harrowing.

It was mid afternoon of our fifth day in The Krajina. Today was our first actual dismounted patrol. I suspected the three others in the patrol were as apprehensive as I was. I was trying not to let the beautiful day interfere with staying focused on soldiering. It was difficult as there was a light breeze blowing the early blossoms off the trees. They drifted lazily across my line of sight as they fluttered to the ground. I focused harder on our surroundings to stave off the adrenalin. We stepped off just after noon and had patrolled to Sirač's northern border. Before long we had a couple hours of patrolling under our belts. So far so good, I thought to myself. We made the turn to head back. Donny Bralorne was on point with me twenty feet behind him on the opposite side of the dirt road. Behind me and staggered back to the right side of the road was Glenn Downton, followed by Earl Bledsoe on my left side forty feet back. We were spread out to minimize our target size. One grenade can kill or wound more people if they are close together. As I walked my brand new flak vest was rubbing back and forth till it bit into my neck. The vest was stiff and inflexible and I cursed its rigidity. On either side of the road were partially destroyed homes. Their formerly white washed exteriors were now branded with racial graffiti and the pockmarks from many stray bullets. I learned the meaning of the crude inscriptions by speaking with the local inhabitants.

The letter U with a cross in its opening denoted the symbol of the Ustaše. The Ustaše was a Croatian fascist movement that originated before the onset of WW2. The Ustaše supported the creation of a Greater Croatia that would span to the River Drina and to the border of Belgrade. The movement emphasized the need for a racially 'pure' Croatia and promoted persecution and genocide against Serbs, Jews, and Romani people. It was rumoured that the organization had renewed its vow. The other prominent marking was the cross with the letter C in each quadrant pointing away from each other. This denoted the Chetniks. Chetnik is the word for guerrilla fighter, which fought for the national liberation of the Serbs against the Ottoman Empire, in the Balkans, and in World War I. It is the name for the Serbian nationalist anti-Nazi resistance movement of World War II, called the Yugoslav Army of the Fatherland. Their faces covered with unruly full beards, the Chetniks would slaughter any non-Serb with extreme brutality.

Those, amongst other graffiti, adorned the walls in an ethnic mosaic of hatred. A swirl of dust blew up into my face peppering my skin, forcing me to close my eyes momentarily. When I opened them the sand under my eyelids scratched away violently at the soft tissue. My brain instructed them to open in quick reaction to the staccato of automatic fire to our right flank. My rifle butt tucked tightly into the soft section of my shoulder as my thumb pushed the safety selector to the fire position without hesitation.

As if it were choreographed our four-man patrol instinctively swung all their weapons to the right in preparation for battle. Everyone's attention was drawn immediately to the point where the fire had come from. In true spaghetti western-style, a man stood to the side of the front porch of one of the homes. He was waving his rifle as he continued to fire wildly into the air. It was as though he was oblivious to his deadly audience. He appeared to be in his mid 30s and was dressed in his cleanest dirty clothes. He was brandishing a lightly smoking AK-47. The grin on his face slid away as his brain comprehended the message that his eyes were sending. The message that there were four assault rifles aimed at various points of his body. The door of the home opened further with a cheer from inside. Glenn, Donny and Earl swung to cover the new threat. I stayed locked onto the guy with the Kalashnikov. From the now open door we could see the smiling faces of a bride and groom followed by a small entourage of well wishers. They too stopped dead in their tracks on the steps. We watched as they went from poor man's frivolity to fear in a split second. These people were no strangers to violence and it was clear we were unexpected guests. It added a whole new dimension to the term wedding crashers, I mused, allowing myself to drift off momentarily. Earl was the first to move. He stepped without looking at me, knowing that I was covering his every step. He cautiously advanced toward the guy with the AK. The joyous occasion had turned to a tense one for the wedding party. My eyes darted back and forth from the shooter's face to his overall body language. I did not want to miss any sign that would prelude his possible attack. This was my first contact in a real-time semi-combat engagement. Years of training brought the responses and reaction time out to their maximum. All the training in the world, however, could not stop my heart from pounding out of my chest.

We were beginning to earn our combat experience. This was our first test on our own as peacekeepers. With hand signals and misunderstood English, Earl patiently disarmed the shooter. He was surprisingly cooperative. I too, would be tempted to relinquish my weapon had I been in his shoes. Even though the situation appeared to be diffusing we did not lower our guards. Once Earl had secured the AK and slung it over his shoulder we eased our stance marginally. Donny drew a big smile across his Cape Bretoners face. As if on cue, the wedding party gave a cheer and they resumed their festivities. Our patrol took to the road again. I filed into the rear guard position, turned on my heels, and walked backwards to cover our move away from the makeshift church. We continued patrolling into Sirač with each man once again watching their side of the road. Once in Sirač we entered the community hall. We all let out a sigh of relief.

Over the next couple of weeks we would learn that this was normal behaviour. It would take some adjusting but we would actually become calloused to it.

The L-tee and I drove endlessly it seemed. Bill was a heavy set guy and his pear shape masked his powerful frame. He was as strong as an ox through and through. He was soft spoken but was not afraid to piss in someone's cereal to get them motivated. Bill had graduated from officer's school in the middle of his class. He did not have anything to prove like some of the snotty officers I had encountered over the years. Overall, Bill Burke was a likeable guy and we became friends through the war.

Every dawn brought something new to arouse the senses, whether it was the sight of main battle tanks driving through a farmer's field or the smell of cordite from newly exploded shells drifting in on the breeze. With each trip I made in Sector West, my personal look into Croatia was bombarded with new messages for my mind to catalogue. Some of the messages were by no means new. I had smelled cordite and seen tanks in the past. The difference was that now they were all brought together to perform in this moving portrait of war. It was a real life war drama, which would soon involve 900 Canadians, playing a major contributing role.

The wind was refreshing as Burke and I cruised down the road. Our new UN flag was popping and snapping as it responded to the buffeting air. Depending on the wind, smell was usually the first of the senses to respond. This time, however, it was sight that got the less than desired honour. For the most part the grass that grew along the side of the roads was long and unkempt. It could hide many treasures or conceal some of the deadliest of killers. As we drove along the grass ahead appeared to be toppled on both sides of the blacktop. I slowed in response to the change so we could observe the different condition. Following the bent grass our eyes beheld a slaughter. In either ditch were Serb soldiers. Their bodies twisted in gruesome poses exactly where they had been rolled. The blacktop which was faded grey from prolonged exposure to the sun now had many dark, almost black, thick splotches of dried blood on it. The remainder of the scene around this massacre looked normal for The Krajina. The homes were riddled with shell holes and most had collapsed roofs. Trees waved lazily in the wind and birds flitted from branch to branch. They chirped as though these butchered wretches were not even here. We looked around speechless trying to determine what had happened as I kept our jeep rolling. I surmised that the soldiers were walking in single file on either side of the road and had been caught in a perfect ambush. It did not look like any of them had had a chance to defend themselves.

There were no visible weapons, which did not surprise me. They would have been scooped up immediately. In a mere moment, as quick as the ambush would have taken to happen, we had driven through the melee grounds. It occurred to me that they could have been executed there on the spot. That too could explain the tight in-line formation of the corpses. It was a bit overwhelming. Was it an ambush or a crime scene? I would have lots of time to ponder the scene as we drove for another nine hours. I busied myself with watching for bad guys and where the Hell we were going, only stopping momentarily to relieve ourselves or to stretch. The UNPA was vast and we covered most of it in a day. There were brief stops to confer with other crews from our company but mostly we just drove and observed the joke of a peace agreement.

Burke and I drove hundreds of miles of roads together, charting as we went. Making maps, as the UN and our Int. Sect could not provide us with any of the local area. Intel was guess-or-by-golly as virtually no maps existed. The one I carried was rolled up so as not to crease it. It was a National Geographic map I had purchased in Germany. Normal military maps we used were detailed down to within 100 metres. The map I used was detailed down to 200 kilometres. A slight 'margin of error' was noticed. I felt blessed that I had a fantastic memory for geographical features. It would save my bacon more than once as I would be regularly driving around the former Yugoslavia alone.

After a week in country Frank Steadman and I went into Daruvar. I was going in to get some film developed and Frank asked if he could join me. We drove the forty something kilometres and arrived around noon. I dropped off two rolls for developing and purchased four more rolls from the store owner, Halil. I had made his acquaintance on a previous trip with the L-tee. After my purchase we went for a walkabout. Frank had not been to Daruvar since we rolled in on the train. We walked with weapons at the ready and checked out the sights.

"Casey, come here!"

I walked across the road from the bombed out hospital in Daruvar. We had been in country a week.

"I won the lottery!" Frank brimmed with stifled energy.

"Holy shit, Frank, how did you find that out? We don't even have any satellite links yet," I said to him.

"Look."

He was going to burst with excitement. He got in close to me and looked around as if he thought we might be stuck up by thieves.

"Look, Casey, there must be millions in here."

I looked and I had to admit my eyes did pop out a bit. He held a leather bag that resembled a large doctor's satchel. In it were stacks of money. All bundled neatly with bands around them.

"You shouldn't have even touched this, Frank, it could have been booby trapped," I scolded him. As I reached in to have a closer look he quickly pulled the bag back. "Don't worry, if it's what I think it is, you can have my percentage," I said knowingly and jokingly at the same time.

"Your percentage?" His eyebrows rose, wrinkling his brow.

"Come on, I'm kidding, it's all yours, just let me look." He reluctantly opened the bag for me to inspect.

"It's what I thought, Frank."

"What's that," he asked suspiciously.

"It's worthless, you couldn't even buy a half empty skunky Pivo with this money," I confirmed.

"What?" His question was filled with angry disbelief. I patiently explained. "This is the currency they used when Yugoslavia was a country. Croatia uses Dinars now, you've seen them. They are newer looking and different colours."

"What does that mean?"

"Frank, it means you have toilet paper in your butt pack that's worth more." His face looked like I had just killed his first puppy. He was completely deflated. I instantly felt bad. I should have let him enjoy his new found wealth. As far as I was concerned there was nothing in this shithole worthy of getting excited about. He had found something and I was his killjoy. I had to do some damage control.

"Hey look at it this way Frank, you have a cool war story and an awesome souvenir."

"Ya I guess you're right. I just really wish it was still good."

"Well the truth is, is you'd have to hand it over, because that much money could end up being your death warrant if the wrong people found out."

"I never thought of it that way." He was feeling better. And so was I.

"Come on let's go."

With that I crossed back to the other side of the street and started walking back toward the only serviceable hotel. Frank took another look in the satchel, took one bundle of bills and tossed the bag into the ditch. He started walking on his side of the street just back from me in perfect spacing. I could not help but notice he was lost in his thoughts. "Pssst, hey, when we get to the hotel I'll buy," I offered to him. He smiled and gave me the thumbs up.

Two days had passed and I went back to Daruvar to retrieve my photos and negatives. Halil was a nice enough fellow and he took pride in his developing. That was all I could really ask of him. His English was choppy and heavily flavoured with what I believed was Turkish. In my travels I was constantly taking photographs. These I would have developed for my personal collection so I could pass on the copies to the other lads for Intelligence. On this particular visit to my photo-developing friend he relayed a story to me through his bloodied face that a couple HV soldiers were extorting money and any photos UN soldiers were bringing to him for developing. These, I concluded, they would use to find enemy positions. I was enraged by this fact. Halil was an honest fellow who was just trying to make a living in a not so pretty world. It was not acceptable

for the jackasses to shake him down. This would also not make a favourable news story should the media get wind of it. Not to mention that if the Serbs found out they would believe we were Ustaše and the Croats would believe we were Chetniks. Either way we would be the losers.

The following evening, I arranged to be in Daruvar to pick up my photos. Luck would have it that these two rogue soldiers were in providing Halil with a fine shake-down. As I strode in they had just begun to put the slippers to my friend. Blood was smeared across his face and his hair was messed up. Some of the products from his counters were strewn about the room. Without a second more thought the closest one to me got a full throttle butt stroke to the side of his head. My rifle butt impacted just above his cheek. The skin instantly split open and a stream of blood streaked out as he crumpled to the floor. He was out like a light. I turned to the second soldier. He was ready for me and did not appear to be afraid. He quickly closed the distance between us in an attempt to render my weapon useless. I jabbed the muzzle into his groin and he cursed in Croat. Simultaneously, using my right elbow, I leaned forward and stung his neck with all my might. He grabbed me to stop himself from falling. I lost my balance and we crashed to the tile. He managed to twist and get the upper hand. His hands now had a vice-like grip on my throat. I could feel my esophageal cartilage crinkling in his hands. My face was bursting from the strain of the battle. In a last ditch effort, I got my legs in the fetal position under his abdomen. I thrust with the force of ten men into his guts. He involuntarily squeezed all of his oxygen out of his lungs from my push spraying my face with spit and blood. I extended my legs fully and the force shot him up and off of me. He went reeling toward the large glass door that adorned the south wall. The glass shattered and he tumbled out over the low railing of Halil's balcony. I got up with the aid of my new friend and stepped out to look over the edge. Below, the soldier lay motionless in the concrete surrounded hedge. He lay motionless, although breathing, as I walked out and drove away.

I never paid another dime for my photo developing and those two butt holes strangely enough never bothered Halil again. My photos would be a good asset for the boys coming in soon. I did not need them compromised. With the main body of Canadian troops expected to be arriving within days, we would all be learning lessons that would have us paying attention and protecting things dear to us.

A LESSON IN FAITH

"Those who can make you believe absurdities can make you commit atrocities."
~VOLTAIRE

As I steered my Iltis around the final corner entering Sirač, my eyes almost bugged out of my head. Staring me straight in the face was an ominous black hole. The black hole was encased by an inch or so of steel. My eyes followed the steel encased black hole the twenty feet back to its origin. Concurrently, my senses and AFV recognition training acknowledged that I was in the sights of a Soviet T54/55 Main Battle Tank. The black hole was the muzzle of its 105mm main gun. There was nothing to do but hope that I would not be snuffed out in an exploding ball of fire. The consolation to the predicament was that it would be a quick death should they engage my soft skin jeep. My foot had not had time to let off the accelerator, which was a good thing, I thought. I quickly jogged the wheel to the left. The main armament of the tank remained motionless. A breath of relief left my mouth. The tank, although menacing in its stare, was unmanned. My Iltis manoeuvred left around the corner in response to my hand direction on the steering wheel. I scarcely took my eyes off the tank as I steered for the Sirač community hall. With a short skid I stopped crooked at the front door, I was not worried about civilian drivers being able to park, as there were none. Well not unless they were driving a tank. I forced a smile at that thought. I pushed the door of Company HQ open with my rifle.

"Has anyone noticed the T54/55 at the corner coming into town?" I questioned anyone who may have been listening. A voice echoed out of the cloakroom.

"Ya we know it's there Scotty. They will be leaving by lunch," Donny replied as though he believed what they had said. I shrugged and grabbed a swig of water from my canteen.

"Gonna take some gettin used to, this whole peacekeeping thing eh?" I commented with a chuckle.

"It sure is, buddy. This morning I woke up to that thing clattering by the front door. I didn't know whether to shit or go blind," he said laughingly.

"No doubt," I laughed in response while sliding my canteen back in its carrier on my flak jacket. "Have you seen Burke anywhere?" I asked.

"He was with the OC out back," Donny replied thumbing the air toward the rear.

"Okay thanks."

Exiting the building I wondered how long it would take to shave the edge off the anxiety and basic confusion that we were experiencing. It was so different to be in a war zone in the first place. Peacekeeping instead of warring made it even more difficult to adjust to. The state of mind required at this particular place and time was being melded on a daily basis. Only experiences could make us what we needed to be. I personally hoped the experiences would not be too painful. The photo shop was an easy learning curve compared to what the future had in store for me. I was about to be shocked by the ugliness of racial hatred and civil war.

The next morning Burke and I went out on a recce.

"Where to, L-tee?" I asked, seeking direction for our days beginning.

Without speaking, Bill thumbed the direction to the right side of the Iltis. The road took us out the east end of Sirač and past the community's cement plant. The gravel road was narrow and enveloped by over hanging trees. Rocks pinged off the fender wells as we exited the canopy that covered the narrow road. Daylight returned as the canopy of foliage broke. Standing like an ancient ruin in the centre of the opening before us was a stone monastery. It was known as the Pakra monastery. We were now approximately fifteen clicks east of Sirač and seeing the religious structure I immediately let off the throttle. Our inquisitive, almost touristy, nature took over.

"Let's check it out, Scotty," Burke said with enthusiasm.

"Roger that L-tee," was my guarded response. My gaze shifted to the neighbouring hills surrounding the area.

We dismounted before the dust had a chance to settle. Weapons at the ready we spread out and cautiously stepped through an opening in the stone fence that surrounded the holy edifice. There was an eerie silence, a silence that follows death. The steps leading up to the large iron and wood door were weathered and worn from decades of parishioner's use. With a sharp creak, that would have given Vincent Price a chill down his spine, I slowly pushed the door open. I quickly scanned the approximately forty by eighty interior. My first impression was one of an acknowledgement of Balkan history. The stone and wood combination was attractive. My second impression, however, was one of dismay. The church had been completely ransacked. It was clear that someone had looted this place with little regard for its sanctity. I could see where the beautiful tapestries had once hung. It was obvious, by the mess, that anything of value had been plundered. Nearly all the pews were missing. The remaining ones lay askew and had been broken into large splinters. The pulpit, nearly thrown through a north east facing window, hung precariously from a jagged windowsill. In the musty air clung a scent that I had not smelled since cleaning out the meat room of our old ranch with my dad years ago as a kid. Lt. Burke stood momentarily in the doorway before following me in. We both surveyed our surroundings.

"I'll check the back", I said pointing my rifle to the rear of the church. I made my way past the altar to the rear where I assumed the priest quarters would be. Opening the door to the in-house portion of the Lord's building, all holiness vanished in one rushed putrid gasp. The smell I recalled from the ranch hit my nasal passages like a hammer.

The smell of hanging meat. There before me was what I believed to be the Padre of this holy establishment. Dangling, from the less than ornate chandelier in the ceiling, was a taught rope, the other end of the rope had been strung around the priest's neck. His face was bloody and grey-blue from the obvious lack of oxygen. Frighteningly, his face had been pummelled by fists and boots before he died. His robes were so caked with dried blood it was hard to tell where they ended and his peeled skin began. The fresh air colliding with the rotting flesh of the corpse only disturbed the flies momentarily. Their buzzing wings drove straight at me and I turned back with a jerk. Instantly repulsed by the scene, vomit filled the back of my mouth. I forced myself to swallow it back down. Looking down I noticed I was standing in a stream of dried blood. Turning away, I closed the door to the scene. My strength was diminishing at the thought of lowering him from the ceiling. Somebody strung him up, somebody else could cut him down, I thought. My mind was reeling from the indignity inflicted upon this holy man. This display of evil had occurred on consecrated land. At this very moment I questioned how good could possibly ever conquer over evil. I walked back to the front door where the lieutenant now stood nonchalantly observing my moves.

"Clear," I said mechanically. We left the confines of the building and walked back to the roadway. I was relieved to be out of there. We clambered back into the Iltis. "Impressive in its day I bet," Bill said admiringly looking back at the workmanship. "Yes, sir, impressive," I replied. I was trying to spare my friend the gruesome reality inside the stone walls.

"Let's head back West, it looks uninhabited out this way," Bill ordered over the pounding silence. I was relieved to just get out of the area.

I sat silently for the rest of the day unless spoken to. I was locked in a personal battle with faith. I had not been raised with religion. Regardless of that, I could not get my head around how anyone could commit such a vile and disgusting act. The Padre was a man who had selflessly devoted his life to caring and saving others. Sure I did not know him personally but he was a priest just the same and I understood what that meant. If a human could do this, I thought, they were capable of anything. Thoughts of the Nazis came to mind. Both the world wars had started in the Balkans. I knew that the Yugoslav people had been some of the most prolific augmenters of slaughter in Concentration camps located right here in Yugoslavia in WW2, killing their own people by the hundreds of thousands, more so, than in the more well known German death camps like Auschwitz or Dachau. Now I was exposed to this depravity in, the once again at war, Yugoslavia. Was history repeating itself again?

Back in Sirač, as evening fell upon us, I happened upon the local Hrvatska Policija commander in the bar. I stepped out on a limb and instructed him to remove the body of the priest and bury him appropriately or I would have to report it to the UN.

As was becoming normal, I was either awake before the sun came up or someone woke me before it had a chance to come up. I had gone to sleep at 01:15hrs and this time Lt. Burke woke me at 0335hrs, putting an end to the couple of hours of tossing and turning re-living the discovery of the priest hanging.

"Come on Scotty we have to go out to Gornje Borki and do a recce for that portion of the sector today." I pulled back the protective Velcro cover and looked at my watch.

"Great two hours and fifteen minutes. Are you fucking kidding me?" I looked up in startled response to what I had just said aloud.

Thankfully the L-tee. had already left the doorway before he could hear my comment. I had gotten in late after doing a documents run to HQ at Camp Polom. It was common place for me to be out late and alone. How the Hell was I going to function, let alone be aware of my surroundings, if I could not get any sleep. I shook it off and welcomed the end to the dreams. I quickly poured a coffee down my throat and had a piece of toast. As I was just finishing the pre-trip inspection of my jeep, Bill showed up packing his Junior General's Kit and piled his fighting order into the back seat. A Junior General's Kit contains all the items officers need to keep themselves organized, like pens, pencils, ruler, maps, and any other documents that pertain to mission tasks. Fighting order is the harness infantrymen wear that contains all the essential things they need immediately in combat, extra magazines full of ammunition, canteen of water, bayonet, knife, fork, spoon (KFS) set, C-5 knife and a butt pack that in peace time carried raingear, socks and foot powder. Here in Croatia I filled mine with extra mags of ammo. I fired the Iltis up and we exited the camp.

The trip to Gornje Borki was quiet. The sun was getting ready to come up and begin warming the earth. It's red glow silhouetting the ridge to the east. Although it had not broken over the crest of the mountains it was bright enough to see without headlights. I preferred to drive without them as it made us less of a target. White light even from a small flashlight can be seen for miles. The route would take us on the same road that the monastery was located on. Cringing at the thought, I tried to enjoy the beauty of the over-hanging branches above the road. I could smell the fragrant sap in the trees. It reminded me of riding my bicycle down the dirt roads at home with the scent of the Blue Spruce and Jack-pine trees accompanied by bumble-bees and Whiskey Jacks flying by. I tried to race them as I steered along. I focused on anything to avoid thinking of the monastery's gruesome inhabitant. We raced by in a hail of rocks and dust and my skin shriveled with goose bumps. In the same way kids hold their breath in childhood games when crossing bridges, so I held mine going past the church. After a quick kilometre I re-focused on the road. We were getting closer to the remote village. My daydream was terminated by the now overwhelming smell of decay that was floating on the breeze. I scanned the woods for anything out of the ordinary, a glimpse of something shiny, or movement, anything that would show signs of an ambush. Shape, sheen, shine, silhouette, and movement were the key elements in divulging your own position. Consequently, it was also what we looked for to find the enemy. The foliage by the road opened up and a few homes appeared on either side of it. I pulled the jeep to a stop at a wooden bridge. Lt. Burke and I were on our guard. I stepped out of the driver's seat and grabbed my C-7 rifle, the Canadian version of the M-16 rifle used by our American neighbours. I routinely laid it in the crook of the mirror bracket and the door frame, as it was easy to access from there should I need to engage the bad guys while driving. Bill grabbed his and stepped out as well. We were alone. Should we get into a firefight with any hostiles there was no covering fire, no F-18s fighter jets or 'fast air' as we called them, no mortars or artillery, just us. We depended on each other's skills to keep us safe. We each trusted the other profoundly. Through this trust we forged a friendship. We protected each other not just from the bad guys but from ourselves. When times were tough we would not let the other quit.

I side-stepped the bridge and carefully chose my footing to have a look at the underside. The soft earth squished under my feet. We had to be very careful when stepping off the pavement as the Serbs and Croats had indiscriminately laid anti-personnel and antitank mines. The ground on either side of a bridge or "choke point" is the perfect place to use anti-personnel mines. It is the unwary who veer off the beaten path that are bitten by this type of trap. In our use of mines, all mine locations had to be marked on a map with their exact location. This was done so our own troops would not step on them and so they could be removed later and would not be a continual hazard after the conflict. Like wars all over the world this was not practiced in the Balkans. Many military leaders were not educated in this practice, only learning as they went after being thrust into combat to protect their independence.

As I moved forward Bill covered my movement by scanning all the windows and doorways. I cautiously moved up to the underside of the bridge and had a look to see if it was booby trapped. It was clear. Retracing my steps, I got back onto the hard surface and gave the 'all clear' thumbs up. I found some old sandbags stacked up at the end of the bridge. I knelt down to make myself a smaller target and employed the bags as cover. Bill was now looking at his rudimentary map which he had spread out on the passenger seat. I took the moment to pull out my camera, all the while watching. I snapped a photo of him standing by the jeep. The jeep was framed by the bridge. Content, I put the camera away and stood up. I walked backwards to the jeep, covering my withdrawal from the bridge. I slid back into the seat and laid the C-7 back into its crook, only now the butt lay in my lap for quicker response. I started the jeep and we slowly rolled across the bridge. The smell in the air this whole time carried a sickly sweet smell. I was pretty sure it was the smell of death. I did not know how right I was till we pulled into the centre of town. We climbed out once again, and proceeded to walk along the south side of the village. I took the lead and turned in between two of the houses heading to the backyards. As I rounded the corner of the cinder block home my eyes narrowed at the grisly scene.

There in the garden were six sun baked swollen bodies. Four of them had stomachs bloated with rotten air. The other two had been deflated, from having been eaten to varying degrees by wild dogs or other scavengers. The only sound was my laboured breathing and the drone of a thousand flies. My stomach was motionless with no urge to vomit.

We continued our patrol through the village and mentally documented the scene. I could not bring myself to photograph it. This would definitely be something I would live with for the rest of my life, I thought. No need for pictures. As I walked I took a rolling tally. The body count was around fifteen. Amongst the civilian bodies were the domestic animals, cows, horses, and dogs. All executed for being Serb or Croatian or Muslim. I was not sure which they were. All I knew for sure was they were dead. I struggled to find some point of reference for this waste of life. As a boy, I had seen moose, deer, and cattle carcasses of on our ranch. Slaughter was a fact of life on the farm, and as a rite of passage I had taken my place and participated in the process. Here I was, twenty-five, and a very long way from the civility of the ranch. I had seen dead people before in accidents and such, but this was really over the top. The Serbian soldiers in the ditch just days earlier, the Padre less than 24 hours before, and now here before me lay dozens of corpses. Their rigor frozen limbs pointed in odd directions. Sun baked brown rotten skin on their faces. Contorted faces with empty eye sockets that seemingly stared at me as if I was in some creepy horror film. A noise to my right made me instinctively hold my breath. My ears tingled as they absorbed every sound. My pulse shot through the roof and my heart pounded as though it would explode. My arms reacted with force as they went from the ready position to a full on aim at the door to my right. The door creaked again. My rifle actually felt like an extension of my arm. In live fire range training that was how we were to feel our rifles, as an extension. There was no wind. My skin bristled with goose bumps. The door once again creaked. I could hear a slight disturbance inside the house. It was barely audible. In the bit of Croatian I had learned, combined with English, I commanded,

"Ruku vies, hands up!" The door remained motionless. We stood fixed on the entryway.

There was some rustling and my grip tightened awaiting the enemy rush. Suddenly the door moved but opened only six inches. Two rats the size of footballs came running out hissing at us.

"Fuck," Bill exclaimed, as he stepped back.

I fired a burst into the second one and it writhed in a death roll. The first was fleet of foot and disappeared around the corner. My body felt charged with electricity. That was our only contact with the living in that town.

It was later that evening while I was having a cold water shower from a jerry-can suspended from a tree that I realized that other than my command to, 'come out with your hands up', and Bill's profane outburst, we had not spoken to each other the rest of that whole day. Not on the drive back to Sirač camp. Not as we sat and ate a cold meal, nor later on when we drove to HQ. Nothing was said. We were lost in our thoughts at what we had seen that day. My mind would not stop playing the movie reel of the day's events as I lay in the dark. From my cot I listened to the sentries whispered conversations. I think I drifted off to sleep around one in the morning.

I woke the following morning around 04:00hrs. I could not sleep anymore. Visions of the bodies had haunted me all night. Their vacant eyes stared at me. Rubbing my eyes, I muttered to myself,

"Three hours should be plenty." I was getting better with the sleep deprivation. With an eye half open, my right hand slid along the aluminium cot rail until it found my C-7 rifle lying tight beside me on the cot, right where it had been since I had lain down. I swung myself up to the sitting position and I picked my rifle up. I cleared it by removing the magazine and ejecting the round into my hand. I replaced it in the magazine. Even though I had just cleaned it three and a half hours ago I was going to give it a quick check. A soldier's weapon is his life line. It is the second most important tool in his equipment list, second only to the soldier's mind. Everything was as I had left it. I replaced the mag and chambered a round, the breech closed tightly with a comforting metallic sound. I then slid the breech-block back a quarter pull length and ensured that the round was there. Heel handing the forward assist to ensure the breech-block was hammered tight into the chamber. To finish the routine, I closed the ejection port cover and checked the safety. I quickly pulled my combat pants and shirt on. Carrying my rifle in one hand I slipped out the back door of the Sirač community hall we now inhabited. As soon as I stepped out the doorway my rifle was in the ready position. My eyes began searching for anything out of the norm, anything human. I strained for anything that represented a threat, the glint off of glass or the sheen of metal in the bush denoting a rifle barrel. No one at home could envision that taking a squirt could be so dangerous. At the back of the building we had piss tubes dug in for disposing of our minor bathroom jobs. A piss tube is a stove pipe dug into the ground with a couple feet protruding above ground. It's topped with a screen to stop bugs and cigarette butts and any other foreign debris from entering the tube. These were designed to allow the ground to filter our urine in the event of no plumbing. As with many war zones public infrastructure is one of the first things to come to a screeching halt. We had no plumbing at this point. I re-entered the building and went back to my cot in the corner of the main room where we NCMs and Officers shared the space. There was no luxury for the officers to have their own quarters yet. We all knew that there was safety in our numbers. Each of us, regardless of rank, understood that.

I was making slight, perhaps almost futile, adjustments to my personal thought processes in dealing with the environment and the people here. I was also making changes to my fighting order. We were now wearing useless flak jackets provided merely for morale support. We knew they would not stop much more than a 'out of trajectory' piece of shrapnel. The higher-ups in Ottawa must have thought it would look good for TV. They did it to pacify their constituents I am sure. The flak jackets were about as effective at stopping bullets or flak as the rain jackets that had been ok'd by Ottawa were at keeping out the rain. It was joked that the officer who tested the raingear put it on as he walked from his car to his office at NDHQ. He did not get wet in the one-minute stroll so therefore it must work. I completed the changes to my gear. Nodding, I smiled,

"Now for the headspace adjustment. Don't trust anyone who isn't Canadian," I said to myself. "Check. Hell, going to the pisser is dangerous enough," I said still talking to myself. I grabbed a quick MRE (meal ready to eat), nodded to Lt. Burke that I was heading out to the Iltis and stepped back outside.

Donny Bralorne was already outside at his Iltis. We shook hands and glanced over each other's shoulders. I checked my jeep over visually, looking for any signs of tampering, even though we took turns doing sentry duty twenty-four hours a day. A soldier never takes it for granted that his gear or vehicles have not been buggered with. In a regular war situation, as soldiers, we would deliberately do it to our enemies and succeed so why would we be so complacent on a peacekeeping mission to think they would not try to do it to us?

"Sleep alright, buddy," Donny asked. I shrugged and said,

"Just like you did, with one of my eyes closed."

"What's the mission for today? He asked.

"We're going to recce a place to the east of here. A couple of streams meet out in the middle of fucking nowhere. The Major figures it may be a resupply route and that we should check it out," I stated.

"Who's going," Donny asked with enthusiasm.

"Sorry, buddy, it's me and the L-tee. I heard him talkin to your Sunray, you are headin to the south, and the others are hitting the other points of the compass."

"Well you wouldn't want us all together havin a fuckin party now would ya?" Donny retorted sarcastically.

WHIZ-SNAP!!!! SNAP!!! SNAP!!! SNAP!!!

Our laughter was cut short as shots from an indiscriminate shooter cracked past our heads. We readied our weapons and took up kneeling fire positions back to back as we were unsure where the shots had come from.

"You see anything? I breathed the words.

"Nothin," Donny said, the venom rolling off his tongue.

"Fucking cowards."

The two other drivers had scrambled outside and were ready to do battle but it was over. Just as we started to come down another volley of automatic fire arched up into the sky followed by a bunch of hollering. Donny and I walked up the side of the building scanning every inch of the bush and through it onto the street ahead. Earl Bledsoe and Glenn Downton, the other drivers, followed and the four of us proceeded out to the gravel strew street. We traversed the main road of Sirač heading east toward the local bar.

"Zero five and these dumb motherfuckers are out here drinking and blastin the place up? I don't think so!"

Earl and Glenn took up fire positions on the far side of the street with good views of the bar. As Donny and I walked up a couple of Croatian militiamen stumbled out into the street, AKs in hand. The two drunks saw us and the one closest to the door started to raise his rifle, Donny was already in 'ready' stance and had him dead-to-rights. I watched with amusement as the Croats right trouser leg darkened. Too much Staroeško Pivo and šljivovica, the local beer and moonshine, and knowing that he was about to die, was too much for his alcohol saturated bladder. The other was sweating profusely and was not sure what to do.

"Ruku vies," Donny said calmly taking the lead. "Hands up," he repeated in English.

"Anyone speak English?" A woman inside the bar called out that she did.

"Tell these men to lay down their weapons. We will not harm them if they follow orders. We are here to keep the peace. They are no longer allowed to carry weapons in this area," Donny said matter-of-factly.

The woman took a few seconds digesting what he had said before translating to the drunken soldiers. My thumb silently pushed the fire selector to automatic in the event that she screwed up the translation and said we were helping the Serbs and were going to execute them for their crimes.

"Ne pushka, no weapons," I said with mild irritation at her slow response.

She spoke softly, in an almost motherly fashion, to them. There was a short pause after she spoke to the drunks. Slowly Pissboy lowered his rifle first and placed it on the ground. The other fellow was a bit more hesitant and maybe a hair braver now in his drunkenness. He stood his ground glaring at Donny. Glenn, across the street, helped the poor drunken Rambo make his decision by whistling a short soft tune. The glare in his eye softened to resolve when he realized he was dead if he so much as flinched.

"Tell them to step back, please," Donny asked.

The woman spoke and the men backed up. I stepped forward and picked up the AKs. By now two of our Lieutenants walked up to the scene. Without looking away Donny filled them in on the situation. The Canadian officers requested the Policija be called and they could deal with the two disorderly soldiers.

After the police showed up we gave them the info, handed the AKs to them and went back to the community hall. I knew those two would be driven back to the police station where they would continue drinking, this time with the police. Their weapons would be handed back and they would be sent back to the front line, possibly to shoot at us again. All of which was common practice here.

"Crazy shit eh buddy?" Donny said shaking his head.

I nodded in agreement. It was a reality to us on the ground. The UN back in New York still had not realised the scope of what we were involved in. Traditional peacekeeping roles are defined by warring factions that had already come to some sort of peaceful settlement. Such was not the case here for us as we had to deal with random groups of rebel style soldiers that did not want to relinquish power. We were also finding that when either side did not like the way the process was evolving they quite often took it to the battlefield again. If a genuine peace settlement had already been reached, the tasks of peacekeeping would have been neither, onerous or particularly daunting. As the initial days passed and the opposing forces became used to our fleeting presence their battles returned to normal. It was frustrating to watch. With the small advance party that we were, there was little we could do to tame the major fighting. We would have an arduous task of cooling this region down even with a full Battle Group, BG. It would be a blessing when the BG was fully on the ground. Until then it was just us, the Dirty Dozen, as we jokingly called ourselves from the Lee Marvin movie.

To the south of Sirač was the Dragović road. Although the front line meandered and changed daily, it was considered the frontline for much of the first month of our mission. It took time and reckoning, but we discovered that the ethnic groups were spread out in pockets across the Sector. This is why the front line moved constantly. The battles moved from pocket to pocket purging the inhabitants from their homes. It was our elementary education of ethnic cleansing at work. In our second week on the ground Burke and I were conducting a recce of the Dragovič area.

It was a cloudy day and a thick spring fog had fallen over the battlefield. We were cruising at 50 km/h over the shell pocked pavement with the jeep's tires splashing small amounts of water from the craters as we rolled along. Traveling south we came to the intersection of the Dragovič road and the Sirač connector. I turned left and headed south east towards Španovica. Slowing down to 20km/h, we could have a good look at the existing Croat and Serbian arsenals. The info

we picked up today would be beneficial for enforcing the peace plan, although the fog was really hampering our view. We were now five minutes past our turn onto the Dragovič Line. The fog had become so thick that visibility was down to fifty metres. Burke and I both knew that the opposing forces would be on edge with the fog. We were in dangerous territory now.

"Neither side will be able to see our white jeep in this slop." I said with concern.

"I don't like this either," Burke agreed squinting through the haze.

"Well we're kinda committed now, eh," I reported with a sigh.

"We are. Just keep driving slow. At least that way we won't sound aggressive."

"Wilco boss."

We crept along in the abyss until partially destroyed cinder block buildings appeared on either side indicating we were in a village of some sort. Our jeep rolled along past a couple of partially destroyed buildings. Bullet marks pocked their exteriors. Small piles of rubble sat in front of them. The fog grew thicker. Without any warning whatsoever, came the scariest sound I had heard to date. The ear shattering, shrill screams, of an M-63 Plamen rocket launcher. From in between two buildings to our left, came at least twenty searing rockets. The sound and flashes took less than ten seconds. The volley of deadly projectiles had been unleashed right over our heads. The rocket's sparks and residual fuel burning off right over the hood of our Iltis.

"Holy fuck," I blurted as I ducked my head in uncontrollable reflex.

"Assholes!" Bill exclaimed in angry shock.

This style of rocket launcher could fire a volley of thirty-two rockets in rapid succession up to almost nine kilometres away and they had the same devastating impact as a 105mm artillery shell. Within seconds, just ahead of us, another launcher fired a volley of explosive needles. The acrid smoke of the launches hung invisibly in the thick foggy air, the smell the only clue left behind. I continued driving 20km/h fighting my instinct to race out of the area. With almost every mortar, artillery, or rocket attack came the WWI Canadian invention, Counter Battery Fire. I knew the longer we stayed in the area the greater the chances were of our being in the middle of retaliatory fire. Bill looked over at me. His face grimaced with the question he put forth.

"You know what's coming eh, Scotty?" The wrinkles in his forehead gave away his earlier calm demeanour.

We could hear the explosions echoing from their targets only a couple of kilometres away.

"If they follow doctrine, yup I do," I replied. The goose bumps began growing on my arms.

"There should be a firing equation drawn up by now."

"Yes, sir, and within half a minute there should be bombs in the air."

"This jeep runs good at twenty K," he said, giving me a hint at where this was going.

"It does." I agreed.

"Do you think it will do one hundred and twenty K's?"

"Only one sure way to find out sir," I responded knowing it would be a stretch for the sewing machine engine under the hood.

Power was only one thing in the long list the Bombardier product lacked.

"Okay well turn around here and let's make it do that," Bill said without emotion.

"Now?" I questioned, gritting my teeth as I accidentally turned the wipers on full speed.

In the distance we could hear the thuuumping sounds of mortars been fired.

"Yes now would be really good," the urgency cracking his voice.

I had already begun aggressively turning halfway through his delivery. The narrow Iltis nosed down into the opposite ditch almost rolling over. Leaning to the opposite side, as if to help stop the rollover, it came back up on the road flailing mud from its tires as I stomped viciously on the tiny throttle pedal. Carrying straight on would have been an easier escape route. However, we had to turn around or face being cut off from our brothers to the north. My foot was rammed so hard to the floor that it felt like it would bend the flimsy sheet metal floor. We accelerated and were now flying down the road in front of the HV defensive position, navigating potholes and concertina wire, I was trying to stay calm, which is difficult at the best of times when driving an Iltis this fast. The fog was now the least of our worries, as I propelled our vehicle at break neck speed through the soup, as we were now trying to evade an impending mortar attack. Apparently the bad guys were all hiding in their bunkers because we drove down the frontline with not a single shot fired at us. At 120kmh and with the cover of the fog they would have had a hard time hitting us anyway. As I manoeuvred sharply, the jeep four-wheel drifted around the corner at the junction, the first bombs began smashing into their targets only a few hundred metres behind us. The tires of the jeep howled with the torture from the tight turn. With my foot once again jammed tight to the floor the jeep wobbled on its narrow chassis. The concussion of the detonating rounds pounded at our bodies. In my mirror I watched as the fiery explosions flashed bright rings in the air only to be swallowed by the fog. I slowed down and we stopped a kilometre to the north, parking on a hillside facing back toward the battle so we could observe the carnage. We gazed upon the scene at the Dragovič Line with our jaws hanging somewhat open. The battle was in full swing as mortar and artillery rounds pounded the buildings that lined either side of the road. The flashes exploded brightly followed by earth shaking concussions that we could feel as they resonated to our lofty vantage point. The white blanket of fog had now been replaced by a much greyer version. Small arms fire began to chatter from under the smoke and fog blanket. Tracer-rounds flashed upwards through the fog cover and burned till they tumbled from sight. Muffled screams of men in pain and panic echoed up the hillside.

"My God," were the words that escaped from Bill's hanging jaw.

"Better them than us," I muttered, in hope that we would not face the same kind of shelling.

"Amen," Bill agreed.

"Some fucking peacekeeping mission this is." I added in disgust.

"Let's go," he said knowingly patting my shoulder.

We made our way to the western boundary of Sector West. In contrast to earlier in the day it was refreshingly quieter here. The fog had burned off by the time we got to the boundary. Senior citizens were making their way along from one village to the next on farm tractors ignorant of the battle that raged to the east. Others walked carrying only what they could on their backs. I could not help but think they were an uneducated lot, not really capable of understanding what was happening to them. I suppose that was my own naïveté. If anyone really knew what was happening to them, it would be they. How the Hell could I know. I may not have come from money but I did not have my homeland torn apart either. I had a home and three square meals a day. These poor bastards were lucky to eat three times a week. I was feeling somewhat humbled by their loss, when I had so much. I lowered my head in silence. I lowered it in shame for my thoughts.

LOTTO TICKET?

"There may be a few isolated incidents, but a general armed conflict will not erupt."
~ALIJA IZETVEGOVIC

With only one of many peace agreements in place, the Battle Group had its hands full with pushing the HV and JNA apart. The UN could spend as much money on paper and pens as it wanted. The reality was that the actual peace agreements were being hammered out by us on the ground. Every day we would venture out onto the highly contested battle grounds armed with antique weaponry and blue helmets to meet with all levels of ranks from both sides. Speaking with even the junior soldiers in the conflict was crucial. This was done to ensure that the peace message was making it to the lower levels as well. We could not assume that the senior staff of either side would be completely upfront with their respective subordinates. Today, like most of these early days in The Krajina, would prove to be no different. The Lt. and I were accompanied by a local Croatian translator. The UN had secured funds to assist translators in return for their services. This was our first opportunity to employ a translator. I was somewhat apprehensive having a local on board. Personally I did not trust any of the indigenous people. Having them work with us was a necessary thing but it did not change the way I felt about having them in too close. After some conversations with the translators I softened my position toward them realizing they wanted peace as much as anyone. In later days we considered it a treat to have a translator along as we did not get the service on a regular basis.

Our recent intelligence update had told us there was a considerable build-up of JNA troops in the area of Staro Petro Selo. Homes were set ablaze or dynamited marking the ethnic cleansing of Muslims from the town was underway. In response the JNA buildup, the HV was moving more of its forces in to the area. Even though the Croats and Muslims had a loose agreement to fight the Serbs this move was done, not to protect the Muslims, but rather to seize any opportunity to increase Croatian land title. Under the circumstances having the ability to get our peace message across without mistake would be crucial. With the info regarding the increased troop movements, BG HQ at Camp Polom requested a recce of the area. Call sign 21 got the job, so Burke and I headed

69

north towards Daruvar to pick up the translator. We both started to chuckle with the sight of our new verbal addition. Beside the main gate dressed in navy blue slacks, a white long sleeve dress shirt covered by a Canadian issue flak jacket and topped off with a UN blue American Kevlar helmet, stood the translator, all one hundred and sixty pounds and six foot eight of him.

"Look at that long-legged streak of misery," I said, shaking my head in mock dismay. "I've seen more meat in a chicken's in-step," I said with a laugh.

The Lt. whacked my arm.

"Be nice, Corporal, he may try and eat us," Burke chortled.

I swung around outside the compound to avoid having to go through the formality of checking in with security. Narrowly missing his head our translator exited simultaneously as the Vandoo sentry lifted the gate as quickly and as high as he could. Lt. Burke greeted him with a seated hand shake and he introduced me.

"My name is Mirko," he said, showing a grin filled with semi-rotten teeth.

"You can call me Casey," I acknowledged him with a nod. I watched with amazement as he climbed in. With the skill and flexibility of a master Yogi he contorted his extended frame into the back seat of our jeep with ease.

From here we began our swing back down south to the reported hot spot. The skipper briefed our translator on our mission. Listening in I drove with a purpose, sometimes causing our guest to gasp in fear. To go fast was to make for a harder target to hit. We passed a couple of other UN Iltis' from the Vandoos

Alpha Company going the other way. They would be the last Canadians we'd meet for awhile. The farther south we got the more on our own we became. The blue United Nations flag flying high at the top of our Iltis' radio antennae snapped sharply in the wind. An hour later we rolled down a dusty bit of paved road to where we could see HV troops milling about just inside the cover of the tree line on the north side of the road. We could have been cut to ribbons by the amount of troops skulking about in the shadows of the woods. We had caught them completely off guard. Luckily for us, we were greeted by what is typical with poorly disciplined soldiers, silence. As we pulled into their defensive position a handful struggled clumsily for their weapons. Most of them looked at us with a dazed and confused look. Lt. Burke and I maintained our composure so as not to embarrass them openly, anything else could cause a knee jerk reaction firefight. Dismounting we carried our weapons with a relaxed hold of the receiver group. We did this to lower the threat response to our impromptu visit. It was humorous to think our visits could be unexpected when the bad guys knew full well we would be calling. The skipper and I stood and watched with amusement as the human pretzel flapped his gangly legs out of the back seat. By now the local commander walked up to within twenty feet of us and he stood defiantly with his hands on his hips. I imagined that he had seen WW2 footage and was emulating the famous 'Patton stance' with both hands firmly placed on two pearl handled revolvers. I turned my head and rolled my eyes in reaction to his pose.

"No Serb sniper threat or he'd already be dead," I said letting my thoughts out.

"Pompous ass," Bill said quietly.

I moved a short distance away to a group of his soldiers. I tried to get a feel for how the junior soldiers were doing by hand gestures and my terrible grasp of Croat to this point. The Lt. and the Pretzel finished the distance with a few steps and were now standing face to face with the Croatian company commander. Greetings were exchanged and the formalities began. I got a three-part education. First, some soldiers thought we were helping the Serbs and that we should

not be trusted. Second, some thought we were there to help them kill the Serbs. Lastly, and almost more disturbingly, was that some soldiers did not want the war to end because they would have to go back to work. Those were the fellows I was particularly concerned about, as a man with no desire for things to return to a normal peace was dangerous.

As the translator repeated in Croatian what the Lt. was detailing, I could see the local commander becoming agitated. In response, the flurry of words that flew from his lips appeared angrier, due to the spit that sprayed from his contorted orifice. It was really quite simple: we wanted him to move his company-size unit and he wanted to stay put and kill as many Serbs as possible. My eyes picked up some movement to our left flank. Slowly turning my head, and looking down so as not to draw attention, I saw six or seven soldiers setting up in line in the deep grass just out from the trees. Dirty rotten bastards, I thought. It was obvious that we were being set up for a swathing. I calmly turned back to the audible melee and after two attempts caught Bill's attention. I gave him the thumbs down for enemy, and showed him a seven count on my fingers for how many, while nodding my head to the left flank for direction.

With those hand signals I discreetly told him about our company. Lt. Burke held his temper, and quietly told the commander we were on to his cronies in the grass, and to withdraw his ambush men immediately, explaining to him that he would be very disappointed by the outcome if we did not make it back to our camp, how it would be viewed by the international community and the sanctions that would follow. That he would be the one everyone would remember as the reason behind their hardships and possibly for the loss of the war. The translator was sweating profusely with the realization he could be cut down along with us if he did not translate well. I could only imagine that what the translator was feeling was akin to being in the middle of a bar fight. The warlord's eyes showed his surprise. He looked about and saw his men. He snapped his fingers to the men and waved them off. They did not move. It was common for the commanders of these units not to have complete control over their men. His anger at them intensified and they quickly retreated. These rogues would be disciplined as soon as we left and one or two would probably be shot to make a point. That was okay with me.

The verbal onslaught from the HV commander was met by calm collected words from Lt. Burke that continued to passively inform him that they would have till tomorrow morning to pull back and meet up with his higher unit. From that point they would work with local HV and police. Under the watchful eye of the UN, they would disarm and dismantle, or fall under direct control of the next higher HV command who we already had reined in. The commander was obviously furious with the thought of relinquishing his command. With the translator doing his best he and Burke got the warlord to succumb to the next HV command. He agreed to be clear of the area by ten in the morning. He needed the extra time. Lt. Burke made the concession in good faith.

They shook hands and we carefully withdrew. The warlord's face wrinkled as he watched the Pretzel knot himself up again in his bid to get back in the Iltis. The drive back to Camp Polom was less than quiet after Burke congratulated the translator. It was interesting to have him along as it gave me the opportunity to pick his brain for the political reality of what was really happening here from his perspective.

From his rendition of events, coupled with my investigations, I concluded that Slobodan Milošević had more or less orchestrated the collapse of Yugoslavia for his own personal gain in early 1991. There were a number of other players in the dissection of Yugoslavia including Franjo Tučman who was the elected Prime Minister of Croatia, wanting it to stay that way he refused to publicly admit that they were at war with the Serb population. Milan Babič was a Serbian Nationalist strong arm, and he too wanted control of The Krajina. Milošević's plans were picked up and expanded on by Radovan Karadčič a year later in 1992. Karadčič wanted to carve up Bosnia and Herzegovina for as much control as he could acquire. It was as if they all conspired to take what they could at whatever the cost. Essentially, we were here to watch over the Serb and Muslim civilian population, as the Croatian HV had already gained major control over the region, in part, by way of killing those who opposed. In much the same fashion as the Serbs were concurrently cleansing Bosnia. Once Croatia was established as a country, in the eyes of the European Community and the United Nations, the Serbs and Muslims would be considered fair game for removal.

A couple weeks went by and Bill and I were racking up the clicks, along with accumulating many images of pain and suffering. Before the main body of the Battle Group arrived Lt. Burke and I were out doing a recce in the southern portion of Sector West. There was a road we travelled with some frequency. By virtue of it being the only road, it led us to other areas of the sector. On this particular day we were accompanied by two other Iltis' and their teams. There had been some intentional tampering with the road. An abiti had been constructed. An abiti is an obstruction built specifically to deter or completely stop any advance. This one was poorly made, with only four large Aspens, fallen criss-cross over each other. It wouldn't stop anyone with the determination to advance. The officers and drivers provided security and labour in shifts to remove this attempted blockade. It was good for the six of us to work together for a common goal. The joint effort removed any NCO/Officer, us and them, mentality. It took us a half hour with swiftly used axes and sweat to open up the road. We mounted up and drove off through the disassembled roadblock. After driving for about fifteen kilometres we were met by a Combat Engineer sergeant standing in the middle of the road with a puzzled look on his face. I could hear him asking his question before we even came to a stop.

"Where the Hell did you guys come from? Oh I'm sorry, sir," he said as he recognised Burke's officer rank.

I raised my arm and pointed my thumb in the direction we had just come from. Past the Engineer sergeant's bulky frame, I could see the road was pocked with holes and piles of soil across its entirety. There was a detachment of engineer soldiers with handheld mine detectors walking slowly waving them side to side methodically. I blinked in shock. On the shoulders of the road,

two more engineers were lying flat on their bellies. The bayonets in their hands were prodding the ground on an angle searching for that metallic feeling: contact with a mine. The sergeant's concern now became evident to me.

"We've been using this road for the last ten days now, on and off, anyways." I said.

Sweat started to bead under my UN ball cap as hindsight smashed me in the face.

Confirming what we had just figured out, the sergeant said,

"We got word last night from a local that they were afraid to take this road because it was mined. So we came and so far we've pulled twenty-two big boys."

"Big boys?" one of the officers asked.

"Ya, TMN-46's. Anti-tank mines, old Russian junk. These guys meant to blow some shit up for awhile now and in a big way, some of them were double stacked," he replied.

"For awhile you say?" I asked.

"Yuppers, usually you can see traces of where they've been placed, but we could not see where they were so we brought out the mine detectors. They've been here for awhile that's for sure." I looked at the skipper. The look in his eyes told me we had experienced parallel epiphanies.

"Lottery ticket, anyone?" I said trying to deflect how close we had repeatedly been to being blown to pieces.

"Is it safe to proceed from here?" Bill asked. The sergeant scoffed,

"Yes sir, we've already cleared where we're walking. It's our favourite

SOP," he said smiling sarcastically.

"Let's get going then Cpl. Casey."

THUMP THUMP

"In war, truth is the first casualty."
~AESCHYLUS

Three more days and many kilometres of patrolling later, the main body of troops arrived. Lt. Burke and I met the train at the Daruvar train station where we had arrived three weeks earlier. The scene appeared to be orderly chaos with troops rushing around in an attempt to get their gear squared away. Vehicles were being off loaded from the flat railcars, and of course the sergeants were barking orders. The semi-confusion was compounded by the fact the language being spoken was predominately French.

Lt. Burke and I strode through the crowd looking for someone from November Company. We finally found our Pl. Warrant Officer, Rob Goddard. He was from Canada's East coast, and considered a naturally good soldier with a confidence not to be reckoned with. WO Goddard was also gifted in the martial art of Judo. After a strong hand shake from both of us welcoming him to Croatia, the Lt. gave him a warning order and basic directions on how to get to our camp in Sirač. I took a moment and spoke briefly with my buddy, Sam Sullivan. I could not believe my ears as he told me that the guys had no ammo. I welcomed him to Croatia by giving him a couple of my full mags until he received his ammo upload. After watching the crowd for a little longer Lt. Burke and I went into downtown Daruvar to monitor the locals' reactions to the increased UN troop level.

We stopped in at the only hotel that had managed to avoid being completely destroyed, sat down, had a bite to eat with a Staroeško Pivo. The locals eyed us with a look that I could not quite put words to. Perhaps I offered the same in return. My look was one of interest but also one of apprehension. I assumed that anyone of them could be packing heat and was just aching to kill a foreign soldier. They were capable of killing their neighbours, so why should I have believed they would not kill me at the drop of a hat. And why not, we were trespassers in a war torn country, their country.

Before departing we stopped at the make shift police station and Lt. Burke had a liaison meeting with the Croatian police and informed them of our incident at the bar the previous day. One more stop at the photo shop and it was off to Sirač. We arrived back in camp at about 15:30hrs.

"We won't be doing anything special, so if you want to relax for a bit, go ahead," Lt. Burke informed me.

"You're sure, sir?"

"For sure, orders will be at 18:00 hours, but I don't think you and I will be heading anywhere till tomorrow, early."

"Okay well that sounds great. If you need anything you know where to find me, sir." With that I walked to the 5pl. tent.

While Burke and I were doing our liaison trip earlier, the troops had moved from the rail yard to the Sirač school grounds. We had done a recce of it earlier in the week. The officers decided it would work as our Company base. The boys had set up four modular tents that would comfortably house thirty men each. After the shit I had already witnessed I was quite surprised that our officers had agreed to place the tents in tight formation. I thought it would have been better if they were spread out somewhat. I walked into the canvas structure with my gear that I had packed earlier in the day and picked my spot opposite the door. Not beside the door, too much traffic, but still easy to exit should I have to. I folded my cot out and placed my ruck at the head to use as a pillow for now, and I did not fuss with it, there would be time to get comfortable later. I sat back watching the guys get their gear squared away. An hour earlier, while Burke and I were still driving, Canadian Major-General Lewis Mackenzie, who was merely by luck, the UN Forces Commander, welcomed the troops and reassured them that they were in a very safe Sector. Orders were given at 18:00hrs and the men listened intently. The orders detailed shift schedules for sentries, explained where the crappers were, and what to do should we be attacked, amongst other things. I leaned back and watched the guys continue to unpack. It was nice just to relax for a bit. A ghetto blaster at the far end of the tent belted out Stevie Ray Vaughn's, 'The Sky is Cryin'. On another cot midway down the tent Dan McMaster was making a recording on a cassette tape. Closer to me some of the guys were asking questions.

"So what's it like so far?"

My rifle rolled in my hand as I shifted on the cot. I could hear them but something outside was drawing my thoughts to it.

"How do you tell Croat from Serb?" The questions were coming so quickly I could not answer. Completely distracted, I now had one foot on the cot and one on the floor. THUUMP, silence. THUUMP, silence. Hmmm, mortars just got fired, I thought to myself. The barrage of questions continued.

"Are all the houses blown the fuck up or what?"

BOOOM, pause BOOOM.

"That's funny, those mortar rounds sound like they are being fired from the north," I said aloud.

"What was that Case?" Sam asked just a few feet away. From somewhere down the tent I heard someone ask,

"McMaster, what are you doing?"

"I'm recording a tape to my wife," he replied, oblivious to what was happening outside our tent walls. I continued having a conversation with myself.

"Those are incoming rounds now. They sound like they are in town."

"Hey Scotty, where the Hell is Daruvar from here?" I ignored the question. My body instinctively began to recoil. I was getting a really bad feeling about the shelling. Those of us who had been here for the last three weeks had already been exposed to mortar attacks. My mind continued processing the audible information it was receiving and it told me to get another sense involved.

"Those rounds are getting close, better have a look." I got up and I spoke loudly,

"Hey these rounds are getting close, get your shit together!"

I was already walking for the door. I opened the flap just in time to see the explosion of a mortar round as it slammed into the ground 50metres away. It silhouetted two of our Pl. HQ guys who were laying communications wire. Their bodies flew through the air as they were blasted by the concussion waves. The words came out of my mouth just like I was watching someone else yell them.

"Get down the next ones droppin short!!!!!"

Within a split second I was hurled backwards by the very near explosion of a 120mm mortar. My sinuses exploded and snot and spit and blood flew from my mouth and nose. I landed like a ton of shit on one of the guys' cots in the fourth row back from the door. The pain from landing backwards over the cot rail seared through me like a hot knife. I would find out years later that I wrecked four vertebrae in my lower back. I was frantically trying to gather my bearings. Guys were running everywhere now trying to get out of the tent. I could see their mouths moving, they were yelling, but I could not hear them.

"What?" I screamed repeatedly.

I winced in pain and yelped as my right hand got stepped on. I tried to get up and I fell over again. Where the fuck is my rifle? I've got to get out of this tent. My head was pounding.

I rubbed my face and my hand came back covered in blood. There was a soft opening in my scalp just above my hairline. I found my rifle under one of the cots and now half assedly scrambled out of the tent. Most of the troops were loaded up in the APCs and were rumbling out of the school grounds at high speed churning up the grass as they went. I ran to my Iltis and jumped into the driver's seat, fired it up, and waited for the Lt.

"Come on, Come on!!!"

The shells were still bursting in the trees all around the camp. I watched the last APC scream by. I stuffed the jeep in gear and drove the opposite direction from everyone else, directly back into the tent lines screaming at the top of my lungs for Lt. Burke. I sat smashing my hands on the steering wheel as though it would encourage him to come running out of his tent to me. I bailed out of my jeep and ran to his tent. The mortars were now exploding sixty feet above the ground in the trees. Branches and splinters of wood showered the ground all around me, and they were accompanied by searing hot metal shards. I was in a panic. I ripped open the canvas flap of the modular tent. He was already gone.

"Fuck!"

I screamed above the ear splitting din of another mortar as it exploded over head. Dodging mounds of earth that had been churned up by the explosions, I ran back to the Iltis. I was mad as Hell he was gone, but elated that I did not find his corpse either. I jumped in the jeep, jammed it in gear and high-tailed it out of the kill zone. In a hail of rocks and dust I drove like I was possessed by crazed spirits. The tires bit in as I hit the pavement, and the added traction hurled me wildly across the road. I bee-lined across the grassy boulevard, up a slight embankment and jumped the railway tracks that paralleled the road. For a brief moment my Iltis and I were suspended in mid-air. It landed cock-eyed in the ditch and sent a spine jarring jolt through my body. My teeth snapped painfully together in response to the bone crashing landing. The jeep almost rolled over and I yanked the wheel furiously to gain control as a large half hidden ditch impeded my path. The APCs had had no trouble traversing the ditch. I drove back up onto the tracks and clattered down the railway ties, like a tough truck commercial, pushing the jeep to approximately 70kmh until I could finally see a way for me to get through to the company. With a twist of the wheel I jumped off the rails and sped out into the field. Through the enveloping dusk and churned up dust I could see the silhouettes of my unit set up in all-around defense ahead of me. This was the predefined area given to us in Orders should we be attacked. Not recognizing my platoon in the fray, I drove my jeep into one of the lines on the left flank, parked and shut the engine off. Exiting the Iltis I went down on one knee and kept my rifle pointing outward from the Company. My hearing was slowly coming back and I could hear men yelling that they were wounded. After a few minutes I could also hear someone calling out to determine my whereabouts. They were trying to confirm if I was killed, wounded or just missing. After numerous attempts of trying to tell them I was okay, I ran over to where the shouts were coming from and confirmed in person. Lt. Burke was pissed off, but relieved to see me. He pulled me aside,

"Where in the fuck were you?" He strained not to yell.

"I was looking for you, sir!" I responded angrily, the dried blood on my face cracked.

"What the fuck does that mean?" Burke asked in a confused tone.

"Orders were to take all the vehicles out in the event of attack," I added. "You didn't show up, I feared the worst, so I drove into the tent lines to drag you out."

"You drove back in there you fucking knot head?" Bill raised his eyebrows and threw his arms wildly in the air.

"Yes, sir, I didn't think you'd bail on me and enjoy the protection of the APC when you could ride in our soup can." I needled playfully to see if he was really pissed.

"Well I'm just glad you're okay," he said his tone changing. "Next time, fuck the jeep and get in the track, okay?"

"No prob," I replied, seeing he was calming down.

"I'll be back with the jeep." He slugged me in the shoulder.

"Asshole," he shot out, his white teeth showing his smile in the darkness.

"Damn rights, sir, but you're not the only officer with two of them."

I turned and walked back toward the ramp at the rear of our Pl. HQ track. The Coy medic Pierre Langevin was applying a dressing to one of the wounded, Axle Keegan, on the ramp of the track. I could hear the fuss he was creating fifty feet away. A wiry 170lbs, Axle hailed from Newfoundland. He was as much a card as any Newf I'd had the pleasure of meeting. He had received a piece of shrapnel in his ass cheek, which we all had a chuckle about.

"It's nowhere near your heart," exclaimed Pierre trying to settle his patient.

At six foot four inches tall and a long-legged 220lbs, our blonde haired C-6 gunner Quinn Moses, who I referred to as No.1, piped up,

"But it is deadly close to your brain though."

More laughter ensued. Warrant Goddard quietly but sharply ordered,

"Alright lads, back to business, watch your arcs and stay alert. We have to be ready for an attack. We'll be here for awhile so don't get sloppy."

I marched back to the left flank and lay down watching my arcs of fire. One of the guys from 7Pl. came over and confirmed who I was.

"I'm just here till this shit winds down because my jeep's here," I reported.

He nodded and crept back to his fire position. After a couple hours of waiting we slowly made our way back to the school. This time nobody headed back to the tents. Shovels were brought to bear and trenches were dug. The demeanor of the troops was now one of seriousness.

"Anybody want to ask me what it's like here now?" I asked with a sinister grin.

Later that evening I was rummaging around the kill zone that used to be our tent lines. Tommy came over to what was left of my shattered bunk space. As I mentioned earlier, Tommy was a muscled killing machine. He was not big, just strong as Hell. We wrestled many times and he whooped my ass every time. Tommy was only 160lbs and measured five foot seven inches. He was a very good friend and we had worked well together for years in Anti-Armour Platoon.

"What happened to your leg, Scotty?"

I looked at him quizzically. My eyes followed his outstretched arm to where he was pointing at my leg. My combat pants were torn at the knee and crusty with blood down to my jungle boot. The pants were already ripped so I opened the rip a little wider and inspected curiously. The skin was open in a jagged gash just above my knee cap. From it I carefully pulled a thin needle like piece of steel. I shrugged my shoulders. That was all Tommy needed to see. His face went pale. "Let me know if you want me to get you somebody else to help you to the medic," he said through pale lips as he turned and walked away.

During the evening mortar attack a dozen of The Men in Black were wounded, although not seriously. I chuckled and gazed up through the spaghetti strainer that was the roof of the tent.

"Thank you Lord."

While the clean-up of the tent lines continued pairs of guys were concurrently digging in. Ross and Sven were paired up digging a trench right beside the sidewalk at the front entrance to the school.

"We trained for this exact poop in Germany, eh guys?" I said as I walked up on them.

They paused briefly from their bantering.

"Ya I'm glad I put so much effort into my shovelling back home," Sven shot out sarcastically.

"That's not quite what I meant. I meant diggin in, in a school yard, or in front of city hall. You know places other than in the bush in the middle of nowhere."

"For sure, all the times we parked in peoples' driveways," Ross responded knowingly.

"That's the one. Even though we didn't dig in, we were sensitized to doing operations in built up areas."

"Speaking of Germany, I love kasekuchen," Sven said wiping the sweat off his brow. I crouched down to one knee and faced half away from them, my eyes searched the surrounding area as we continued our bullshit session.

"Amazing eh, if you parked a track in someone's driveway back in Canada they'd blow a gasket. In Germany the Frau comes out with cake and coffee," I commented.

"Mmmmm coffee cake," moaned Sven. "I love food."

Without warning it was Ross' turn to vent.

"That's because people back home don't give a shit about us grunts. That's why we have shit equipment, that's why guys in the units in Canada are getting their wives to claim welfare."

"I'm with Ross, I'd bet most people back home don't even know we're here and the ones that do know, think it's a nice safe peacekeeping mission," I stated matter of factly.

"Definitely, if they had any idea what it's like here they'd be doubling our pay," Ross added.

"Maybe they could pay in kasekuchen," suggested Sven.

"The way you think about your stomach you should have a thirty-pound shit bag hangin over your belt," Ross fired nastily.

"Well if you did more diggin and less whining we'd be done diggin already jackass," Sven shot back. Their bantering was continuous and I laughed at their antics.

"You two are meant for each other."

"Don't you have somewhere to go, Casey?"

"And miss this? Absolutely not," I said pausing for a moment.

"I do have to go before somebody hands me a shovel though," I said chuckling. I continued my fun verbal abuse. "Besides I've been here longer than you Numptys, and Warrant Goddard said this was remedial PT for you slackers."

They made some remarks but the words trailed off as I was walking away. I had been here longer, it was only three weeks, but it was fun to give them the gears about being FNGs just the same. I walked back to the CQ tent and met Ray there.

"Hey are you taking the Warrant out anywhere?" I asked him.

"No I'm in with the CQ today," he replied.

"Oh nice, sucks to be you," I said rolling my eyes with mock pain for his daily tasking.

"Tell me about it," he agreed drawing in a breath.

"Where is the little fella anyway?" Ray pointed down the right side of the tent.

"Thanks I'll go the other way. Good luck buddy."

He just shrugged his shoulders. I walked down the side of the tent until I bumped into Warrant Goddard.

"You look like you're hiding Corporal Casey," the booming voice came like a freight

train.

I changed the subject away from the obvious to avoid getting a shit detail.

"The L-tee told me you wanted to see the T-54/55 with the mine roller."

"Ya, that would be great Casey. When do you think you'd be ready to take me?"

"I've got a clean appointment book, so whenever you want."

"Ok I'll meet you at your Iltis," he said like an excited kid.

"See you there, Warrant."

Like I had any other option. After all, he was the Platoon Warrant. We drove off the end of the pavement and out to the cement plant. I turned into the driveway of the plant and noticed it looked like any concrete yard back home, with a chalky dust covering everything. The major difference was this plant had a main battle tank on the boulevard. We clambered up onto the tank. Like when Lt. Burke and I had been here previously, it was locked up tight. The wind blew in and kicked a fine dust into the air, coating our skin. We got some good pictures of us standing with it. The tank had a mine roller attached to the front of it. Each side had three solid steel wheels on it. These are used to set off any anti-tank mines before the actual tank drives over it.

"Hard to believe we're actually here sometimes eh, Warrant?"

"When you're standing on the turret of a Soviet main battle tank, it's definitely surreal," he replied.

"We are going to have to make sure this makes it out of the sector soon and doesn't end up hidden somewhere," he said with concern.

I agreed but it was cool to actually see some of the real tanks and other vehicles we studied in Armoured Fighting Vehicle Recognition up close and personal. After taking our photo's we returned to camp. The paved areas of travel carried their own inherent dangers that you could plainly see. As we learned days earlier the gravel roads could be just as dangerous as the soft ground. It was what you could not see, off the pavement that was really dangerous. The concern of course was the indiscriminate use of anti-personnel land mines. We paid particular attention to where the locals walked. They had inadvertently cleared the way for us. If they had walked there, then these areas would generally be clear to walk on. The removal of land mines is generally left to the skilled hands of the Combat Engineers or Hold Fast as they were called on the radio. The Battle Group was covering a great deal of acreage, and the Engineers were spread thin as they were responsible for more than just mine clearance. Trenches and bunker locations needed to be dug just to add a couple tasks to Hold Fasts' responsibilities. This was done with a variant of the Leopard tank chassis, called the Badger. The Badger was outfitted with a dozer blade, an auger, and an excavator style digging arm with bucket. Concertina wire had to be stretched around main camp locations. Water and sewage lines had to be dug. Needless to say the Engineers were very busy.

With Hold Fast being over tasked, the infantry units had to do a lot of the minor engineer jobs themselves. During infantry battle school these skills are taught as part of regular training. Soldiers from each platoon were selected to do mine clearing jobs. The technique they would use is called 'prodding'. This task was by no stretch easy with the soldiers lying on their bellies side by side separated by only an arm's width. With their bayonets on an angle to the ground they would slowly prod them into the ground. Upon finding a mine, a small flag or a strip of bright tape would mark the location. The actual task of removal would be left to the Hold Fast call signs.

This was done because the explosive device could have an anti-lifting device under it. They were better outfitted to deal with these problems.

Call sign 21 was to move from the school grounds to the Sirač sports field in a few days and it was rumoured that the area was mined. The L-tee and I sat and observed the groundskeeper and any other passers-by watching as they walked the entire field and the outer areas. They showed no concerns and no patterns to how they walked about. After a considerable time observing we determined the area to be clear. However, as a precaution, the area our tent was going to be placed in was prodded. With land mines ever present in our thoughts, I decided to do some upgrades to my Iltis. The Iltis was light by way of using very thin metal and absolutely no armour plating. I had come to the conclusion that I had to do something for protection against mines. Using a short handled shovel, I filled a dozen sandbags. Selecting and placing each one carefully on the floor of the jeep based on how much sand I had scooped into them, manoeuvring them into position to leave no part uncovered. I had seen the damage done by mines, and I hoped to limit the abuse to myself and Lt. Burke should we hit one. It was far from anything the Yanks had but better than anything provided by our own government.

"What the Hell is that shit, Casey?" Asked WO Jensen in his usual, 'you're such a fuckin idiot tone'.

He always had a way of making many of us feel unintelligent.

"They are sand bags, Warrant." I tried to send him off with the sarcasm.

"I'm aware of that, but what are they for?" he asked, his nasty enthusiasm growing.

"For protection against mines," I replied confidently.

He laughed and said,

"You'll hit a mine and get killed by a flying sandbag, dumbass."

He turned away, shaking his head. I continued with my self-made task. That evening a French jeep in Sarajevo, hit a mine and killed the passenger. The driver survived, because he had sandbagged his side of the floor. The next morning, I walked by WO Jensen's jeep as Frank was putting sandbags on the floor.

"What you doin, buddy?" I quizzed.

"The WO came up with this idea and ordered me to do it ASAP," Frank sighed.

I smiled knowingly, and patted him on the shoulder.

"What will he come up with next, eh?"

I slid into the driver's seat and wiped the sweat from my face. Smiling, I placed my feet on the sandbagged floor.

"The sun appears to be angry with us today," I said to myself, looking at my thermometer. The temperature was crowding 30 Celsius, to warm for this early in the year.

"Probably die by hyperthermia before a landmine anyway."

I drove off chuckling to myself.

The following day around 1pm, I could hear music playing somewhere in Sirač. It was cheerful music so Donny and I went to investigate. We walked over a small footbridge which crossed the equally small creek that separated the schoolyard from the main part of the village. We climbed the trail that brought us up the 100ft in elevation, to town. Weapons up, we crested the hill and walked straight into a procession of farm tractors. One of the tractors was pulling a trailer.

"What the Hell is this shit?" Donny's voice sounded with mild anxiety.

"Looks like someone's gettin hitched Cletus," I said mocking the Southern US accent.

"That is a smoking hot limousine," he said pointing to the one with the trailer. We both laughed out loud. The crowd looked our way.

"Ooops, that was kinda disrespectful."

"Aaah don't sweat it, if it was an hour from now we should be concerned"

"Why an hour?"

"Cause you know as well as I do. By then they'll all be drunker than shit house rats," I explained.

"Good point."

We watched and waved. When the procession had disappeared we sauntered back to the school. About an hour later one of our sentries started hollering.

"Stand to, Stand to!"

This is the alarm call for soldiers to make ready for an attack. Gun fire erupted in town. It sounded like one Hell of a fire-fight. A section of guys made their way up to squash whatever was happening. Donny and I looked at each other and burst out laughing.

The mortar and artillery threat was still very real in everyone's mind. So when the platoons were assigned their respective camps over-head protection, OHP, had to be built. OHP in this case would come in the form of complete bunkers. Our Pl. bunker was constructed over the course of two days. Sturdy timbers that would be used as stringers were measured and cut to twenty feet in length. Logs for the walls were cut to ten feet in length. Five feet would be embedded in the ground with the remainder above ground standing upright. The stringers would stretch between the uprights to form the flat roof. Corrugated sheeting was the next item to be used in the building process. The sheeting was nailed to the walls starting from the bottom and working upwards. The roof sheets were then nailed on. OHP kits were stripped for their tarp sections. These were then taped to the steel sheeting. The tarping would give us protection from the weather, but would also keep sand from filtering onto the occupants during shelling. The final and most labour intensive part of the bunker build was the sandbags.

Over one thousand sandbags were filled, carried, and then stacked in position. Each bag weighed an average fifty pounds. The walls of the bunker were four sandbags thick, or three feet. When the walls were completed the last two rows of bags were tied in by staggering them into the bags used for the roof. This was done for strength and overall integrity. When the bunker was completed we sat back and discussed what we thought our survival chances would be if we had to use it.

"Well this is built to withstand a direct hit from a 105mm arty round," Warrant Goddard conveyed to those of us as we lay on the roof resting.

"A direct it? Lard tunderin, tinks we'd aft ta be needin a pile of Tylenols fer dat bye," commented Axle in his thick Newfie accent.

"Yes buddy, our ears would be ringin for sure," I agreed.

Ray Gondole who showed up after all the work was done posed for the inaugural photo. We all had a good laugh while we busted his balls for posing. In Ray's defence though, he was driving the WO back from HQ. Shortly after the bunker was constructed the sections mounted up and went on patrol. We were back to focusing on the mission at hand.

6 Platoon or call sign 22, moved into the area surrounding Omanovac. The four section APCs and their soldiers deployed to get on with the task of removing the JNA units from the area. Upon our arrival weapons were pointed and voices were raised temporarily. Within an hour of dialogue and 22's refusal to go away the JNA packed up without firing a shot. Each section mounted up and escorted the Serbian soldiers and their vehicles outside the Sector West boundary. For the remainder of the day 6Pl. patrolled the large area around Omanovac. To the north of Omanovac, 5 Platoon, call sign 21 was conducting similar operations disarming HV troops. This was a difficult undertaking as the HV had worked very hard to

arm themselves with weapons. They had fought many fierce battles against the JNA and to say the least they were more than a little less than inclined to just give up their hard earned foothold. Convincing them that we as peacekeepers were not going to allow the JNA back onto their turf was difficult. We also told them we would not tolerate any attacks perpetrated by them against the JNA or Serbian civilians in The Krajina either. After hours of explanations backed up by our refusal to leave without collecting their weapons they finally caved in. Again our platoon patrolled the area all day reinforcing our peace position. As the sun began to set we turned toward Sirač and made the 70 kilometre journey home.

Back in our tent the guys from 21 and 21A sat back and discussed how the day had gone. Everyone was pretty excited as they each gave their account of hands on peacekeeping, the tension and repeated explanations. Trying to get the interpreters to understand what we needed to have happen. It was cool to listen and watch the guys tell their stories as the evening wound down. The troops tried to get some rest.

The following morning Lt. Burke and I saddled up into 21W, with the 21C carrier driving point, we tucked in behind them. 21A and 21B brought up the rear. We followed the road back towards Omanovac. We would be conducting patrols in the same area, with an expansion of the patrol range by the afternoon. Via radio we were in contact with Sunray 23, 7Pl.'s commander. They were almost back in Omanovac. He reported that things were not looking good. The JNA units had returned and had brought reinforcements.

Our platoon rolled into the rural area north of 7 Pl's location only to find the Croatian HV had done the same. The previous day's diplomacy was thrown out the window overnight. We started from square one by getting out on the ground and having face to face discussions with the HV command. All three section carriers made their way up and down the roads that divided the warring parties. Our Pl. HQ carrier 21 and my Iltis 21W stayed with the HV HQ. By supper time and after two refueling stops our portion of the Sector had once again been cleared. This crazy job of peacekeeping in Yugoslavia was similar to the war in Vietnam, in that we gave up land once spoken for, only to find ourselves having to win it back repeatedly. For today, Sector West was once again secure. Tomorrow would be another day.

A few days had passed with the usual daily patrolling of the cease fire lines. We had received a tip from some locals that a body was found up in the hills. To Lt. Burke and I this was nothing new, however, it was the first for most of the guys to see a corpse. That's how I remember it, the first time for most. So as with any report we had to check it out. It was a bit of a drive up into the hills and for this early in April it was quite chilly. There were still some traces of snow in the shadows. As we rolled to a stop I shivered and blew steam from my mouth.

"Should have put the doors on, Scotty," Lt. Burke acknowledged.

"We'd just be cheating ourselves if I did that, sir," I commented cynically.

"Oh most definitely," he joked along.

"Besides it's hard enough to see through those plastic pieces of shit let alone defend ourselves" I said straight forwardly.

"Very true," he replied flatly.

As we walked we surveyed the area. The road had brought us to a dead-end. There was a sick irony in that. The landscape was comparable to anywhere in wooded Canada. Spruce trees stood tall all around. An abandoned horse-trailer was off to one side. Lying in the back, face up were the remains of an elderly man. We assumed in these temperatures he had been dead for awhile as the only visible decomposition was limited to his face. To put it bluntly his face had been removed by insects and larger scavengers. We knew he was probably a senior citizen because he was balding and the hair he did have was grey. He was wearing a heavy military olive-drab wool overcoat. Upon further scrutiny we found a hole the size of a pinkie finger in the fabric just above his heart. This old man had been shot and killed for whatever reason, probably because of his ethnicity I personally deduced. Plain and simple, he was murdered. Just like the priest, only this guy got it quick. One of thousands I thought to myself. Commanders from both sides gave the orders to execute hundreds of civilians all across The Krajina. Somebody executed this guy and I prayed that they would be held accountable.

It was interesting, in a ghoulish kind of way, to observe the guys who had just arrived. This was their first encounter with death. They stood quietly in a semi-circle gazing with veiled curiosity. After a few minutes of death's contemplation, the task of breaking the solemn mood with typical Canadian dark humour was

Axle's.

"Yis, byes. Bernie ere's got quite the shit eatin grin don't he?"

Nervous laughter erupted and the gloves were off.

"Ya, he must have played Leper ice hockey, cause there's a face off in the corner," said another, followed by more nervous laughter. Other than verbal nonsense no indignities were offered to the body. It was just the way to deal with the uneasy emotions that accompany thoughts of our own demise. Right or wrong, dark humour gives that release. A member of the Hrvatska Policija arrived in true form, filthy and wreaking of šljivovica. He was certain that the deceased had fallen victim to the Chetniks. This bit of police work was followed up with a complete repertoire of racial insults which our impartial Croatian translator aptly translated for us. After much eye rolling on our part we placed the body into one of our body bags and sent the ranting cop and his package on their way. To finish up the day the section mounted up and we headed for the hotter side of Sector West.

The following evening, I drove into the sports field parking area which was adjacent to the 5Pl. bunker. The standard two sentries met me with coffee in hand and a funny look on their faces.

"What's shakin, boys?"

"It's a little damp inside in case you were thinking of floppin out," Randy Dempster called out.

"No I'm here to grab some shit off the skipper's bunk and header for Omanovac," the days with no sleep, evident in my groggy speech.

"Good cause the water's up to the top of our boots and deeper in some spots," stated Randy unhappily.

"A water line broke when the sports field keeper came and tried to water the field," Les Roberts explained.

I took a swig of coffee. It was a welcome taste.

"The guy that put Baileys in this should get promoted." I winked at Roberts. Les was famous for having a bottle of Baileys on hand.

"I'd settle for at least a week off in Dubrovnik," he nudged playfully.

"I'll put in a good word for you as soon as I meet up with the L-Tee."

My words drifted off as I walked through the concrete archway into the playing field area where our modular tent was located. I tried to hop from dry spot to dry spot. Everyone's barrack boxes were floating about and the cocoa matting was completely submerged. It would be stinking to high heaven once the water subsided. I quickly checked my gear and threw my floating barrack box on my cot. I was thankful that I stowed my kitbag on my cot every time I left or it would be soaked like most of the others. I manoeuvred to the other end of the tent to grab Bill's 'junior general kit' off his bunk. I turned quickly and got what Axle would've called a 'booter' as the water spilled over the top of my boot.

"Shit," I cursed aloud. I slogged the rest of the way back out, no longer trying to stay dry.

"Didn't maker eh?" Randy scoffed.

"At a hundred 'K' they'll dry quickly enough." I replied trying not to let it get to me.

It did not take long before my mind switched to more important things as I swung out onto the road and headed west. The sun had gone down and I was free wheelin as fast as my little Iltis would take me. It was at that moment I was glad for my attentive driving skills. Hammering my brakes, I skidded to a stop. My hands immediately began to ache from the vice like grip I had on the wheel. I blinked my eyes to make sure my focus was right. In the glow of my headlights sat three black circles, three inches tall and each a foot in diameter. They looked as harmless as large Frisbee's. Harmless, they were not. They were TMA-3 anti-tank mines.

"Fuck," I yelled with an anxious jitter.

I repeated the profanity three more times. My head felt as though it would burst from the immediate adrenalin rush. It was too late now and I knew this predicament was not good. I slammed the transmission in reverse, side stepped the clutch and floored the throttle. The Iltis lurched backwards and shuddered from the abuse. My mind raced and kept saying over and over, 'AMBUSH!'

This was how ambushes were done. Set up a couple of mines to stop any passers-by, whether they stopped by exploding or by chance. Then you open up on the prey with a vengeance. The Iltis' little four-cylinder engine was screaming at full rpm as I backed up about 800 metres. I then shut the engine off and killed the lights. Nothing happened. I was partially relieved, because now I was wrestling with the decision to continue or turn around. I was required in Lipik ASAP to pick up the L-tee.

"Well Scotty, don't let fear and common sense stop you," I muttered, trying to convince myself to go before fear set in.

With that, I left the lights out, put it in gear and crept forward. When I guessed I was close enough I switched on the headlights and gunned the engine. Holding my breath, I picked my route and grabbed another gear. I think I even closed my eyes as I waited for the explosion and the machine gun fire. Once again there was nothing. I let myself breath again. After a kilometre of driving I began to laugh uncontrollably.

"WOOOOOO!" I screamed at the top of my lungs.

It was a nervous release. It's amazing how your body corrals energy. I arrived in Lipik ten minutes earlier than I had expected. I climbed out and went into the UN Liason tent and splashed some coffee into my metal canteen cup. I sat down on a rock at the opening to the tent. I felt okay but my body was shaking. I gulped at my coffee. I gave the anti-tank mine info to the Vandoo corporal standing waiting for his OC. They would be in better position to call the Engineers sooner.

Lt. Burke came out from the other end where the officers had been having an 'O' group. "Corporal Casey, you're here," Bill acknowledged my presence as he came into the front portion of the tent.

"Yes sir, I am."

We walked out to the jeep and Burke continued our conversation.

"Well that was entertaining. 7pl. reports they had a company size JNA mechanized infantry unit roll through to the south last night."

"Holy poop," I said raising my eyebrows.

"Ya, it's a concerning move. Let's head back to Sirač."

"Ok sir, I thought we'd go back via Badeljavina."

"Oh? That will add half an hour to the trip won't it?"

"Yes it will, but I don't really want to drive through the ambush kill zone again."

"Ambush?" his voice cracked.

"I'll tell you the story on the way. We'll have time. Oh ya, congratulations." I offered patting the new Captains rank slip-on situated on the front of his flak vest.

"Thanks," he said beaming with his new promotion to Captain.

"I'll still be callin you L-tee though, and I drink Pivo if it's all you can find." I commented with a mischievous grin, as it was customary for newly promoted NCOs and Officers to by beer for their brothers. He just shook his head as we pulled out onto the road and he told me the short story of his promotion. It seemed only appropriate for the officers to be captains as it commanded more respect from the local warlords. I agreed with the thought process behind it.

One of the primary tasks of peacekeeping is to maintain the separation between conflicting sides. Separation can be determined by a few things: geography, ethnicity, and the size of the bad guy's forces to name a few. Part of our mission involved disarming the civilian population and moving the actual military forces out of the UNPAs. To assist in disarming we set up checkpoints at key locations in The Krajina. Each checkpoint was constructed with the same principles in mind. One, it must slow traffic down for better control. Two, it must have clear fields of fire. And three, it should be temporarily defensible.

Sandbags, forty-five gallon drums, concrete blocks, white paint and lumber were just some of the supplies needed to build a checkpoint. In the case of a permanent checkpoint, a bunker would be incorporated to provide the controlling unit with shelter from heavy munitions should they be attacked. The attached bunker could be built above ground or it could be dug in. If the water table permitted and the digging was easy, digging in was preferred. Once the bunker was in place a sentry shack with overhead protection from the elements was constructed. Chicken wire would be stretched across all windows to thwart any chance of grenades being thrown inside. Rations, water, and ammunition for two days would be stored inside the construction. Outside, in whatever direction the roads intersected with the guard post, an obstacle course of forty-five gallon drums would be placed. Usually in groups of three or four these drums would be situated in a manner that would force all traffic to weave in and out thereby reducing their speed. The drums, once in place, would be filled with sand, cement rocks, or any other material that would make them a formidable stopping block should someone attempt to ram through. A control arm would be built and placed by the guard shack. It would be built so it could be raised and lowered easily.

Upon completion of the construction the entire set-up would then be painted with white paint to show its UN neutrality. Because peacekeeping is a twenty-four-hour mission, lights would be mounted to provide unobstructed fields of view from the darkness. Coils of concertina wire would be staked to the ground and stacked three coils high on angles that would manipulate vehicles, but more effectively pedestrians, like a funnel to the sentry post for inspection.

The Sector was divided up between Alpha and November Companies equally. The responsibility within N. Companies 'Area of Operation' was again divided by platoons and again by sections. The breakdown provided each section with a checkpoint like the one mentioned previously. With these downloaded responsibilities more ground could be controlled effectively. As many major routes as possible were given 'high priority' for checkpoints. Then areas where the bad people could sneak around the back of the Sector were next. Whiskey-Charlie-One-One, WC-11, was an example of that type of remote cut-off checkpoint. It was out in the middle of nowhere. It covered an intersection that connected a one hundred kilometre loop outside the Sector. Although WC-11 was quiet it did net some smuggled weapons that would have otherwise found their way into the wrong hands. Besides patrolling all four Sectors, November Company was also responsible for setting up Sector North for the Argentineans. Because Sector West was cut off from the Northern Sector by a large rocky ridge a Radio Re-Broadcast, or RRB, station had to be set up to ensure that our guys were not out there with their asses hanging in the breeze. An RRB is simply an outpost that broaches the coverage of the two radio signals. Any message from one side of the RRB to the other must in essence be transmitted twice. You tell me the message then I pass it to HQ and vice versa.

I thought it was a bit of a stretch but while the guys were not out patrolling or running checkpoints they could do what they wanted in regards to physical training. Some opted to go for organised runs, with weapons of course. It was not until later in the tour that guys ventured out without them. Going without a weapon was a bit of a stretch from my point of view. I barely had time to sleep and eat let alone go for a run. Regardless, the guys who had time made use of it. They ran and did circuit training on the sports field. We had a small assortment of weights that had been brought in the back of one of the APCs to work out with as well. It was not the YMCA but it did the trick to help stay in shape. Sgt. Franklin's section had been tasked with providing security to a unit in Daruvar on a rotating basis at the one functioning hotel. This was a great tasking for the lucky ones that got to partake. When the lads were not on shift they could use the facilities at the hotel, like the pool, weight room, and sauna. The hotel was functioning and housed mainly journalists and upper echelon UN personnel. This was a sign that our presence here was having an effect on the stability of the region. That is not to say that out on the land outside of Daruvar things had returned to normal. We witnessed the instability outside of town regardless of the population that was moving back into the local area.

MAIL CALL

"No weapon has ever settled a moral problem. It can impose a solution but it cannot guarantee it to be a just one."
~ERNEST HEMINGWAY

The mail came in and a shoe box size parcel was sitting on my bunk. I was hoping that this was the package I was waiting for. Parcels from family were good for the soul. The few that I received almost always contained baking from mom's kitchen, a letter reporting the latest events in the community and the standard I love you and be careful. I appreciated all my letters including the letters to, "Dear Canadian Soldier." These were generally handwritten letters from Canadian school children to show support for the soldiers deployed in theatre. For many of us they provided an escape from this evil place. I pulled out my Russell knife, issued hunting style knife, and used it to carefully slit the tape of the parcel. It contained four boxes of Kraft Dinner, a package of razor blades, a deck of cards, and two bags of Smarties. Lifting the bags of chocolate candies, I smiled. Lying flat on the bottom were two porn magazines. I smiled an almost devilish smile. Oh yes, the women on the pages were beautiful. These rags were more than just visual stimulants though; they were trading material. A couple of the guys walked in.

"Hey guys, check these babes out." I offered, handing each a peek.

"Don't fuck up the pages with drool because I'm donating them to charity."

"Charity my ass, Casey, you'll have these pages stuck together by noon."

"Don't be jealous, Mikey. I'll let you see them when I'm done," I said laughing.

"No thanks." He replied handing the magazine back, disgustingly holding it by a corner, as though it were already soiled.

"What the Hell is the mandate this week?" Mikey asked.

I shrugged at the question offering very little solid information,

"I'm not sure, the basic shit, but I don't have a clue what the big picture is."

"Ya me either, protect UN personnel and equipment, civilians and civilian establishments. Bla bla bla."

"You got it. And kill any mother fucker that messes with The Men in Black,"

I said with John Wayne bravado.

We all laughed at that.

I took the magazines and slid them into my combat pants map pocket before anyone else showed up. I stored the rest of the goodies in my barracks box. Walking with a spring in my step I exited the tent and climbed into my Iltis. Reaching up under the dash to the left of the steering column I pushed my Bic pen into the ignition and turned on the main power. During my earlier mad dash over the train tracks my key rattled out and was lost. As with anything in the prior Liberal governmentally funded Canadian arsenal we learned how to overcome the adversities of inferior equipment. It fired up and I was off. I was brimming with excitement. After a half hour drive I turned onto the Dragovič road. Another five minutes' drive and I pulled over on the right and parked by a bullet riddled decoy of two soldiers on a motorcycle. It was humorous to think how many Serb soldiers shot this thing. The Croats, I am sure, laughed too. I smiled more when Iljac stepped outside to meet me.

"Dobar dan," I wished him good day. I noted three men standing smoking in the shaded tree line adjacent to the house.

"Dobar dan," he replied cheerfully.

We stepped inside their platoon house. The blankets over the windows made it quite dark and it stunk of body odour, cigarettes and feces. Once inside we shook hands. I refused to shake hands outside for fear of appearing to be favouring the Croats, which I did not. I honestly did not give a shit about either side. I wanted to stay alive and I was merely using Iljac to get what I wanted. In a sense he was using me too. It was the combat version of 'Let's Make a Deal'. He stepped behind a table that was set up as a desk and pulled an AK-74, the updated version of the AK-47, out from beneath it. He smiled and levelled it at me. My smile dropped. There was no way I could bring my rifle to action. I had slung it when we entered. He had me dead to rights. I resisted the urge to flinch. At that moment my blood pressure must have blown off the charts. I stared at him and without moving my eyes I quickly re-evaluated my surroundings. There was nowhere to defend from. Shit. Diplomacy, I thought.

"What the fuck is this, Iljac?" I half yelled, forcing him to reveal his bluff.

"Vut is dis? It is good vepon. Have you book?"

"Of course I have it. I'm Canadian, I always keep my word."

I was starting to think this was a bad idea. All of this risk for a handgun. I could see my flag draped coffin surrounded by my relatives, the flag being folded and handed to my wife.

"We're sorry Mrs. Casey your husband died, In the Service of Peace."

No he did not. He died trading skin mags for a sidearm. The crowd began laughing around my casket. I shook the vision off immediately.

Knowing I had nowhere to go it was time to force my hand. Kill me or get on with it. My smile returned.

"Iljac, put that thing down before I'm forced to kill you."

Now it was his turn to smile knowing I did not have a chance for that. It worked. He put the AK on the table.

"I vaz show for you. You like?"

"Ya its dobro, but I want a pistol."

With that, I pulled the Penthouse porn magazine out of my map pocket and threw it on the table. He turned and grabbed a CZ-99 handgun. He placed it on the table with two loaded mags. I held my calm composure but I was inwardly excited. A CZ-99 was one of the most reliable combat handguns in the eastern bloc at the time. His eyes narrowed as he retrieved his prize. He flipped through the pages. I picked up the piece and slid one of the mags in. I jacked a round in the chamber, flipped the safety off, and kept it in my hand. I still had to get out of here. He was so engrossed with his prize that he did not even register with the sound of the gun being cocked. He knew I had nowhere to go should I pop him.

"Hey, do you have a bayonet for that rifle?"

I was pushing him to see if he would throw one in. He did not want to haggle. Not looking up from the pages of beautiful American girls he said,

"Yis me git. You come vit yedan girl book"

Not wanting to risk coming back here I decided to ante up by pulling the second mag out.

"Not one, yedan, I have two, dva, girl books today." I thought he was going to blow a load in his camo pants right there. I tossed the Hustler magazine onto the table. I looked away disgustedly as he swiftly undid his belt. Seeing my expression, he laughed and pulled his personal bayonet off. He came around to my side of the table and put it in my free hand. He smiled, turned and walked into a room at the back of the house. I gripped the butt of the pistol anticipating a shit storm. He emerged from the back with two glasses and a new bottle of Sliv. He cracked the lid off and we had a couple of shots.

"Hvala, thank you, I have to go now," I said.

"Molem, molem, Kanada is dobro," he said shaking my hand again. Easing a blanket aside I looked out the front window. I put the safety on, slipped the pistol in my belt and stepped into the sunlight. I slipped my rifle off my shoulder and took a quick look underneath my jeep. The three smokers were still chatting away. I spun the Bic pen again. The engine fired up, I backed up and drove away. I now possessed something the Canadian government did not want to pay for: equipping the average soldier with a secondary weapon.

HOTEL CALIFORNIA

"Have you ever thought that war is a madhouse and that everyone in the war is a patient?"
~ORIANA FALLACI

I had a difficult time getting up the next day as my back was killing me. Perhaps it was from the night we got shelled at the Sirač School. With the skipper's permission I took the day off from driving him around. He obliged, and a couple of Tylenols later, I was enjoying the morning on my cot. An hour later Sgt Glass stopped by and said he needed one more guy for a patrol. I got up and threw on my gear without question. I downed two more Tylenol and in less than five minutes I was standing in 1 Sections carrier, call sign 21-Alpha.

Getting out and patrolling with the boys was not R&R but it was a good break from high-speed low-drag jeep wheelin. I stood in the back hatch and watched the scenery go by on the left side. We passed through Pacrac and kept heading south through Okučani. The road gradually led us over a main four lane highway. This four lane road was the arterial link between Zagreb, the capital city of Croatia, and Belgrade the capitol of Serbia. Within in a kilometre of the highway we rattled into Covac. Covac was currently a Serb held village. As we rolled in I began a mental count of the armour we were seeing. There were three JNA APCs. Of the three, one in particular made me take a second look. What caught my eye was the SA-9 Gaskin which is a variant of the BRDM2 APC. The SA-9 Gaskin uses the BRDM chassis but has the Strela-1 surface-to-air missile system mounted on the roof. I tapped Sgt. Glass on the shoulder and pointed it out. Over the ICS he directed Earl Bricker in the direction of the SA-9. This was a special find because of its lethal ability to knock down aircraft. We as United Nations did not have air power on a regular basis. The UN made it clear that there was a US aircraft carrier on stand-by and fast-air could be called upon should it be an outrageous emergency. I was not quite sure what an outrageous emergency might be considered to be.

It was visibly quiet around all this armour. I could not feel any negative energy. It actually felt like a friendly neighbourhood. As we dismounted the soldiers who belonged to this equipment came out to greet us. They were full of smiles. One of them was approximately six foot six. He had dark hair cut like a mop top from the Beatles' glory days. He wore large frame wire glasses and was smoking a pipe. On his right hip, he wore a brand new tanned leather holster. He must be the chief, I thought. The holster was large enough to house a small machine gun. I envisioned what type of weapon I thought was in it as I had never seen anything like it. We took the time through some broken English/Serb that they would have to be on the road heading out of Sector West by morning. But that was tomorrow and they were friendly enough. So for today we opted for some educational exchange. They were as interested in our C-7 rifles as we were with the Sa-9. They showed us inside and all around it. In return we unloaded one of our rifles and let them check it out. It was then that the commander opened the flap of his tanned holster and drew a Scorpion machine pistol. Without clearing it he handed it to me. It was a well balanced weapon for its unique design and it felt good in the hand. I was impressed with it. Before handing the weapon back I called everyone to the anti aircraft missile launcher for a photo op. Earl Bricker quickly scooped the Scorpion out of my hand for the photo. We all clambered aboard and sat down. We posed and smiled. It was not until after the photo was taken that I noticed a farmer was standing in the picture. He looked like this was normal activity. I supposed that it probably was normal. It made the photo that much better.

We reconfirmed that they would be gone by first light. We also told them we would be back to make sure they got the message. Many of the guys shook hands all around and mounted up and left. The men of 21-Alpha continued patrolling the Serb held region for the rest of the day. We took back roads that led us to the Sava River. From here 1 section followed the river south to a large built up area. On the far bank of the Sava was the city of Stara Gradiška. I could see the apartment buildings and homes from our side of the water. Some of the inhabitants stood on the water's edge and waved the three finger-wave of the Serbs. I stared back at them without lifting a hand. I did not want them to think they had my support, nor did I want to appear friendly at this point in my day either, so I halfway nodded. The track rattled along and the dust swirled in our wake. We were racking up the kilometres patrolling the backwoods of the western edge of Sector West. The flat terrain was concealed by a large forest of deciduous trees mixed in with some conifers. The Sava River's gentle journey between its banks was in complete contrast to our own. Our APC rattled and jogged noisily. The calm waters also told a very different tale compared to the recent history on the land surrounding it. Our continuing journey led us to the small city of Nova Gradiška. As we entered the city, our tracks, although adorned with rubber blocks, still a metallic ring resounded off the sides of the buildings. Each of us in the track scanned every nook and cranny. Every window and door was scrutinized for any signs of an attacker. It was stressful to be here, not just for us but for the citizens as well. I am sure they were always on edge when they heard the sounds of combat vehicles within their city limits. They could only believe that violence would follow. That was what past and recent history had taught them. I was concerned because we were alone. Only eight of us were in this bright white rolling target. Gradually more and more residents came to the street. The hands they were waving were free of weapons. I was happy about that, so much so that I risked a wave or two. My wave was a regular wave that we would do at home, not the Serb or Croat waves. In a few short minutes we exited Nova Gradiška. I breathed a sigh of relief. Our patrol continued north on the four lane back toward Okučani. From there we made our way back to our camp at the sports field. The day was a success as we had had contact with a major Serb outpost. We had used diplomacy and got them to agree to leave Sector West. The patrol had also netted the intelligence of their surface-to-air missile capabilities in the region. Once we got to the sports field we geared down, cleaned our weapons and treated ourselves to a Pivo. Tomorrow would be a new day and maintenance had to be done.

The sound of sledgehammers clanged through the concrete breezeway into our modular tent. I carried a jerry can of water from inside our tent for the rest of our section. The boys were chattering away while they broke the torque on the bolts that held each portion of the track together.

"Who's thirsty?" I asked.

Hammers fell and the metal sound of the torque wrench being leaned against the carrier's metal wall were words enough.

"I hate doing this shit," said Tom Gorman.

The evidence of the sweat pouring down his face underscored the truth of what he had just said. It told a different story from his physical conditioning.

Tom was a bull of a man. He was an avid rugby player and had excelled at football. He and I had a good rivalry going when it came to football.

"Yis bye, she's the worst part-o track maintenance," added Axle.

"Its gotta be done though," came from another.

We were all sweating. Although I drove the platoon Iltis I tried to lend a hand with the carrier as often as I could. It was not much and I acknowledge that. It was generally because I was on another task. The water break ended and we got back to it. It was my turn with the hammer. The track on an APC is made up of four parts: the main body, track pad/growser, and two end connectors. Two guys would operate the torque wrench. One would place the socket on the bolt and the other would muscle the bolt loose. Once the bolt was loose, a third soldier would beat the steel end connector in towards the centre of the track. When the connector was flush the bolt would be re-torqued. This process would be repeated for the entire length of both tracks. It was back breaking monotonous labour for many soldiers and was akin to chain gang labour. This was regular maintenance as the tracks would loosen over time from rattling down the roads. Because we were peacekeepers and not an actual warring party we used the rubber track pads. We did not want to destroy the country any more than the locals already had. Once completed the sections would mount up and get back to the chore of patrolling.

The following day my Iltis was in for a complete service including tires. The REMEs arrived at our camp and performed the service on site. Because the jeep would be down for a while Capt. Burke took command of our carrier and performed his duties that way. This gave me the opportunity to go out with one of the other sections. I opted to take a patrol with 3 Section.

The ride was warm. I took my post standing in the open hatch of 21-Charlie watching for bad people, and enjoying the breeze. The odd bit of exhaust fumes filtered back and caught my nose making me think of trucking with my dad. We drove through a village that had been razed to the ground. Dust swirled up from our APCs tracks as they churned up the pieces of rubble that had rolled out to the road. Every building had crumbled to piles of bricks, wood, and twisted pipes. A couple of the ruins were still ablaze with smoke billowing out of the ruins. The fire reached angrily at the sky as it searched for more oxygen to continue its plan of destruction. In one of the rubble piles a couple of old women scrounged for anything of value. They stumbled and crouched in an attempt to dig for scraps of anything to make their miserable lives better. One of the ladies stepped on her tattered dress and fell onto a sharp pile of stone. Her friend rushed to her aid and held her bloodied face up off the broken bricks. I thought of my mother and how it broke my heart to watch the scene of despair. As we drove through I continued to contemplate the suffering here. What would it be like if this was our home? How would it be different for me? I closed my eyes and wiped the depressing thoughts from my mind. This was not our mess. It was their mess. I had to stay focused. As sad as the situation was and despite the compassion I had for them, many people here did not like us. That was a fact we all had to be cognisant of.

"Watch for bad guys," I said to myself out loud.

"What?" Walker asked, hearing something.

"Ahh nothing, just talking to myself," I said distracted.

"Sounds normal, dumbass," he grinned.

Grinning in return, I shot him the bird over my shoulder. I turned my mind back to the buildings and the tree line and watched for soldiers. We drove for another ten kilometres along the edge of Serb held territory.

Ahead, the roof of a building came into view. The structure sat on the top of a knoll and just off the road. As Klassen, the driver of 21-Charlie, pulled to a stop he simultaneously lowered the ramp and we dismounted. Klassen stayed with the track and clambered up into the commander's cupola, where he trained the .50 cal machine gun on the building. A 4x8 sheet of plywood dangled precariously from the eves by some tattered twine. Upon it, painted in black, were the words, 'Hotel California'. Spreading out, we silently moved up to the structure and took positions on either side of the door, minding where we stepped. The wind in the grass, my racing heartbeat, and the slight creaking of my flak vest were all I could hear. The sergeant gave the signal to move in. With weapons at the ready, Charlie Stephens pushed the door open and walked in, I followed, and I was followed in turn by Sgt. Penderson, and then Walker. The wind whistled through the willow type trees making the hair on my arms bristle in response. I peered through the broken windows. The building appeared to be uninhabited. I believed it was an old school house. As we entered I recalled the sign on front of the school, 'You can check out anytime you like, but you can never leave.' the words of the song sounded more eerie as I stepped over the bodies of two dead Serb soldiers. The flies, buzzing a gruesome song of their own, were already hard at work. The four of us spread out and walked carefully from room to room looking for survivors.

"They've all checked out," Stephens said, mocking the name of the establishment.

"Clear!" Walker hollered from a far room.

I lightly kicked open the front door to look outside. A Yugoslav flag lay on the steps, its broken flag pole hanging over the railing. One corner was saturated in blood that had been leaking from one of the corpses. I examined it carefully for an anti-lifting booby trap. Carefully, I pulled it from the pole, gave it a quick wringing out and I stuffed it in my right leg map pocket. The weapons from the dead were collected and secured. We exited and moved out to the carrier. The day was going to be like this. Hell, the whole mission was like this. Moving from village to village, looking for survivors, civilians or soldiers. One thing I was certain of: we were going to find more dead.

The daily patrolling of the UNPAs continued. Our 900-man Battle Group was still on its own to conduct its mission. No other countries had arrived to assume their responsibilities. The traditional role of peacekeeping was being redefined on a daily basis at the UN HQ in New York. The re-definitions filtered down to us after we had already made the changes. In effect, we were bringing on the UN changes as we went about our daily patrols, and letting the UN believe it was their idea. The UN thought it was calling the ground level shots, but in reality, we were. Our mandate was changing to include 'Pink Zones' that lay on the outskirts of the UNPAs. Of course with the exception of our own combat vehicles, through our active patrolling, we had managed to push almost all of the military style vehicles out of the four Sectors. The Serbs controlled the regular army vehicles keeping them within the JNA. The Croatians had done what they could at the onset of the war by building their own army vehicles. Their relics were strewn about the countryside.

Imagine being thrown into a civil war and you have to fight against your country's standing army. You have no tanks and no APCs. What do you do? Well, you raid the local steel mill and welding shops; that is what you do. With a little know how you can build your own mechanized army. Take any big rig highway truck, cut all the fancy stuff off and weld sheets of plate steel to where the cab used to be. Cut small slits to see through and of course four inch round holes at intervals for firing ports and, voilà, instant APC. If you are really creative you can even use a city transit bus, which I saw at one point down by the Dragovič Line. Slap on a coat of olive drab paint, splash on some brown splotches for a camouflage effect, and for the finishing touch, highlight the front by adding stylish shark teeth like a WW2 P-51 Mustang. One was colourfully adorned with the name CEDO-TREB which translated, meant 'Chetnik-Whacker'. The rigs we saw were interesting to say the least. A few were even well thought out. The better ones employed sloped armour with the intent to deflect bullets or anti tank rounds. Another had been constructed with spaced armour. Spaced armour essentially, is two plates of steel welded in such a way that there is a space between them. This is done to negate the kinetic energy of an anti-armour explosive round. In this case the new armour engineers filled the space between the plates with sand. I cannot imagine how much the improvised tank must have weighed, but I am sure it was heavy. It may have looked like a scene from Mad Max, but under the circumstances the engineers of these road warriors fabricated functioning combat vehicles with limited resources. Sometimes they were fortunate to abscond with JNA vehicles.

A week later we were travelling down the Dragovič road and that proof came screaming right by us. We stood with mouths hanging open as we were passed by a Bov-3 outfitted with twin 30mm cannons. The Bov-3 was the new four wheeled APC of the JNA. We were impressed that they actually had some real fire power. It was not the twin guns or the fact that it passed us. It was the huge American flag flying high atop the turret that caught our immediate attention. The Croatian commander of this Bov-3 was a smart one. He knew that the Serbian forces did not want any US involvement so he hoisted the American flag gambling that he could drive around with impunity. By using this form of camouflage they were able to drive through 'No Man's Land' with ease, charting enemy positions and movements at their leisure. It was quite remarkable to watch. As impressed as we were by this improv we had to end their free reign. A roadblock was set up and when they made their eventual return we intercepted them. The meeting went exceptionally well. They respectfully pulled down the flag and handed it over. In broken English they explained what we figured to be reality about their use of the flag. Capt. Waddell explained that he would be informing the Serbs about their conduct and that it would be dangerous for them to continue driving without the flag and to stay behind their lines. All went with smiles and handshakes. We wished that all the negotiations were that pleasant.

A few days later I was sitting on the roof of our bunker, soaking up the sunshine, when a UN jeep pulled into our camp. A sergeant loaded with enthusiasm, and an ear to ear, smile jumped out and walked up to me.

"C-C-C-C-Corporal Casey?" he said with his usual stutter.

"Hey Sergeant, what's up?" Sgt. Kellogg walked up to me. He was N. Coy's Int sect. commander. Because of his size, chippy attitude and the fact he worked with secret information, he was nicknamed, 'Secret Squirrel'.

"I've been informed that you ha-ha-ha-have some really good photos of the armour around here."

"Yes, I believe my photos are pretty good." I said trying not to sound conceited.

"C-C-Can I get a looo-look at them?" he asked.

"Ya sure, when do you need them by?" I questioned his time frame.

"Well I'd like them ASAP. I want to put t-t-t-together an updated AFV package for the B-B-B-Battle Group. Maj. Devlin has heard your pictures are decent and thinks they wowo-wo-ould be valuable for all the troops to refer t-t-t-to."

"Wow, that's a nice compliment. I can get copies made cheap when I head into Daruvar tomorrow."

"That would be great. C-c-c-can I get a looo-ook at them right away so we c-c-c-can choose the ones for copying?"

"You bet," I said, "I'll meet you in the kitchen in ten minutes."

In the time I had been in Croatia I had assembled a pretty healthy assortment of photos. Everything from main battle tanks to armoured personnel carriers to ground mounted recoilless guns. I had been collecting them just for my personal collection of memories. This was an opportunity to make them available to the whole Battle Group. I felt like my photos would be benefiting everyone.

The days passed by, patrol after patrol. Cyrus Vance, a special envoy to Boutros Boutros-Ghali the UN Secretary General, was brokering peace agreement after peace agreement. We knew from daily 'O' groups that Milan Babič, the self proclaimed Serbian rebel leader of The Krajina, had threatened that there would be UN casualties when we entered the Former Yugoslavia. So far short of a few minor wounds the Battle Group had not encountered any major troubles. It was laughable to watch the news on the one t.v. our Company Quartermaster brought from Germany. We had hooked it into a satellite link. That was not all that was a joke in regards to watching the tube. It was as if the reporters were reporting on a totally different war than we were watching. The Serbs were doing this and the Croats were doing that. When in reality they were quite often killing their own people and blaming it on the other side just for the media. We had to be impartial, which is not difficult when the World Community has tied your hands behind your back under the guise of being peacekeepers.

The weather was getting warmer as summer crept into full swing. Cordon and search operations were conducted, yielding many weapon seizures. These seizures were usually accompanied by the removal of the soldier from the Sector by their respective police force. He would then be de-commissioned as a soldier and sent home. This I thought was a joke, because I knew he would be back on the front-line by sun down. Liaisons were organized to afford Croats and Serbs alike, the ability to return home. Each village had an ethnicity that outweighed the other. That was what determined which ethnic group would remain and which would have its ass handed to them on a plate. This is also why we witnessed refugees walking in all directions. They had no idea where to go because the civil war had no structure as to where the front line was. So they would wander aimlessly, trying to stay alive. Most, however, had no homes to return to. The opposing side would force the inhabitants to leave their homes then systematically destroy the house so the owners would have nothing to come back to. The interesting thing I noted right away was the fact that the houses were not exploded, but rather imploded. The inside walls would be brought down inside the home by explosives, leaving the outside walls standing. It would be much easier to clean up the mess if it was contained in one pile versus blown across the countryside. Whether it was Croat, Serb, or Muslim it was done with extreme prejudice. There would be no peace here for many years I thought. The hatred here was too deep for this to be over in a year or two let alone our sixth month tour. I could not comprehend the hatred. Maybe some people in other countries around the globe might understand the depth of it, but this Canadian boy could not.

PHOTO ALBUM

Quit school to get schooled

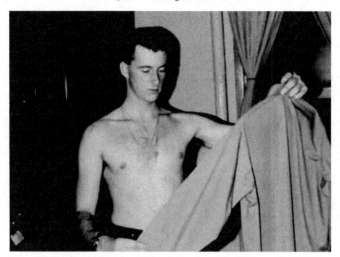

Serving in Denmark

Ranger and I

The East West Connection (day 2 in Croatia.)

top: The bridge at Gornje Bork

middle & bottom: Mad Max vehicles

The morning after being shelled when the main body arrived

Disputed T-55 with the charred remains inside

Dr. Spock's tank

Entire village razed to the ground

The Dirty Dozen

The infamous house

Arrival at the Sarajevo Airport

Posing with French troops

118

Following another shelling
(day 2 in Sarajevo.)

The Holiday Inn fiasco

First Canadian aid plane

Damir and I posing with the truck he refused to drive

Weaving through obstacles, *note steel dragons teeth

top: Unloading humanitarian aid

middle & bottom: Small truck hitting landmine in front of PTT building. During and after. The crew was shot as they ran away by unknown gunmen.

Working with the boys in Anti Armour platoon, *note hull down position

My truck after receiving heavy fire

Manning the C6 machine gun on patrol in Sarajevo

View through a TOW missile sight

top & middle: Tank shell hole, Pakrac and Buducnost sign, *The Future

left: Major General Lewis MacKenzie and I at the N Coy reunion

WALKING THE LINE

"We have war when at least one of the parties to a conflict wants something more than it wants peace."
~JEANE J. KIRKPATRICK

It was a warm sunny morning when we started south west through Pacrac. From my position in the rear hatch I scanned the countryside over the sights of a C-6 machine gun. My Iltis was down with engine trouble so Burke and I jumped in our APC. I enjoyed these days doing regular grunt duties. It was relaxing and far away from running around like a cannonballer looking for the next checkpoint. The crops were growing nicely in the farmers' fields. I so longed to be standing in a field of hay with the warm sun touching my face. I tried not to think about the farmers. They were more than likely dead, their crops left to fall over and rot. Again, I cleared my mind, and took from the landscape what I could.

The wind was making the hay dance in the morning sun. I was happy to be here. Every so often the radio would buzz in my headset with a 'Contact' or 'Shot-rep'. I struggled not to let the war interfere with my new found serenity. Unfortunately, the smell hit my nasal passages first. The images of dead soldiers that lined the ditches came second. I opened my mouth, thinking it would minimise the stench, to my taste buds dismay, it only made it worse. The smell of freshly cut hay would be a heaven sent thing right now. There straight in front of us half blocking the road, half in the ditch was the burnt out hull of a T-54/55 tank. We slowed down just enough for Axle to scan the chokepoint for mines or ambush. I did the same. Once there appeared to be no threat I quickly grabbed my camera from its nest under the hatch opening and snapped a couple of photos. We passed by the scene without stopping. Questions filled my mind. What had happened there? Who were they? The answers would come. We arrived in the section of Croatian front line we had been tasked to patrol.

Here we checked in on Croatian positions and got the story about the tank. Three HV soldiers had commandeered the tank and were furiously making their way to the Croatian side of the battle when a Serbian controlled M-84MBT engaged them. The Croatians were killed immediately, thus ending their efforts to add the tank to their arsenal. This had taken place nearly two weeks earlier and the fighting was so intense over it that none of the bodies either in the tank or the rescue teams could be removed. It took a week of continued negotiations. Finally, we organised a plan for the bodies to be removed.

November Company had been in Croatia two months and there was little I had not seen. The fields full of bloated animal carcasses, streets and alleys littered with dead soldiers, and civilians gunned down in their backyards while gardening. And the hanging priest still haunted my nights. Through our presence though, I noted, a change was coming. Recently some local villagers had returned to Sirač. Not in throngs, but enough to show signs of life, aside from soldiers. It was mildly uplifting. Ray and I sat in the shade of the community hall across the road from the Privredna Banka in Sirač. As we sat there a BRDM-2 with its cannon rolled up on the wrong side and parked in front of the bank. Ray and I looked at each other.

"Who's gonna mess with a guy robbing a bank with that puppy?" I asked with a giggle.

Ray answered immediately as he raised an eyebrow,

"Sure as Hell ain't gonna be me."

We had a laugh at the thought.

"If it was me," I said, "I'd use the BOV-3 with the three 30mm cannons."

"Well, keep in mind their money ain't worth shit and you'd need a dozen MLs full just to get a million bucks." Again we laughed.

"You know what's really funny?"

"What's that?" Ray asked.

"It's the fact that, that's a Police vehicle."

Ray nodded and shook his head. Marked on the side in six-inch-high white letters were the words Vojna Policija.

"They could probably use that in LA or Chicago," I joked.

The vehicle was only permitted in the Sector because it was a Police vehicle. What a joke I thought.

We had been out in the thick of it all day. The Croats were making a big push to the south of the Dragovič road. The Serbs were not interested in lying down and giving up. Our guys were doing their best to stop the fighting. Without getting right into the battle it was almost pointless to be out there, however, the officers did their best to liaison between the sides to broker a local ceasefire. The fighting raged and our blazing white targets were right in the middle of it. As we drove down the, imaginary line of peace, mortars whistled overhead. Shots zinged past our vehicles and into the opposing wood lines that lined most of the roads. Ricochets made their agonizingly close sounds as they careened off our APCs metal exterior. Driving into a destroyed village that still harboured some Serb resistance, a barrage of mortars began exploding to our right flank. The buildings were taking fire all down that side of the street. With every impact the shards of wood and brick flew by us. Our driver swerved through the kill zone and once again we escaped with only minor injuries. If Canada awarded the Purple Heart, for being wounded in combat as the Americans do, dozens of us would have been awarded it by tours' end. Canada used to award the Wound Stripe to its wounded warriors, but abolished it decades ago.

As night fell we dropped back to our platoon areas and waited for the fireworks display. We could not be out running around in the dark. Under normal battlefield conditions we would be more comfortable under the cover of darkness but our mission here did not allow for it. So with our hands tied we holed up for the night and listened to the daytime battles turn into night time skirmishes. Donny Bralorne and I were sitting on the hoods of our jeeps.

"Pretty cool, eh?" Donny said to me as we watched the tracers arc upwards and then fall to earth.

"Yes, it's pretty impressive. I wonder how many of these dumb bastards will be dead by first light," my lack of emotion quite evident.

"You're such a shining light Casey."

"I'll take that as a complement."

We sat and watched the tracers for a while longer.

"Well Scotty, I'm gonna call 'er a night."

"No prob buddy, have a good sleep."

"You too," he said.

I shifted my body up the vehicles hood and leaned back against the windshield, staring off into the dark.

"Morning Corporal Casey," called Capt. Burke.

Startling the shit out of me, and in knee jerk form, I levelled my C-7 at him.

"Little late for that don't you think?" He said, smiling.

"Agghh, you're lucky it hurts too much to squeeze the trigger," I said in agony.

Again he laughed.

"Well that's what'll happen when you sleep on the hood of an Iltis."

Groaning in stiff pain was my only response. My back was killing me. Sliding off the hood I asked,

"Do I have time to grab some coffee?"

He offered quickly,

"It's against the Geneva Convention to deny food and water."

Before I could respond he threw me a zip lock bag with a toasted bacon, lettuce and tomato sandwich. He held out his other hand with a steaming cup of coffee in it.

"I saw you out here fifteen minutes ago, but let you sleep. We don't have time for you to get cleaned up. You can eat on the way."

And with that he slid in behind the wheel.

"L-tee?" I raised my brow and voice.

"If anyone asks, we are in a war zone and it's only right that I should know how to drive this in case you get wounded," he replied, knowing what I was going to say.

"Don't get too comfy though Scotty, cause once you're finished breaky you're gettin behind the wheel again."

"But my beauty sleep?" I said jokingly as I looked in the small jeeps' mirror.

"Even if you slept for a year it wouldn't help that face," Burke let out a bellow of laughter.

That evening, I sat in the kitchen portion of our tent, listening to the BBC. After two months in this country and listening to grunts jabber on, it was soothing to listen to the melodic sound of the British female journalist reporting the news from around the world. Her voice had a hypnotic quality. She went on about the 'no fly zone' imposed by the British and US governments in the north of Iraq to help protect the Kurds there. She reported on the Serbs intimidating Croatians and Hungarians from returning to their homes in Vojvodina. She went on to report on the same in reverse, of Serbs being refused to return to homes in The Krajina. She switched gears and moved on to cricket and the football scores. Manchester United was doing well. Her melodic voice washed out the reality of how terrible things were all over the world. I sat and listened to her for another half hour. I was not interested in the news. I sat quietly imagining what she looked like. I wondered where she was from. Thoughts of my wife and the horrible state of our marriage interfered with my day dream. I suddenly felt very alone.

Today we would be heading to the southernmost portion of Sector West. Capt. Burke decided to ride in the track today. From earlier patrols in the Iltis, Burke and I had seen a large amount of JNA and HV armour in the region. Being in the carrier would offer us a little bit more protection than the jeep. The section mounted up and we were joined by the three other section carriers in our platoon. It was chilly on this late April morning.

"Any idea where we are going exactly?" Sven asked me. He was still wiping the sleep out of his eyes.

"We are heading to the very south of the sector, no place in particular, just patrolling the area."

"Gotta love the Sunday drives." The words he offered reminded me of home.

"Even if it's Thursday."

"Is it Thursday?" he asked.

"I have no idea, Sven, it could be Tuesday for all I really know."

"It all sure blends together, eh?"

"Sure does, eh," I agreed.

A few minutes went by and our platoon of APCs clattered out onto the road. Axle pushed the throttle to the floor and the engine belched black smoke out of the stubby exhaust pipe on the right front corner of the carrier. It flowed directly to the back and I caught a full breath. Again it reminded me of getting up early with my dad when he was logging. He would fire up his old Kenworth and the engine would clatter and the smoke would pour out of the chrome stack. That was one of the few happy memories of my growing up. The track lurched to the right as Axle gave the tiller bar a strong pull, as he negotiated a row of land mines that had been placed on the road. There was no sign of anyone around to claim the mines. Capt. Burke tried his best to mark the location so Holdfast could come and remove them. I was glad Axle was paying attention. I looked down through the back hatch and saw Campbell leaning on a rucksack, his headphones sealing out the noise of the carrier. He was listening to the ICS and monitoring the Company radio net as well.

After another hour down the road we encountered a built up area. Most of the homes had the common signs of battle. Bullet holes riddled a couple, three had been imploded, and one had a RPG splatter mark across the front. Sven looked at me, the concern playing out on his face. Three of the homes on the left had blood sprayed up the walls at the four-foot mark. From there it had dried black as it drizzled down the walls. In the blood were a dozen or so bullet holes. This could have only come from one thing, an execution.

"You feel that, too?" I yelled to him above the roar of the track.

"Yaaaa," he yelled back.

There is a sense soldiers get over time. A sense that tells them something is not right. This was one of those times. There was no one in the street or in the yards as we entered the village. We came to a T-junction, and turned left, as it appeared to be where the larger portion of the village was laid out. Axle drove the track about two hundred metres into the village. It was not till then that we saw the first life form. A soldier stepped out of the bush. His energy was dark. It was ugly in that mind. My hand deftly slipped the safety off, Sven followed suit. A couple more soldiers came out of the woodwork and they had their weapons at the ready. We had not surprised this bunch. The tension was instantly very thick. As we continued into town more soldiers appeared.

"This is getting bad," I thought aloud.

Sven nodded, as we were now looking at seventy plus enemy troops. Then the hair stood up on the back of my neck. In between every house, in various degrees of camouflage, were T-54/55 tanks.

"One, two, three, four,...ten, eleven, twelve, Holy shit look at them all," I counted aloud.

I leaned forward and clicked the ICS open.

"A few more than we saw a month and a half ago eh L-tee?"

With his face showing major concern he nodded.

"Are you getting a count?" His voice crackled through my headset.

"Roger that, I count sixteen so far and about seventy dismounted." I reached down into the hatch and found my camera bag. I had strapped it to its nest in the bungee netting on the wall. I cautiously brought it up onto the deck, never taking my eyes off the scene in front of us. I set it on a ration box we had tied to the deck. I pulled my British combat scarf from around my neck and laid it over the camera leaving the lens exposed. I was taking a big enough chance having it out. I did not need to make it blatantly obvious. I clicked away in the general direction of the tanks. I would not know how the photos would turn out for a few days. The usual bloated animal carcasses littered the grassy areas. The tracks behind us followed along and we exited the town on the eastern edge. Our patrol continued for another half hour till we came to a junction and turned south again. The energy was slowly subsiding from the Serbian tank laager. Burke keyed the radio side of the ICS control,

"...All call signs 21 this is 21Sunray...we will be making a 15 minute stop up here... Stay on the hard stand and keep your spacing...You can dismount in all around defence...."

"...21Alpha Roger...Over...."

"...Bravo Roger...Over...."

"...Charlie Roger...Over...."

"...21Sunray...Out...."

We dismounted and while some guys provided cover, the others took the time to relieve themselves. Then they switched. It took a couple of minutes but the conversation started.

"That was incredible," said Ross as he strode up to me.

"No kidding. There were more tanks in that place than Canada had in its whole arsenal," I blurted incredulously.

"Did you see the one with the rubber matting being used as side shields to detonate RPG and anti-armour shots?"

"I saw that. I hope I got a good shot of it."

"You were taking pictures you crazy bastard?" Frank said in disbelief.

I was grinning.

"You're retarded. Did you see how many of those wing nuts there were? Most of them looked like they killed their own families."

"Ah relax, we're representatives of the United Nations," I chirped cynically.

"Whatever," Frank said exasperated.

Tommy chimed in like a southern belle,

"Frank you don't think those nice gentlemen would do harm to lil' ol us now do ya'all."

"Oh man, you're as retarded as he is," Frank remarked shaking his head as we low-fived and laughed at his displeasure.

"Did you see the first guy we encountered?" Frank asked.

"Did I see him? He damn near burned a hole through my head with those eyes." Our break ended and we mounted up. The trip back to Sirač was uneventful. We patrolled about 270 clicks. It does not sound like much, but when your vehicle top speed is 35-40 kmh. and your average speed is 20kmh it takes a few hours to complete a day's ride.

I parked my jeep and walked over to 5 platoon's HQ APC. Tyler was sitting on call sign 21's ramp. He had his helmet off and his feet up as he was monitoring the radio. Tapping his pen to imaginary music he looked up and smiled.

"Well how's Mrs. Campbell's little boy today?"

"Well he hasn't managed to stir up too much shit today," Tyler said chuckling.

"Keep your chin up lad, the days still young. You could piss someone off real soon."

Lifting the right side bench seat, he reached in and pulled out two Cokes. He handed one to me.

"What do you make of this war, Tyler?"

"It's an ethnic thing," he replied.

"Gotta agree with you there, buddy."

"I'm sure there's more to it but it's definitely fuelled by racism."

"Ya, the names Slobodan Milošević and Radovan Karadčič come to mind," I added.

Those two were in the hot seat for ordering ethnic cleansing, the environmentally friendly name for genocide.

"And those are only two that we know about," Tyler scoffed at the reality.\

I amped the conversations tone up a bit.

"This war could easily be fought back home in the same way, eh?"

"How do you figure?" Tyler looked at me and asked inquisitively.

"Think about it, at the base level. Serbia, at the base level in terms of its distance, ethnicity, its way of life and its overall disdain for the rest of the country. Take, take, take, and give little in return. The people's desire for a 'pure' state that reflects only their values. That's Serbia or Quebec. You follow?"

"Continue," he replied.

"So one day Slovenia has had enough, that's BC, so they break away, luckily with no bloodshed," I explained my theory.

"I'm listening." Tyler confirmed.

"Alberta and the Prairies are Croatia. Seeing what BC had done, they decide to do the same. Only they aren't so lucky to get away without a fight. Oil money right? Ontario is Bosnia."

"Carry on."

"So the war starts, now English speaking and French speaking neighbours are killing each other in all the western provinces, because of their ethnicity. Claiming enclaves as their own, much the same as here in Croatia and in Bosnia."

"Jeepers you really put some thought into this hypothesis, Scotty."

"Not really, it's just a similarity I noticed. I don't even know if there is any real basis for my thoughts. I just don't want this shit to happen to us one day. And if the Separatist's have their way it could be a reality. And it scares the shit out of me."

"Have you forgotten? We are here side by side with the FAMOUS Vandoos."

"Ya, thanks for instilling confidence, Tyler."

"That's what friends are for."

"Oh, there's the L-tee. Gotta go. Have fun brother."

"You too, see you back at the tent."

I was truly concerned about Canada. I honestly believed that a similar type of conflict was a very real possibility back home. I hoped that our way of life and Canadian values would avert that sort of thing but the thought still lingered in my mind.

The one thing that I had learned about Croatia was that this was a place where anything could happen. You could be getting kisses, hugs, flowers, and a handful of thank you's one day. The next day you could be totally ignored as if you did not exist, and the very next day they were trying to kill you. The damndest thing was you did not know which until you were in the middle of it. To further confuse matters, they could be performed by the same person or people. Today would prove to be no different.

A BRDM-2 passed us at break-neck speed with the whole crew waving and full of smiles. Twenty minutes later our patrol encountered them in Sirač parked at the local watering hole, IKO's Bar. They were still in a high spirited mood out on the street with Pivos and AK-47s in hand. We were greeted by their commander.

"Do Vijenia, UN. Good evening, UN," he translated needlessly.

"You, Burke," he said obviously referring to Bill after reading his nametag.

"You drink vit me, no?"

"Good evening to you, sir, but no I can't drink with you."

The conversation went reasonably well considering we were dealing with a belligerent drunk, who was holding a Scorpion machine pistol in his hand.

"Ok you no drink šljivovica, you have shit friend for party next veek."

I raised my eyebrow while containing my laughter at his poor use of English.

"What my Captain means is, I will drink for him; he is too soft for sljiv."

The L-tee shot me a dirty look. To which I smiled coyly back at him.

"I'm takin one for the team Sir, so watch my back will ya?"

The drunk Scroat, as we referred to them, rhyming it with scrotum, smiled and put his arm around my neck,

"You, no Chetnik!"

"Nope, me no Chiklet," I could not resist mocking him in his drunken state.

"Shtand ve drink," he commanded.

"Dumbass." I snickered as I was already standing.

Ah yes, a friendly drink between men, he probably thought. The first few shots of šljivovica went down just like gasoline. For the next two hours I listened to how the world did not care about Croatia and how the Serbs raped and pillaged. The ranting went on longer than I remember. At least the 'šljiv' was making it tolerable. I had become his lifelong friend in the over indulging. The evening ended without incident. The next day would prove to be different.

Four Extra-Strength-Tylenol just barely took the edge off of my blistering hangover headache the next morning. I grabbed a Pivo from my kitbag and guzzled it.

"That oughta do it."

A couple of hours later, Burke and I rolled up to a Croatian roadblock.

"This shouldn't be too painful, it's your drinking buddy up there," Bill let out a laugh.

Drinking buddy or not, we were met by raised weapons and voices alike. The Scroats were hollering at us and pointing their weapons at us. Without being told to, I got on the horn.

"...2, this is 21Whiskey...sitrep, Over...."

"...2 send, Over...."

"...21Whiskey we are stopped at a Croatian Charlie Papa...approximately two kilometres south of Badeljavina...one BRDM-2 with four dismounted-infantry...we are going to liaison, Over..."

"...2, Roger, keep us posted... Out...."

We both exited the jeep and approached the group. They were accusing us of transporting Serb soldiers through their land. It was physically impossible. With Bill and I and all our gear we did not have room to squeeze in a coffee break let alone a couple Serb soldiers. They asked forcefully to search the Iltis. We politely refused to let them. They became more agitated. We had formed a reputation for standing our ground. The Croats as well as the Serbs knew we did not scare easily and if we were pushed we would fight with conviction. So there we sat in the stalemate. I radioed our situation in and Coy HQ was going to direct one of 7 platoon's APCs our way for back up. We had been at this impass for ten minutes. It was time for us to show that we would not be bullied and hope that reinforcements would arrive in time if we got in a shoot out. If the Scroats were not going to let us pass, then we would detain all traffic by taking control. I turned my Iltis across the road and we stopped all traffic. The road was soon blocked to them as well. After a half hour of this impasse, the commander from yesterday's debauchery came stumbling over, drunk again, or still. It was clear early in, that this was a poorly disciplined unit.

"UN, you go now," he ordered harshly.

His men kept their weapons aimed at us the whole time. I had my weapon at the ready and assumed a ready to move body position. I had already searched the immediate ground around me and located my route should this escalate to a firefight. Directly in front of me was the BRDM-2. Two men stood to its left-rear side, the commander on the ground to the right side front. The 12.7 machine gun in the turret was manned by the fourth. Our Iltis was behind us to our right and it would not give much cover from the 12.7 anyway. In front of us and to the right of the BRDM was a small knoll. That would be my escape route. It would also give me a good position to return fire, as long as I could make it there. I gave Bill the look, motioning at the knoll. He nodded knowingly. My finger danced lightly on the trigger of my C-7. I had already switched the fire selector to automatic. It would be wise to get as many rounds down range as quickly as possible if we were to have a chance of making it to the knoll. Another ten minutes passed since the stand-off had begun. The warlord was losing his edge. He was sweating profusely. He knew we meant business and were not going to succumb to his wishes. Seeing the weakness, Capt. Burke commanded sharply,

"You will now move your men and vehicle. You will leave now. This is a United Nations controlled area."

In our usual style, Bill was determined to show this local warlord that we would not be pushed around. The point was to be made, even if there were only two of us. His men began fumbling on their feet. They were unsure as to what to do. It was great to watch, but nevertheless somewhat volatile, in that they were unpredictable. The warlord waved his hand in disgust at Bill's suggestion, turned on his drunken boot heels and stumbled back to his BRDM. There was a five-minute pause, and then the Croatian APC fired up and drove down into the ditch. They then roared past us and disappeared in a flailing of mud and hand gestures. I scanned the round firing ports that ran down the side of the APC and watched for protruding AK-47 muzzles that may have been pointed at us, there were none. The Croats were gone in seconds and the tension lifted.

"Well that was a heap of fun, eh Scotty?"

"Ya, great times, sir."

"I wasn't completely sure how it was going to turn out," he offered.

"Me either."

"Had the tables been turned, I would have killed us in a second, buried our carcasses right over there, and had a beer to celebrate."

"Well sir, lucky for them, we show restraint and discipline. If this was our war things would be very different."

"Yes Scotty, it would be."

We carefully controlled the couple of cars and farm tractors that remained, out of the checkpoint traffic jam and went on our way. We carried on with our patrol of Sector West and headed into Sector South. Within an hour we met up with 2 section's carrier 21B, and Lt. Burke had a chat with Sgt. Glass. They had observed a small exodus of civilians walking south through the bush between Okučani and Stara Gradiška. The group was made up mostly of elderly civilians, with a few middle aged women hidden in the middle of the group. Women still capable of rearing children would often be raped then murdered so they could not continue their genetic line, be it Serb or Croat or Muslim. Other than their names, I honestly could not tell the difference. We were hearing stories of rape camps, designed merely, to feed the low instinct desires of men. The rag tag bunch appeared to be carrying what they could on their backs. My thoughts were filled with momentary sorrow for these displaced people. They had been in their homes only a day before, merely to be cast out as living garbage the next. Their homes dynamited or set ablaze.

Sgt. Glass reported that his section had monitored the fleeing expedition for half an hour. The refugees did not run into any resistance and had crossed the border into Serb held territory, which signalled that they could have been Serbs fleeing Croatian hostilities. Lt. Burke inquired about the welfare of 2 section's men and Sgt. Glass confirmed all was well. They shook hands and off we went.

Exhausted, the L-tee and I returned to Sirač sports field, arriving two hours after the last patrol got in. It was dark and we had to slog our way in between the cots and gear into the kitchen portion of the modular. Everything was laid out and orderly. Rifles lay on top of flak jackets and blue helmets adorned the top of each pile, just as firemen lay out their gear, for quick access to engage in a fight. The guys were stretched out relaxing, playing cards and bull-shittin.

The television was on, up in the corner, and it was tuned to Sky News. Bill and I arrived at the grocery table only to find we were too exhausted to eat. We looked at each other, turned and walked away empty handed. I flopped out on my cot, without taking my gear off. My eyes rolled back in their sockets and I exhaled deeply.

FLIGHT OF 21-WHISKEY

"Man is the only animal that is cruel. It kills just for the sake of it."
~MARK TWAIN

The following day Lt. Burke had some details to take care of at Camp Polom. While we were there he asked if I would be interested in showing the Administration Officer and a couple other officers around part of Sector West. I did not want to lay about HQ so I happily agreed to the tasking.

"REMFs, my favourite," I grinned mischievously.

REMFs or Base WOGs, as we called them, were military personnel who stayed inside the wire. The main camp areas were denoted as the Rear Echelon. The people that stayed there picked up the acronym, Rear Echelon Mother Fuckers (REMF) or With-Out Guts (WOG) was another derogatory slang term used in reference to people who stayed in the cozy base camps. Military personnel, who stay in the Rear Ech, were doctors, dentists, pay clerks, quarter masters. The Vandoos pulled security duties for the entire camp. The WOGs enjoyed life in a nice secure camp and very rarely ventured out into the deadly world that surrounded them. These gentlemen, however, wanted to quench their imaginative thirst.

"I know just the place for your look at Croatia, gentlemen."

We exited the camp and made our way to the south. I was heading for Dečanovac. It was not that anything overly terrible had happened there. It was just that it would provide a good circle route for the tour. Along with being frequently patrolled by the Vandoos and November Company, it also harboured just the right 'tourist' attraction for REMFs. As I drove my Iltis, I calmly pointed out items of interest to the officers in the fashion that a tour guide would.

"Now if you look over to your right gentlemen, you will see that the houses have been imploded based on the owner's ethnicity."

All three looked with interest.

"How do you mean imploded?"

"Well it is easier for them to clean up a house that has collapsed in on itself, at the end of the war, rather than one that has been blown all over Hell's half acre. The ones they don't blow up with dynamite they set fire to."

My explanation was met with nods. Camera's clicked away.

"Over here you will see what's left of an entire village that was razed to the ground."

More ooohs, aaahs, and camera clicking. We drove along for half an hour; all the while the officers had lengthy conversations about the situation here. I calmly sat there and endured the school book discussion of how countries get themselves into these predicaments in the first place. It became more evident to me that they had formed their opinions based on text books and chatting around the dinner table in the secure perimeter of the camp.

My nose caught something floating in on the wind as we drove and it perked my mischievous side. You REMFs want to have something to remember? Something to chat about while eating your dinner?

"Well then, let's give you something, shall we," I said under my breath.

This was the point where my tour became gruesome and to the point.

"Now of course you'll smell this before we get there, but if you look in the ditch," I was slowing down.

"Right about here."

I stopped the jeep and killed the engine. The stench of rotting flesh was overpowering.

"Yup here they are. You will plainly see three bodies."

"This is the sad harsh reality of war, gentlemen. These are not soldiers. They are civilians. You will note that two of them are senior citizens and the other is an adolescent boy. They were killed because of their ethnicity."

My description of the scene was met by the sound of the wind. The Admin officer whispered a prayer for them. Overwhelmed by the putrid aroma, the officer behind me leaned out toward the centre of the road and puked his breakfast onto the asphalt.

"Oh boy, are you okay, sir?"

"Let's go Corporal," said the Admin officer holding his hand over his nose and mouth. I intentionally fumbled with the ignition.

"Just take a bit to get it runnin, sir."

My delay was just enough, as the officer on the right was now overtaken by the foul air and decaying corpses, and he too fired a volley of vomit from the back seat. I tried unsuccessfully to contain my smile and leaned down toward the dash giving the bic pen the proper turn. The jeep's engine magically came to life.

"There we go; cantankerous piece of shit," I offered my mock displeasure.

"That's fine Corporal, please take the short cut back to Camp Polom," said the Admin officer, his hand patting my shoulder somewhat frantically. The shortcut, I determined, meant 'drive as fast as possible and don't stop anymore.'

I lurched away from the ditch, to add to the enjoyment one gets from viewing a rotting corpse, and turned around. Nobody said a word the rest of the way back to Camp Polom. I drove up to the gate and the Vandoo sentry checked each of us visually and waved us in. His nose wrinkled when he got a whiff of puke from the back seat. Cleaning it up would be worth it.

"Well gentlemen, that concludes our service with United Nations flight 21-Whiskey. I hope that you enjoyed the tour of The Krajina."

The officers dismounted, mumbled their thanks, and walked away quietly.

"REMFs," I murmured quietly to myself and looked in the mirror smiling. "They were such a lovely shade of green too."

The battle climate had levelled off during the past week. It was nowhere near as crazy as the first few weeks had been. That is not to say that The Men in Black were getting shot at any less, it was just slightly more controlled. Our Battle Group had been on the ground for just over two months now. During this short flat period, we ventured out on a speculative limb that we were making change. It was either our good influence or the bad people were merely re-arming for a new offensive that created the lull in the action. As luck would have it, it was the second. Even with the brief break in hostilities the danger level was still high and it would only increase as we entered the third month. As was commonplace, the end of the week would usher in a breakdown in the fragile peace we had established. The Serbs were now making a push on the south-eastern flank of Sector West. Vukovar, a major centre one hundred and fifty clicks south east of us, had been under siege a year ago and we did not want a repeat. The JNA had rolled into that predominately Croatian city after an artillery siege that lasted days. The fighting was fierce and reduced to hand to hand in many cases. Within a few short weeks the city of Vukovar was reduced to rubble. The death toll there was reported to be in the thousands. Because of the escalating conflict to the south-east the racial fight was in effect recharged here throughout much of Sector West and our plate was now heaping once again. Indiscriminate shots from one side or the other turned into raging ethnic infernos. As in Canada's peacekeeping past, it was our task to extinguish the fires of hatred. The whole on again off again process was very taxing on everyone in November Company. Added patrols and increased patrol distances only worked to stretch the framework of time. Moments turned into hours, which turned into days, which caused most guys to lose track of time altogether. With dodging small arms fire, and being virtually on my own, my nerves were worn raw. Because of that, my piss poor attempt to keep a journal only got worse. My photographs would have to serve that purpose.

Within the week we had suppressed the racial tension but not before hundreds more on both sides had been slain. The bodies piled up and my strength to deal with them dwindled. Some of us had been tasked with the unpleasant duty of assisting with bagging some of the bodies for burial under United Nations cooperation. The scene was morbid to say the least. We were assisting in the removal of civilian deaths. As with the town of Gornje Borki earlier, the corpses littered the streets and homes. My camera sat idle in respect to the dead and I did not want to have to clean it later. The remaining living citizens would take them to local cemeteries for burial. There was a lot of crying and praying by the people. Many walked about in what I thought could only have been a catatonic state. This was especially noticeable when an elder would bring in the body of a child. It made me think of my own little girl at home and I immediately flicked the emotional switch to 'OFF' with a mallet. As difficult as this was, I was thankful we had not been here a year earlier and gone to Vukovar. I felt blessed that I only had to deal with my own little piece of Hell here in The Krajina. Over the next week or so, my mind kept replaying the kaleidoscope of ugly images, and they tormented my every waking moment. The scene was so grim that we have not spoken of it since. At that moment I understood why my grandfathers never spoke of many of their experiences in war. I tried to rationalize that this war, and all the atrocities in it, was just normal, and that I was no longer just reacting to my environment, but I was actually a living part of it. My mind twisted and turned as I tried to suppress what was happening to me. There would have to be an end to this craziness, I prayed going home would bring that.

Accompanied by Capt. Burke, we drove out to 6pl's location. It had been playfully labelled as 'Hill 141.' The platoon had dug in and occupied the hill for its key observation point. We were going to drop in for a visit on our way to check out each platoon's position and to exchange intelligence on daily HV or JNA activity. I turned my wipers on high as the drizzle we were driving in turned to a torrential downpour. The water was pooling on the road, making it difficult to steer and our little Iltis hydroplaned repeatedly. Pulling off the pavement our tires slid wildly across the grass spraying mud and dirty water in a rooster tail. I stopped short of the platoon's bunker and we dismounted making a mad dash for their modular tent. The storm had darkened the sky and we walked into an even darker tent. We stood for a moment, sopping wet, and waited for our eyes to adjust to the lack of light.

"Boy, you can sure tell these guys are not from our platoon, eh, L-tee?" I said referring playfully to their lack of electricity.

"Certainly sub-standard accommodations for this day and age, I must admit," he played along.

"Ya, ya, what brings the dredges of call sign 21 crawling out in this type of weather?"

6pl. Sunray, Capt. Dillon directed his question boldly at us.

"I thought you guys from Sirač were afraid of thunder and lightning?" added the 6pl 2ic.WO Benner.

"Uninformed as usual. It's not the thunder and lightning, it's the lack of Pivo and chips that scares us," I directed the comment with mock contempt.

"Go find the lads Casey, and leave your 'L-tee' alone with us so we can abuse him at liberty," the 2IC ordered jokingly, putting emphasis on the L-tee part.

"Yes, Warrant."

With that I turned and bolted for the bunker. Over my shoulder I heard Burke, "Thanks for the back-up, soldier."

I stepped into the darkness of the bunker. Inside the guys had a lantern burning for low light and warmth.

"Donny. How's it going, eh?"

I had not seen Donny Bralorne in a couple weeks. Our job as platoon commander's drivers kept us ridiculously busy.

"It's going, Scotty. You got here just in time. Are you stayin for a bit?"

"I'm not sure. Why? What's the occasion?" I asked not sure about the hype. "The light show should be starting anytime now. Almost every night, one side or the other, lobs a shit load of mortars into Pacrac," Donny explained as he was looking out the firing port of the platoon's bunker.

"Oh goody, I just hate it when I miss the indiscriminate killing of civilians," I rubbed my hands ghoulishly. As if he had willed it, the familiar sound of mortars thumping echoed up the hill. Within seven to eight seconds the deadly projectiles began their whistling descent into the built up area in front of us. The rule of thumb for determining distance was to count the seconds from the sound of the firing thuump to the explosion. We estimated the mortar tubes to be about eight to nine kilometres away. It did not take long and a single mortar fired out of the village back in the direction of the enemy barrage. The dark humour comment was about how 'pretty' it was. Mostly, we just sat and watched, shaking our heads in disbelief. From many patrols through Pacrac I knew that there were ten times the number civilians compared to actual soldiers down there. Surely, that should have meant something to the guys firing the rounds into the town, but the shelling, like the rain, did not let up and it pounded down even as the captain and I left.

It seemed that the rain might never stop. It had been continuous for two weeks and had no sign of letting up. We tried to get some sort of weather report from the intermittent t.v. reception we were getting, but to no avail. The only thing that seemed to come in on the television was reports of how General Mackenzie had been taken hostage by the Serbian forces in Sarajevo. These reports were discredited within hours as Gen. Mackenzie was seen on CNN claiming that plans for a Canadian peacekeeping force were being organized for deployment to Sector Sarajevo in the very near future. Yet again, the media correspondents were reporting a skewed version of reality. Two days earlier, a couple of UN appointed translators informed us about what was being said on Croatian media sources. It too, could not have been more different from the truth.

By the end of the week we were hearing rumours from our officer staff about going to Sarajevo. We were picking up whatever we could from the officers and the rest from the media.

The media, of course, was the last resort for accurate info. Many of us had learned that when it came to media views, we could only believe half of what we saw on t.v. and only a quarter of what we heard. The BBC, however, provided the best coverage and could more or less be trusted for accurate reporting. The following couple of weeks were beset with stress as we waited for confirmation orders for a Sarajevo mission. All the while patrolling of the four Sectors continued. As we neared the end of the third week of June the Capt. and I had been back and forth to BG HQ at Camp Polom a dozen times. It was on our last visit that we received confirmation orders that there would be a Canadian peacekeeping mission in the newly formed Sector Sarajevo at the start of July.

ROBIN HOOD

"How far that little candle throws his beams! So shines a good deed in a weary world."
~WILLIAM SHAKESPEARE

By the third week of June I had been in country for over three months. I had travelled through all four Sectors within all three of the UNPAs. The other contributing countries were now getting set up in their respective Sectors. I was fortunate to be a platoon commander's driver as it afforded me the mobility to go almost anywhere I wanted. Today was no different. I wanted to pay a visit to the Nepalese sector to see about getting a Kukri knife for myself as a memento. The Kukri was a knife of WWII fame. It was the preferred weapon of the Ghurkha soldiers. Tales had been told since the end of the war of the Ghurkha's silent killer skills employing this knife to remove the heads of enemy soldiers before they could scream. I was thankful to be on the same side of this war with the Nepalese, and took it upon myself to get one of these famous knives. Not one purchased through Soldier of Fortune magazine or some other cheesy company selling fakes.

The idea had spread within N. Coy and a bunch of the guys put in orders for them too. Sgt. Franklin was not busy so he asked if he could join me. We left the platoon lines and headed off to the south. We had a quick stop to make at Coy HQ to drop off some mail and then we were off. After driving for about an hour and through a few UN checkpoints we encountered a Serbian Bridge Demolition Guard, BDG, at a key crossing on the northern section of the Saba River. We slowed and weaved through the landmines and dragon's teeth. One of the JNA soldiers met us as we walked up. He was smiling and flashing the usual Serb two fingers and thumb wave. Being a smart-ass, I smiled and waved the Vulcan wave from Star Trek fame. With his thick Serb accent, he said,

"Beam me up, Scotty," he said, laughing at my antics.

He had another good chuckle when I showed him my military ID proving my name really was Scotty. The tension normally experienced with these unexpected visits eased for all of us with the present laughter.

Mr. Spock led Sgt. Franklin and I down to what could not be mistaken, even in its muddy dug in position, for anything other than an M-84 MBT. Most equipment used by Eastern Bloc countries was either bought directly from the Soviet Union or was a locally manufactured almost exact copy. The M-84 was a direct copy of the T-72 Soviet MBT, which was considered the most formidable machine the Soviets had on the battlefield. The M-84s were employed here at the bridge. These guys had good equipment and it was evident from the level of their morale. We got the guided tour of their position and an in-depth look at the inner workings of an M84. Mr. Spock climbed up on the turret. I followed. He opened the hatch and ushered me inside. I took to the opportunity like a fifth grader at an Aquarium dolphin ride. I jumped in with both feet, right up to and including over my head. Much to my surprise he pointed to the firing mechanism and began giving me orders. I could not understand his exact words but I equated it to receiving Fire Control Orders. He repeated his commands. He wanted me to aim at what appeared to be a T-54/55 HV tank in the woods approximately a kilometre to the north east of the bridge.

"You shoot! You shoot!" he ordered.

I laughed and said,

"I can't shoot, I'm UN. I don't shoot him and I don't shoot you." Again he ordered me to fire. Once again I explained why I could not.

He was becoming more agitated with my refusals. The other members of the tank crew became edgy in response to their comrade's energy. I looked at Sgt. Franklin and without speaking a word we agreed it was time to scram. I slid my hand across my belt and touched the butt of the CZ-99 pistol concealed under my combat shirt. I thought of the trade I made with the HV soldier months earlier. At this moment I was very glad I had taken the risk of acquiring it.

"Please don't be stupid, buddy," I told him quietly, as though only to myself.

My rifle was with the Sergeant. Foolishly I had allowed myself to be put in a confined space. I should not have climbed in to the tank in the first place. This was not a training range in Germany. It was a real time war zone. I was furious with my poor judgement.

"Really fuckin smart, Casey," I whispered as I calmly climbed up out of the turret.

Sgt. Franklin exaggerated the movement of looking at his watch,

"Better be moving out Casey, we have to check on the rest of 5Pl."

We moved with confidence even though we were a bit nervous. Once on the ground I strode up to Spock. Saying thanks in Serb and shaking hands with him helped to cool things down. We made our way out to the jeep and I made a controlled but hasty departure. I watched the mirrors to see if the main gun on the tank would be trained on us. Twenty minutes later we arrived at the Nepalese camp. After a short search I found the soldier who would procure the knives. He provided me with a Kukri knife for each of the guys who had given me fifty Deustch marks. I had been carrying DM 2,450. Nice spoil of war had the Serb tank crew killed us. Franklin and I drove back to camp and I doled out the knives to the happy customers. They would be nice souvenirs.

The tour was about to enter its fourth month and the heat was becoming insufferable. The temperature was climbing daily and with it came humidity. The air hung stale in our tent. The cocoa matting that we had laid out on the ground was holding the moisture from the ground. To make matters worse the temperature was fifteen degrees hotter inside than the temperature outside. The insufferable temperature woke me from a sweat drenched nap. My nose wrinkled from the mouldy scent of the canvas. I quickly went to either end and rolled the flaps open. A breeze blew in momentarily refreshing the air. I walked back to my bunk and kicked the lid of my barracks box closed. The heat was making me crazy. Staying here was not an option. I put my flak jacket on and grabbed my skid lid. With rifle always in hand I made my way out to my jeep. I had to do a delivery to the guys at WC-11 anyways. I loaded up the mail and the other supplies the troops asked for. Batteries for flashlights, foot powder, three boxes of rations, two crates of ammunition, and two air mattresses. The latter were for floating in the river.

I made my way along the road through Sirač and out past the cement plant. About three kilometres out of town I spotted a house off the trail. I had not seen anyone around it before. Today, however, it was inhabited. I skidded to a stop and waited for the dust to clear. I am not sure what made me turn around and go back. I just had a feeling. Dismounting, I cautiously walked the two hundred metres to where an old woman stood holding a wooden pitch fork.

"Dobar dan," I greeted her. She stood there frail and hunched over. She looked at me through cataract glazed motionless eyes. The fear she was generating was clear. I was not interested in intimidating her. Easing my hand slowly into my map pocket I pulled out a dry chocolate cake ration pack. It was a troop favourite. Putting my rifle into the crook of my arm, to free up both hands, she watched me as I ripped it open. I broke a small piece off and put it in my mouth. I then offered her a piece. She took it and put the cake in her mouth. She chewed the cake slowly. She smiled when the sweet taste of the chocolate hit her tongue exposing a mouthful of rotten teeth. Reaching out she took my hand and led me to the back of the house. There, in a rickety wooden chair, sat what was left of her husband. He was alive but barely. He was emaciated beyond anything I had seen before.

"I'm sorry you folks have had to live through this again," I said knowing they had lived under Nazi rule decades earlier.

Their blank stares confirmed they did not understand what I had just said. I raised my hand with my forefinger extended.

"One second, I'll be right back."

"Ne Razumije," she said.

"I know you don't understand."

With that I raised my forefinger again.

Again they just looked at me. I ran out to the jeep and grabbed a box of rations. I placed it on a block of wood by the back of the house and opened it. I quickly sliced the brown plastic packaging open with my Russell knife. Next I carefully laid out each of the items inside. The elderly couple looked on in amazement. It was apparent by their expressions that they had not seen many of the items in this MRE in quite some time. I smiled and as I made a physical gesture for them to keep this as a gift,

I said, "This is for you. The whole box is yours. I want you to have it."

The woman began to sob.

"Hvala," she said, as tears welled and rolled down her cheeks.

"Molem," I replied, smiling.

Her eyes showed even more surprise when she realized I was leaving the whole box, not just the single ration pack. I walked back out to my jeep, climbed in and drove to WC-11. It was not much but I felt better for it. I drove the road to WC-11 without thinking about the heat.

"Hey we ordered three boxes of rations," declared one of the troops.

"Shut up you fat fuck, you don't even know what it means to be hungry," I snarled.

"Wooo a little testy are we?"

"Ya, fuckin eh I am! We have so much when others have so little." I went on to explain about the old couple.

"Hey no prob, Scotty, we'll get by."

"Ya buddy we can order more."

The skies began to transform from blue to grey as though it were foreshadowing the turbulent battleground ahead of us. For the past two weeks the Company was in a UN style limbo. Our patrols were cut back somewhat to provide us with the time to square away our equipment for the impending Sarajevo mission. Set up of the 'Phase Two' platoon houses went ahead while we waited for movement orders. We would inhabit these homes when we returned from the Olympic city. I continued to run from checkpoint to checkpoint amongst other duties. The doors for my Iltis lay in their canvas bag unused for the entire tour to this point and I speculated they would stay that way for the remainder.

The last week of June was upon us. Capt. Burke and I were in at BG HQ as he had to finish up some of the last minute details for our road move to Sarajevo. While he was in at the Orders group I was out scavenging anything of value for the platoon. I walked from each tent to building all the while talking to the WOGs on duty so I could eyeball anything of value that was not nailed down- no one's personal effects of course, just the kind of stuff that the desk pilots could afford to be without, while we were in Sarajevo. I cut my scrounging early because I had managed to acquire a box full of Mountain and Coleman stove repair parts, along with other items that could be handy to the platoon, from an acquaintance in Quarter Masters Stores. I slung my rifle across my back and carried the goodies out to the parking lot where we were parked. APCs were coming and going out the front gate and I watched them with mild interest, more to see if they were November Company guys or Vandoos. Camp Polom was a busy hive of activity. One of the Battle Groups 5-ton tow trucks in our Mobile Support Equipment platoon was parked along the downhill curb of the main road of the camp. A small blonde female soldier was surrounded by the others in her crew. She was cute enough and very athletic and always seemed to draw a crowd of horny grunts and WOGs. It was annoyingly amusing to watch as she basked in their lustful thoughts of bedding her. I could not help but think of what fools they made of themselves. I walked by and avoided making eye contact with her. I did not need the distraction, to be honest. I had gone for months without sex, including not giving myself a rub and tug, and under the circumstances I was okay with that. Upon arrival at the parking lot I began storing my box of treats in the back of the Iltis. It was then that I noticed, over by the white canvas Post Office tent, a news crew which was making a lot of noise. In fact, there were a dozen news crews. They were lounging about waiting for the 'O' group to conclude, after which they could ravage any shred of news for the day's story. They knew we were going to Sarajevo. The speculation was high as to when we would be heading out. I sat and watched them. They looked like ravens on a gut pile back home at the dump, all squawking away at each other trying to be heard. I had to move my jeep for the 5-ton wrecker as it needed more room to make its turn back out of the camp. As I was backing it into my new parking space a Canadian Broadcasting Corporation (CBC) cameraman began filming me as I parked. Anna-Maria Tremonti, a well known journalist from the CBC followed in his footsteps. With all the officers in the 'O' group she decided to drum something up in the mean time. Speculation was that we only had a few days before we left for Sarajevo. She picked up her microphone and eyed her camera man to make sure he got the shot. She made a bit of small talk and then asked for a brief interview. I was impressed with the fact that she was even here, firstly, because I had not seen anyone from the CBC since we got in country and secondly, and perhaps chauvinistically as a consequence of my youth, because she was a civilian woman. The CBC reporter was accompanied by an officer from Canadian Forces Public Relations, CFPR. After the small talk she began by asking,

"What do you expect to find when, you get to Sarajevo?"

My reply was unexpected by her and of course by the CFPR officer.

"I'm expecting to find a city that's been given a blood soaked enema."

Miss Tremonti raised an eyebrow not sure how to react to what I said.

"Pardon, I couldn't hear you."

The REMF captain from P.R. gave me the sternest look a desk pilot could muster.

"I expect to find a lot of destruction and chaos."

Miss Tremonti-upon hearing my second response-asked a question that could have arisen only from within her own feelings I thought.

"Are you scared?" she asked, looking at my face for any tell tale signs of fear.

I smiled.

"Am I scared?" I repeated her question.

This was something I had put a considerable amount of thought into. Initially when we got to Croatia I was apprehensive. My dad's words resounded in my head once again. 'We're already dead, son.'

"No I'm not scared. All you have to worry about is dying, and if you worry about that shit you'll go crazy."

She scribbled in her notes. The camera which had been hanging on the cameraman's shoulder was now pointing at me. This interview was going like a firefight often did. Even though the bullets are flying in thousands of feet per second everything around you is like molasses.

"Do you want to go to Sarajevo?" she asked, the words escaping from her lightly coloured lips.

For a brief moment the interview had seemed to switch to slow motion. I looked into her eyes and discerned that she asked the question with fake concern. With that I gave her the most generic comment I could think of. It was so clean, and at the time, void of real emotion.

"Well it's not that I want to go, but in the aid of other people I will." She nodded. That was it. That was the line she was looking for. She gave a look at her cameraman that said,

"Got it."

He folded up his gear and walked away.

Before Anna-Maria left however I made a comment for her to take to heart.

"I'm not really impressed with how the media is reporting what's going on down here. I sure hope you tell the real story about us here," I said matter of factly.

She looked at me and then at the P.R. dork. I saw his disgusted look as they turned and walked away. I liked Miss Tremonti; she had an honest quality about her. As they moved to their next victim I could not help but notice how clean their helmets and flak jackets were.

With the impending Sarajevo mission, Canada Day was celebrated early. It was a typically warm day and a typical one for me in particular. I was running errands between BG HQ and the four platoon HQs. Capt. Burke was forming his battle plan for the move and needed me to run messages back and forth to the other Pl. Comds. This was the most secure mode of communication at our disposal. So needless to say I was running across The Krajina like a madman. While I was running these dispatches the guys played volleyball and enjoyed other sports activities. Canadian flags waved on the sports field portion of the schoolyard in Sirač. Beverages were consumed and the cooks assigned with our unit were doing a stellar job at the grill. They prepared a BBQ that still has no rival today. N. Coy was very lucky to have them and we showed our appreciation daily. To add to the festivities both of Canada's major breweries, Labatt and Molson's graciously provided a sea container of their products for our celebration. The troops were overwhelmed by the fantastic gesture of both companies. Showing our appreciation, in the true spirit of the Canadian soldier, the supply ran out quickly.

Two nights had passed since the Canada Day celebration and M/Cpl Hanson called the section together for orders. We assembled under the light of a lantern in our modular tent.

"I called you guys in for a meeting, not Orders, so you can put your field message pads away."

"A meeting? What the Hell does that mean? I asked with a raised eyebrow.

"Give me a second and I'll explain."

We all crowded in on a few of the cots to hear the story.

"Okay you guys are fully aware that in a couple days the company is tasked to go to

Sarajevo, right?"

There were nods all around.

"Well, we will be requiring some people to stay behind and take care of stores and such.

You know, to take care of things here while the Company is down in Sarajevo."

He paused and lowered his head. I leaned back on my cot so as to drift into the obscurity of our surroundings. There was no way in Hell I was going to miss this mission. I waited for him to start calling names. I knew mine would be near the top alphabetically. I could not be left behind. Then he spoke and I sat dumbfounded at the words that passed from his lips.

"Listen guys, I'm scared," he paused and looked at each of us before continuing. "I'm scared to go to Sarajevo so I'm volunteering to stay behind."

I looked at Ray, he looked at me. Without saying a word our eyes said the same thing.

That was not enough for Ray and he uttered our thoughts aloud.

"What did he just say?" Ray whispered.

"Did he just say he was scared?" I semi-confirmed with my question.

M/Cpl Hanson continued, "I'm scared, so I've drafted up this petition so that if you're scared too, then all you have to do is sign and you won't have to go."

I leaned over to Tyler Campbell and whispered,

"Is this guy for real? Did he just say it would be okay to sign a petition to refuse to perform our duty? Can you say Court Martial?"

My dumbfounded expression was being replaced by mild anger.

"I'm not signing that shit!"

"Me either," whispered Tyler.

Hanson looked at each of us and held his petition on a clip board out for anyone interested to sign. No one moved. The uncomfortable tension was too much for him and he got up and left to canvas the rest of 5pl. I was madder than a cut snake on hot pavement.

"I can't believe that just happened," I continued, the anger boiling out of my verbal onslaught.

"I passed every test on my 6A, I missed the last eight days of a three-month bag drive because my wife almost died giving birth and this chicken-shit mother fucker is wearing a leaf?"

I was referring to his rank of Master Corporal which has two stripes topped by a maple leaf.

"And they wonder why I have a bad fuckin attitude. He should be stripped and sent to Greisbach for mutiny!"

Greisbach was the military's version of prison and it is located in Edmonton, Alberta. It has the reputation of making civilian prisons look like an amusement park.

I grabbed my rifle and stormed out of the tent into the darkness. I did not go far, just far enough to be out of range of the light from the tent. I sat there for over an hour, seething. When I felt I could tolerate being near that piece of shit coward I returned to the tent.

Almost immediately after, the order came through confirming that the Canadian BG would be deploying to and securing the Sarajevo airport. The BG sent a small recce advance party to the besieged city. Major Devlin and his driver Jarrod Gainer were part of that advance party. They had been down there for a couple days when news got back to us that they had been shelled.

Jarrod had been chewed up a bit by shrapnel and had been medivacced to a hospital in Belgrade. The Major was okay. The news hit us all pretty hard. We did not know how bad-off he was. There was a notable increase in the tension level amongst The Men in Black. Peacekeepers or not, pity the dumb bastards that crossed us now.

According to my luminous watch I woke the following morning at 03:35hrs. Underneath me, my sleeping bag was soaked with sweat. I was lying in my skivvies and olive drab t-shirt. A poncho liner is a thinly quilted, camouflage, nylon blanket and at some point in the night I had kicked mine on the floor. It's warm, light weight design, and the fact that it could be rolled into a small package made it nice to have on patrol. It was also perfect for times when a down-filled sleeping bag was too much. Tyler Campbell was on his cot, which was only three feet away. He was half propped up on his side facing me. His eyes were half open.

"Fuckin hot, eh buddy," he whispered.

"No doubt, man," I whispered back.

"How come you're awake?"

"I haven't been able to sleep since I got here," I told him.

"An hour here, an hour there. How about you?" I asked.

"A little more than you but not by much," he replied still whispering.

"Can't stop thinking about going south?" I asked him.

"Nope it's right there every time I turn over."

"Ya me too." I confirmed.

"I'm sure it'll be okay," he said, not quite believing it.

"I'm gonna go visit the guys on sentry." With that I slowly eased myself up off my cot and slid my combat pants on. I vigorously shook my boots out and slipped my feet in. Grabbing my rifle, I stepped into the kitchen part of the modular tent. I deftly slid a magazine in and made sure the rifle was on safe and slung it upside down, muzzle facing the ground. I grabbed three yellow melmac coffee cups, poured them full with fresh hot coffee and stuffed some packets of sugar and whitener in my map pocket. I walked back to the main door. Quietly I took the four or five steps up to where the sentries were on watch.

"Morning, you guys want a coffee?"

Ross Varney answered first sounding like Randy 'The Macho Man' Savage, "You know it brother, bring on the black gold."

We always joked around about the wrestlers in the WWF. Ross was from Sarnia, Ontario and I considered him a good buddy. He was almost always smiling and it took something pretty shitty to wipe the smile off.

"Anything happenin?" I quizzed.

"Nah, couple of shots to the south, but overall pretty quiet."

"What ya doin up so early, Casey?"

"Campbell shit the bed, couldn't stand the stench anymore, so here I am."

It was good to laugh, even if it was quietly. On the forty-foot-tall, high frequency, antennae that stood beside our bunker the United Nations and Canadian flags flapped in the breeze. The wind felt refreshing. I looked away from Ross and Gerry out toward the distant trees that stood between us and Sirač. The glow of a soon to be rising sun appeared above the ridge to the east. My mood changed involuntarily. We would be leaving in a couple hours for Sarajevo. I had a sip of coffee and wondered if today was the day I would die.

'Hell' was how the media described Sarajevo. I would have my own slant on that soon. I tipped my cup to the boys and strolled out to my jeep. I climbed up on the hood and leaned back against the windshield. The cold glass felt good on my skin. My mind drifted back to sitting on our old Farmall Cub farm tractor, pulling an even older dump rake around the hay field. I could smell the hay just like I was really there. Just then, I recalled what my dad had said when I asked him about death. I could hear him say, "We all gotta die son, we're already dead."

He was absolutely right.

"I'm already dead," I said aloud.

I sipped some more coffee and smiled.

The days leading up to our deployment to Sector Sarajevo involved re-examining existing equipment within our platoon and within the Company. The rumour coming down the pipeline was that Sarajevo was surrounded by Serbian heavy artillery and an overwhelming number of tanks. In an effort to add some strength to our basic infantry peacekeeping arsenal, a weapon was coming from Germany. Bring on the TUBs. The military is famous for its use of acronyms. TUB was the platoon nickname for the M-113 TUA. 'TUA', Tow-Under-Armour is the TOW missile launcher encased in an electric armoured turret. The Conservative government, following in the footsteps of the Liberals, "cheapest equipment for the military" way of upgrading, purchased a turret conversion for the ancient M-113 APC. This turret would house the TOW missile system. The TOW missile was designed to destroy any armour threat on the modern battlefield. It had proven its effectiveness in Israel and Desert Storm. In my opinion as with many other Canadian soldiers the TOW should have been used on a newer firing platform like the German Marder armoured fighting vehicle. Anyhow, as Canadian soldiers, we were so used to doing so much for so long with so little that we did not bitch, we just turned up the sarcasm and the TOW Under Budget (TUB) was founded. When the plan to bring us to Sector Sarajevo was born Brigadier General Mackenzie directed the Battle Group commander, Colonel Michel Jones and N. Company OC, Major Peter Devlin to have four TUAs shipped to Croatia so they could be employed in Sarajevo. Gen. Mackenzie had been in Sarajevo for some time and understood the tank threat we would encounter. The order to have these tank killers brought into the mission was done without consulting the UN for approval as it would almost certainly have been denied for fear of looking like an escalation. Thank God for officers with the balls to make crucial decisions that take the survival and welfare of their soldiers into consideration before anything else. Gen. Mackenzie was one of those officers.

I was fortunate enough to use the new system during my time in Anti-Armour Platoon (AAP). With so few gunners, and the fact that my jeep would be parked, I was employed on the TUAs to cover off some shifts. The TUA would prove to be a valuable asset to our mission, providing us with anti-armour security and extended sight range from its powerful scope. It would send a message that we were capable of destroying tanks at a greater distance than they could engage us. All we had to do now was get there and maintain our position in Sarajevo. The journey would take us 300 kilometres into Bosnia and Herzegovina.

ROLL 'EM

"Yugoslavia is a multinational community and it can survive only under the conditions of full equality for all nations that live in it."
~SLOBODAN MILOSEVIC

On the 28th of June the sun had not even broken over the eastern hills when we mounted up. Each platoon drove south to take their respective places in the convoy. We rendezvoused with the platoons from the Vandoos. We were assembled into packets and prepared to launch our journey to Bosnia-Herzegovina. Bill and I sat quietly in our Iltis as each packet crossed the start line with the first one leaving at 04:00hrs. Packets would leave at intervals. This was done to minimise casualties from air strikes and to be able to adjust to battlefield requirements should a packet be attacked. The trip was quite scenic. The former Yugoslavia was a beautiful country before the war. At one point we traversed a narrow canyon that had a medieval castle on a cliff. It stood as a testament to its era. My camera clicked away.

Unfortunately, the scenery could not be fully enjoyed under the circumstances. We saw the scenery but we were more importantly looking for any signs of ambush. The air was thick with heat, humidity, and with tension. It was tense merely from the nature of the mission's vulnerability. We all knew that 750 of us would soon be further cut-off from any support and completely surrounded in a condensed city pocket.

Short of minor breakdowns and the heat, the day had gone without issue. With the first day drawing to a close we sat on the shoulder of the road, waiting. The convoy would have to continue our journey to Sarajevo the following day. As we sat there a local parade was in full swing. It was bizarre to watch. It was not your average hometown parade. It was a rag tag bunch of drunken Serb regulars making their way to reinforce the front line to the south. In true form the locals came out and were handing out alcohol to their heroes. An M-39 anti-aircraft gun parked right in front of me. Two men dressed in camo fatigues passed what looked like a 60-ounce bottle of dark whiskey up to the commander of the AA gun crew. He happily obliged by downing a few good mouthfuls. Already drunk, he narrowly stayed on board as his vehicle moved to stay with the parade.

They passed by and we set out to look for a place to set up for the night. There was really nowhere to go so we slept on the side of the road. Sentries were assigned to patrol up and down the column. We leaned our seats back and got as comfortable as we could. Burke and I tried to drift off to no avail. The seat finally became too painful and I opted for the gravel of the shoulder. Rocks dug into my skin with every turn. My poncho liner gave little resistance to their sharp edges. Finally, morning arrived and the convoy started off again.

Throughout the three hundred kilometre journey we were met by cheering crowds. We concluded that each crowd believed we were going to fight for their particular cause. We learned this through basic translation and hand signals. The odd shot would be fired at us from obscure locations. It was somewhat unnerving. Our first major stop in our long road move was at the Banja Luka city limits. This was a rest break and refuelling stop. Our white vehicles lined the side of the four lane highway. A twelve-foot-high hedgerow was to our immediate right across a ditch. To our left and across the three other lanes was a wide open field. Ahead of us was an overpass which we would be taking. I got out and stretched out the aches and pains of one of the worst sleeps I had ever not really had. It was before noon and the heat was already making dark sweat stains on most of the soldiers' combat shirts. Some of the troops asked if we could dress down to just t-shirts. The idea was declined because we were Royals and we would be dressed according to code. We would not be like the Vandoos who had already shed their combat shirts. I am the kind of person who sweats just brushing my teeth in the morning. So I did not care one way or the other because, hot is hot. You can only take so much clothing off before it becomes a moot point. So I drank lots of water and soldiered on. I cycled into my position at the re-fuelling truck. The soldier from the Vandoo transport platoon was smiling and whistling and looked as though he was enjoying his job, which I found interesting, as he was standing beside a really good target for bad people to shoot at. When fuelling was completed the Pl. Comds, Pl. WOs and we drivers got together for a group photo.

It was shortly after the photo that I noticed something shiny, glinting through the hedgerow to our right. I stood on the hood of my Iltis to offer me a better vantage point above the hedgerow. Upon further inspection, with jaw hanging slightly ajar, I found an Isayev S-125 Surface to Air Missile(SAM) sitting in ready mode for launch. These missiles were capable of reaching speeds of Mach-3. They were very manoeuvrable and deadly against low flying aircraft. Even the fastest NATO fighter jets were not capable of out running these babies and would have to launch Electronic Counter Measures to evade being destroyed. Surrounding this missile was an entire air base and the remaining battery of Isayev S-125s. I could not believe my eyes. There before me was a squadron of MI-8 Hip Soviet model troop carrying helicopters and a compliment of support personnel. I managed to get a couple of photos before we had to mount up. I mentioned it to Capt. Burke but outside of that I never thought much about it until later on. A member of the BG Intelligence Section called me in for a 'debrief' on what I had seen and to acquire copies of my photos. To our knowledge, that Serbian air base was supposed to have been dismantled as part of the peace agreement. Obviously it had not been. I was not surprised by that fact. I felt things would have been different if this area had been in one of the UNPAs. With the stretch and refueling complete we mounted up and continued our advance to Sarajevo.

I was still mesmerised by the beautiful scenery. It was a shame that these people were destroying such a magnificent landscape. I thought it might even be a good place to build a home at some point, however in its present shape that would not be a wise choice. Besides, I had lost so much respect for these people and their destructive path. I just did not understand how there could be so much hate. Maybe it had something to do with the intense heat. Daily temperatures in June/July were in the high forties. God knows it made us all irritable.

The road move to Sarajevo was definitely a time that I was a glad to be driving a jeep. Although there was zero protection from enemy fire I was out in the wind. Add to the heat the fact that we were wearing full gear with flak jackets and it was barely tolerable. As I always travelled with the doors off we captured the breeze unlike the poor bastards in the carriers. Even with the hatches open, as well as the man door in the ramp, a small access door for exiting without having to lower the ramp, the guys could not escape the heat. The carriers were also jammed full of equipment and the lads were forced to wedge themselves in amongst it. All the needed equipment and eight soldiers per carrier. To say the least, conditions were cramped and miserable. To make matters worse the APCs were antiquated battle wagons from the 60s. With the long move and excessive heat, it did not take long before break downs started. Fortunately, we were blessed not only with great cooks, but with two of the best mechanics the army enlisted. With tricks that would make farmers and NASCAR crews get out pen and paper these guys kept us rolling. They too worked in the blistering heat of the day which was doubled by the engine heat. The Royal Electrical Mechanical Engineers, REMEs, could not work the wrenches and watch for bad guys at the same time. So security was provided without being ordered for them as they had to work at feverish pitches to stay with the pack.

We encountered a few roadblocks while on our journey. None were more concerning than he who commanded his domain with a drunken iron fist. Many warlords were drunken abusers of the people in their local areas. They may or may not have had any military background prior to the wars beginning, and merely took up arms and took to killing anyone who would not succumb to their new power. Col. Jones tried to make peace with this particular warlord by assuring him we were just passing through and had no quarrel with him. However, he was an obnoxious drunk and would not listen to reason. He told Col. Jones that if we tried to continue he would order a full scale attack on our convoy.

As evening was drawing near, our BG commander decided it would be best to avoid confrontation, and we withdrew till morning, hoping that a sober mind would prevail. With that we pulled back a full 28kms in the direction we had come from and set up camp for the night. We withdrew so far for a couple reasons, both tactical. Firstly, the warlord would have to organise for any opportunity to get to us. Secondly, the area Col. Jones chose was a premium, defensible location, affording unobstructed views of any enemy advance. Wondering what might be in store for the following day kept almost everyone awake for the night. I spread my sleeping bag out this time and lay on top of it. The gravel from the night previous, felt like it was still embedded in my skin.

I awoke the next morning to the rustling of our sentries waking up the others. An anxious air seemed to be drifting amongst the platoon as we saddled up and headed into the eye of the storm. We knew the warlord had had all night to reinforce his position. The question was, did he? The tension mounted as we drew nearer to the warlord's territory. My hands fidgeted on the wheel. I looked at my rifle continuously, examining its body checking for any signs that it might fail me in the impending battle. We rounded the final corner that we had been stopped at only hours before and I cursed inwardly. The sun had come up and was shining right in our eyes. I flipped the sun visor down and quickly put my sunglasses on, Ray-bans I had purchased, years ago on my first European tour, when 1 RCR went to Denmark. I was proud that I still had them and they were in good shape. Superstitiously I hoped that they would protect me from the bad guys.

As expected, he had blocked the road, in anticipation of our return. Col. Jones went forward and was met by a somewhat less intoxicated warlord. He was still just as belligerent as the previous day. The worst part of the stand-off was that we were sitting ducks, lined up in a perfect row on the road. Occasional sniper fire from poorly disciplined warlord forces plinked into our ranks. As the situation escalated, our CO ordered that we deploy our TUAs to over watch positions. Our snipers were also deployed with orders to kill the warlord first, then to kill targets of opportunity. The sabre rattling plateaued with Col. Jones telling the Serb warlord that if he reinforced his position we would advance and kill everything in our path starting with our snipers killing him. No matter what happened, after the start of the battle, he would be the first to die. Col. Jones made him very aware of that. Without giving it a second thought, as the warlord was mulling it over, the Colonel made the decision to exploit the opening of indecision. Our convoy roared to life and we drove through the roadblock. We moved right through without firing a shot or being fired upon.

Later that morning we stopped briefly to allow the packet in front of us to increase its distance from us. Burke and I were both smiling and feeling relieved that the warlord had shown his bluff hand. As we sat there an old woman came running toward me. Down an incline, through the tall grass that was her front yard. She was clad in a dirty light blue floral dress and had a mouthful of rotting teeth. Her hair was askew and oily. She used her free hand to smooth one side down in an attempt to restore her dignity. The emotions she was feeling overcame her and she lost composure. Blubbering tears and ranting words poured out. She ran full out toward me, the bundle of flowers in her arms floundering under the strain of the laboured run. Sweat beaded and rolled down my face stinging my eyes. My combat shirt was half soaked from sweat. Fuck it was hot. According to my Canadian Tire thermometer, it 49c today. She was at the 100 metre mark and closing fast. I slowly lowered my rifle into the crook of my arm and slid the fire selector to auto. As was common practice amongst the Company, I already had a round up the spout. The woman, upon seeing the look in my eyes and the fact that she was looking down the business end of my rifle slowed down. I cautiously waved her in as I took up the slack on the trigger. The haggard woman slowly proceeded, the scent of the flowers only temporarily covering the smell of her body odour caused from months of improper hygiene. She laid the flowers on my lap and took my arm in her hands and began kissing it. The months of war streaming down her face. She had been witness to a husband and son being executed in her front yard before her, and her daughter's, eyes. At gun point she was forced to watch her daughter being taken away screaming into a backroom and raped repeatedly and then shot because she was young enough to bear offspring.

Sobbing, she exclaimed, "Dobra, Dobra." 'Please, Please.'

I was fighting to maintain my cool. She was so close to eating a burst from my C-7. The thought went through my head to give this wretched soul the comfort she was seeking, however, I could not seem to reach out to her. I could end her suffering either through a hug or by squeezing the trigger. I looked into her eyes and I allowed her pain to transfer to me. It was as though she could see into my soul and may have gained some consolation from that. My heart was pounding and I could not stop sweating.

"What the fuck is wrong with these people?" I ask rhetorically.

Bill, sitting in the passenger seat of our Iltis, just shrugged and my question hung in the air met by silence. The woman stood back, as we prepared to leave. I put the clutch in and slid the shifter into first gear. I looked away from her knowing that she was still looking at me. I forced myself to stare at the APC in front of us. I did not want to make eye contact again. I knew I would not be able to contain my helplessness for her situation. And with that I let out the clutch and we moved off in line with the convoy.

By early evening of July 1st, we could see the skyline of Sarajevo. It was right there in front of us. We stopped 38kms to the north. There was nowhere for us to stay in Sarajevo as accommodations had not been completely secured. So there we sat tired, sweaty, burnt out, and frustrated. Canada Day was supposed to be the day for our grand entry. Any hopes of that were now dashed. Dejected, we set out sentries. We were so close and the battles from the city raged so no one completely relaxed. We knew through our Int. Sect. that the Croatian forces had been successful in their southern push and were very near to Sarajevo. We were very much in their path. It was rumoured that they might attempt to link up with the Bosnian TDF. If this happened, we would be in the middle of an even bigger shit storm. Out here we would be sitting ducks. We needed to get into the safety of the city soon. I did not realise how crazy that thought was going to become.

None of us slept well that evening. The waiting was making the lot of us crazy. Warfare is described by many soldiers as 90% boredom and 10% terror. You sit around and wait and wait, and then everything goes ballistic. I laid my head on the butt pack of my fighting order and drifted off to the staccato of a machine gun off in the distance. The old woman came to me that night. She kept saying "Dobra, Dobra." I tossed and turned. She was making me crazy. Please what? How am I supposed to do anything more than I am already doing? I did not create this mess. And now you and the world want us to clean it up.

03:15hrs July 2nd, I woke to the sounds of a fierce battle to the west of our position. It was only a few kilometres away and I thought it was more than likely a first light assault by the HV on Bosnian Serb defensive positions. By 06:15hrs we were mounted up and waiting for the order to advance into the city. The battle to the west had been going on for three hours and was increasing in intensity. 07:10hrs we received the move order. As usual we were broken into packets and travelled at safe intervals to avoid being one huge target.

Our packet rattled to a stop on a paved single lane road draped by large over-hanging trees. We used the trees to provide cover from the air and from OPs, observation posts, up in the hills. My eyes scanned the underbrush near the road. I quickly but methodically took each piece of cover apart looking for bad guys. I could not see anything obvious. As we sat there, a few TDF soldiers came out of their hiding spots inside the buildings that were close by. From what I could gather they were all that was left of their unit. I know one thing for sure: they were scared out of their minds. They had a look to them. It only took me a second to nail it down. Each looked like a dog that bites from its own fear. I am surprised they did not engage us. Within a few more minutes some of the locals came out. It was with smiles that they placed flowers on the hoods of our Iltis' and in the open trim-vanes of the carriers. From a scene right out of a Vietnam War movie, a young girl walked up to Ted Jackson and placed a flower in the muzzle of his C-7. It was magical to watch. She did it, as though she knew that back before Ted joined the army, as a teenager, he was the youngest ordained minister in Canada. Ted joined the army, he told me, because he had no life experiences. How could he give advice to people twice his age, if he had no experiences of his own to draw from? Only a private, he was six years younger than I was, yet his intellectual wholeness gave him an air of maturity I was seeking for myself one day. I respected him.

After a half hour delay, we exited the security of the canopy and pressed on for The Show. The Show would be the name many of us would use to refer to Sarajevo. We entered the city limits at approximately 10:20hrs. We drove past a TDF checkpoint and meandered our way through a couple of JNA checkpoints. A kilometre from the airport we encountered one of if not 'the' most infamous buildings during our tenure. Hanging from one of the windows was a Canadian flag. To its right painted in big letters were the words,

'Welcome to Sarajevo' The building became infamous to us because we were shot at routinely from that location. As bad as we thought the first few months were, they were about to be overshadowed by a scene so ugly, Lucifer himself would cringe.

THE SHOW

"If you want to be a sheep, then you can be a sheep and that is okay, but you must understand the price you pay. When the wolf comes, you and your loved ones are going to die if there is not a sheepdog there to protect you. If you want to be a wolf, you can be one, but the sheepdogs are going to hunt you down and you will never have rest, safety, trust or love. But if you want to be a sheepdog and walk the warrior's path, then you must make a conscious and moral decision every day to dedicate, equip and prepare yourself to thrive in that toxic, corrosive moment when the wolf comes knocking at the door."
~DAVE GROSSMAN LTC US ARMY(RETIRED)

In 1984, Sarajevo was a portrait of Olympic beauty, colourful and full of life. Athletes and tourists buzzed around the city with joy in their hearts. In 1992, less than a decade later, the city was filled with death. People raced from point to point to avoid being shot by snipers. Gone were the bright colours and the feelings of joy. They had been replaced by charred paint and the feelings of doom and despair. The act of getting the daily water could get you killed. Snipers did not discriminate. They shot soldiers, women, children and pets. I actually do not like referring to them as snipers. It is an insult to those who do that job with honour. These barbarians were actually just murderers.

Rounding a couple more corners we entered the gates of the Sarajevo Aerodrome. The BG formed a tight leaguer and dismounted. 50. cals were pointed outward and remained manned as per SOP. Each of us was then given interlocking arcs of fire for where we stood. I was uneasy. The packets were too close together. I made my opinion known to Bill. Apparently someone with more rank than me had not learned from the shelling we had taken in Sirač. Luckily only the odd round whizzed by but over-all we were left to ourselves. A few French Marines came out and there were handshakes and smiles all around. In their confident way they proved that things were not volatile at this point just by the way they walked out. We were no strangers to being fired upon either. So we relaxed somewhat. After a bullshit session with them and a photo op it was back to business. Col. Jones was standing off to one side of our laager and doing a press interview. A couple of other officers stood around assisting in looking important. An APC rolled up into the view of the cameras and a few grunts jumped out of the back. One of the soldiers was bilingual M/Cpl. Gilles Tourand an R22ᵉR Mortar Fire Controller (MFC). There had been no room for him with his mortar platoon gunners so they had hitched a ride in another APC. Now they were standing in the middle of the Vandoo Commanding Officers press release looking lost through no fault of their own. Their unit had more or less forgotten about them. Within half an hour they were shuffled off and given a 'bedding in' area for their mortar, which they did in record time. With the 81mm mortars now embedded in position Gilles started the climb to the top of the Air Traffic Control tower. From here he would be able to observe Serb, Bosnian and Muslim mortar positions. The tower was poorly armoured. The sandbags were only partially doing their job. The roof was almost completely unprotected. Within seconds of being in the tower, fire from a 7.62mm RPK machine gun raked over our heads and slammed into the tower. Glass shattered and the guys up there were hollering like Hell. There was little any of us could do. The MFC continued to use the tower as often as possible as it afforded a good view. He did, however, perform a lot of it from the prone position.

We began to relax after a few hours of watching the local urban areas with all their gunfights. During that time, I went for a short walk about. A. Coy, I noted, was already thinning out of the laager and were assuming defensive positions around the airfield. Their APCs boiled out black smoke as they pivoted 360 degrees in some cases out of the laager. They would be staying here and providing permanent airfield security during our mission. I BS'd with some of the guys at the back of the laager and picked up the scuttle that we would be going to an old JNA military barracks. We did not know at the time but it would become our permanent home for a month while in Sarajevo. It would formally be named Beaver Camp. The profile of a beaver, accompanied by the words 'Pro Patria', small metal decorative pins, adorned the collar of our dress uniform. The Latin words 'Pro Patria' translated mean, 'For Country', with the beaver above it simply meant 'Working for Country'. Although the beaver portion of the name was from our Canadian and Regimental Heritage and represented hard work and industriousness, we hated the name for our camp. It sounded lame. We left the airport and wove our way through the city streets. Bullets ripped past us throughout the twenty-minute journey to the JNA barracks. No one returned fire as it was impossible to see where the shots were coming from. Stress levels were through the roof. Our tracks clattered around a corner where magnificent trees stood at the opening to the small JNA base. The barracks were in shambles. The carriers lined up and ground guides dismounted in order to back the tracks up safely. There was a large metal canopy that was selected for our vehicle parking. The noise of all the APCs backing in under the canopy was deafening. The metal clad building only acted as an intensifier to the steel tracks on the pavement and the roaring engines. Once all the carriers were parked the signal was given to switch off. This is done so that it is difficult to get a count of how many vehicles are in the hide location. It is very effective. When they were all shut down the remainder of us dismounted and got to work setting up a temporary camp. We would move into the main building tomorrow. For now, we would sleep under the stars, or the cover of the metal canopy. I chose to be just outside the building. Looking at how we had parked and were poorly spread out I could not help but stand there and shake my head. Had we not learned a single thing?

"What's with the look, Scott?" Capt. Burke inquired as he walked over.

"With all due respect sir, did someone really put any thought into this parking job?"

"What's the problem?"

We stopped our conversation for a moment to look in the direction of the city, as a couple of shots from outside the compound snapped by us.

"Come on L-tee, three months ago the company did the same thing and we got the shit shelled out of us," I said not believing this was real.

"Ah I see, well it's not our decision. Col. Jones has selected this as November Company's home."

"Well how fucking convenient. His boys are spread out across a two square mile airport and we get two hundred square metres. That sounds fair."

He knew I was right.

"Well we don't have a choice, so make the best of it, soldier," he said flatly.

"Yes Sir," I replied, defeated. "I still think it's a bad call," I said under my breath.

Hearing me, he replied, "So the fuck do I," as he walked toward call sign 2, the C.P. carrier.

The sun had been down for a few hours and as I rolled over on the asphalt. I did not know what time it was but it was the darkest I had seen in any city. As I fumbled with the Velcro cover on my watch, the darkness was transformed into exploding moments of daylight as the mortars came screaming in. Many guys had been sleeping under the steel canopy. Shards of molten steel pierced the roof and walls of the canopy. Everyone was in a state of confusion and terror. There was nowhere to run and nowhere to hide. I cursed the foolish decision to harbour us all in a confined space again. The saving grace was that the rounds were exploding 50 metres away leaving us just outside of the 'kill zone'. As quickly as the mortar strike occurred it was over and the night air was as silent as death. No birds, no crickets, only the silent smoke wisping around on the wind. We sat in our spots as though we were fixed with cement, each of us holding our collective breath.

"You missed asshole!" was the lone angry comment from the blackness.

We lay back down and tried to go back to sleep. The silence did not help our mental state and many of us listened, for quite some time, until the local militias could be heard firing again, and like a lullaby we drifted off.

In the morning we discovered that the Company had lost two Iltis' and an ML along with two sea containers full of gear. The shells had detonated inside the compound and the vehicles had actually shielded us from the force of the blasts. We were lucky once again that no one had been killed. An Angel was credited with protecting us, and over the next month that Angel would be very busy indeed. Our first patrols left shortly after the sun came up and they would start by beating a UN path back and forth to the airport. Others would be working with the UNHCR to establish Drop Points, DP, for humanitarian aid. In essence, patrols of the city began, before we even had a place to live. We had to make the most of our UN presence. Concurrently the officers were trying to secure some form of accommodations. I was out on one of the first patrols to recce a DP location and I teamed up with 21-Bravo. We drove through the north end of the city out to a location that had been described as a possible DP location. As it turned out the warehouse had been completely destroyed and with that information we returned to the airport. As we wove a path through many dragon's teeth and concrete block barriers, we were learning our presence here was not a welcome thing. This was made clear by receiving a lot of small arms fire. As we got closer to the airport I thought I saw a group of civilians in the brush just off the road.

"Did you see that, Tommy?" I said concern clear in my voice.

"Did I see what?"

"Well it looked like a bunch of people huddled in that field back there on the right." I pointed with my thumb over my right shoulder.

"They weren't soldiers, they looked like handicapped people."

"Nope I did not see them, but somebody said there's a mental hospital that lost its flock and it's rumoured that they are runnin loose," Tommy informed me.

"No way! The Vandoos are locked in at the airport right now." We burst out laughing.

My heart was momentarily upset as I looked back at the brush.

"Can you imagine if some of those poor bastards got a hold of weapons?"

"Oh man what a nightmare that would be for them," replied Tommy.

"Just being here in this shit show, sure as Hell ain't fair for them." I yelled above the din of the APC. I turned my head to the other side of the carrier and watched for any signs of trouble. Our carriers drone and rattling, like always, shook us through and through. My mind finally let the handicapped go and it returned to its growing callousness. A few shots whizzed by and I reacted mildly to their closeness. The other guys in the open hatch all had the same pissed off look. As we dismounted at the airport the thoughts concerning all of us exploded into conversation. Marvin Maise was the first to vent his frustration.

"This is bullshit, we get shot at, but we can't fire back because we're UN. What kind of crazy ass shit is that?" shouted Marvin.

"No, you can't fire back unless the incoming fire is effective fire," said Sgt Franklin emphasizing the effective fire aspect of his sentence.

"How the Hell are we supposed to know what is considered effective enemy fire?" The frustration was evident in Marvin's question.

"Effective enemy fire is when the assholes are shootin at us. That's what I learned in Battle School," Marvin said as he churned a cigarette butt into the ground.

"No shit, the shots are zippin by and the UN says, "Sorry, not close enough." Maybe they should bring their shiny fuckin shoes out here and show us how it's done!" Tony said angrily. We were feeling the anxiety from the UN handcuffing.

"What's it gonna take, one of us gettin greased before we can shoot back?" asked Tommy.

"It's bullshit that they can shoot at us and we can't shoot back. It's like being in a bar fight and havin your hands tied behind your back," added Ray.

I joined in by extending my arms and waved them from the side of my body up over my head and back down repeatedly,

"It's like anything inside of this, is effective fire. If it's outside arm's length then you're screwed," I said.

Sgt. Franklin nodded,

"Casey's got it right, inside the arm swing. It's BS for sure but it's what they want."

"Well they can go piss up a rope. If some Scroat's shootin in my general direction he'll be gettin 'er right back," Marvin said defiantly.

"You'll follow the rules, and if the bad guys are within the zone, then feel free to open up and blast 'em," ordered Franklin.

"No problem. I'll follow the rules of engagement, Sergeant," confirmed Marv.

Under my breath I said to him, "I'm with you. They will be eatin shit sandwiches if they shoot at me too."

Can you shoot back? When can you shoot back? Who are the aggressors and what do they look like? Just some of the many questions we asked over and over from the start of the tour. Shoot when it is appropriate and unless they are wearing stylish blue hats like ours they are all bad guys.

With all the added stress of being in the middle of this Sarajevo shit storm my nerves were a bit on the edge as I walked across the tarmac. The broken glass that had been blown from the boarding catwalk overhead crunched under my feet. With engines running, I could see the heavily armed escorts in their APCs. They were visibly brimming with excitement. Cupola mounted 50. calibres were being swung left to right to ensure freedom of movement. To the south by the last hanger lined up ready to go, sat six United Nations High Commission for Refugees, UNHCR, trucks. Scania flatbed trucks numbered 1 through 5 and a lone Volvo displaying the number 6 on the dash in its front window. When I was a boy my dad had a Peterbilt cab over highway truck and it had also displayed a number six in the front windshield. I smiled; this had to be a sign. Giving the truck a quick once over of the exterior I opened the door, climbed in and claimed it as mine. Laying my rifle on the console between the seats I quickly reacquainted myself with the controls. There was little time to get organized as the aid had to move quickly. It was reported that at the present rate the aid flights that were now pouring in would swamp the airport with goods faster than we could load them out. Turning the key, I fired the diesel engine up and waited for the low air warming buzzer to silence, signalling there was enough air pressure to release the brakes. The passenger door opened and my buddy Ranger piled in. I was immediately relieved to have him with me. We knew how each other would respond to danger. We were a good team. With Ranger riding shotgun we jockeyed into position for the first humanitarian aid run into a downtown DP. In preparation of our run, APCs from our four platoons combined with carriers from Recce Pl., left early and assumed covering positions at key locations along the route. I could see that many eyes from the Vandoos A. Company were now faced towards us and not towards Dobrinja. I imagined that they were envious. The grass of the infield waved in response to the C-130 Hercules aircraft as it roared down the runway in its bid to escape the evil clutches of the Olympic city. Once airborne and still visible against the bright sky, tracer rounds fired from a hidden machine gun in Butmir, arced up toward the plane. I watched as the softball size tracers streaked toward the plane in their bid to bring the plane down. Missing the plane, the tracers fell toward the earth. As I followed them to where they disappeared into the building etched skyline, my eyes came into line with the crew commander of the lead track. He had raised his arm high and dropped it forward signalling for the convoy to move. I released the park brake and slid the truck into gear. Within seconds we exited the relative security of the airport. Our convoy followed the lead carrier as it meandered its way through the various burned out cars and other obstacles that littered our route. Turning into the sun, Ranger and I squinted to see the road and the hidden dangers on either side of it. I had the air conditioning on full blast to ward off the already blistering temperature. I am sure the truck's air conditioning unit was angry with us because we had both our windows open wide. Ranger sat poised for action with his rifle out the window. With each corner or intersection we traversed, we were met with thumbs up from our guys that covered our advance. Moving down the littered streets a sound caught my attention. I could make out a, 'thwack-thwack' above the regular noise of the truck as we tore down the street. My curiosity was remedied when I looked in the mirror and simultaneously watched the wooden side rails splinter as the 'thwack' sound occurred again. The windshield in front of us shattered at the top.

With notable concern, I yelled above the outside noises, "These fuckers are shooting at us, Ranger!"

"Looks like we gonna have us a gum fight," Ranger whooped, like the crazy old coot in the '80s Hubba Bubba gum commercial, as he craned his neck out the window in a bid to determine where the shots were coming from.

"Good news, Sherriff," he said as he pulled his head in the window.

"What's that?"

"They can't shoot worth a shit," he said smiling and spit his tobacco chew out the window. With unobstructed views, the cupola on the lead carrier swung to our right flank in response to the shots raining down on us. To my dismay, the 50.cal machine gun sat silent in its cradle, as the gunner not being able to pinpoint the location. Sweat was streaming down my face from the heat and stress. Controlling the big Volvo, I guided it between a set of dragon's teeth and four PMA-3 anti-tank mines that dotted the road. I could clearly see the three black pressure switches protruding from the top of each mine. Our convoy twisted and turned on its path to the DP. The sun's rays would blind us as it burned down between each building. Then it would dim down again as we passed through the shade of the next structure.

I felt more and more disoriented with each change in direction we took. As drivers we just followed the APCs in front of us. I was not impressed by the fact that we really did not know the route to where we were going. We had been given a photocopied map of the city that was so poorly done it was hard to tell what was street and what was land features. If anything happened, we would be screwed. I did my best to remember key landmarks. That was difficult at best with all the other stuff I had to pay attention to. The thwacking of bullets hitting my truck did not make it any easier to focus on map and compass skills either.

It seemed like an eternity but we made it to the downtown DP. Slowly I made my way alongside the building. There was a protruding canopy off the side that our truck could fit under. I was content as it would provide added cover from sniper fire not to mention shade. Ranger bailed out before I had the park brake applied and he went right to work providing security for us. I climbed down and shook off the stress by busying myself with lowering the cargo sides. The spots where the bullets had ripped into the wood were now clearly visible. I had barely lowered the side rails when a team of UNHCR local volunteers began the bull labour of unloading the trucks. Within an hour all four trucks were empty and we were traversing our way across the city again. Once at the airport there was no time for celebration. We spotted the trucks near the piles of divvied up aid and the forklifts went to work filling the cargo decks again.

In between our aid trips downtown I sat and watched as a group of Vandoos cleared Foreign Objects and Debris, FOD, from the runway. It was a regular task as the props from the many planes would dislodge shrapnel and the likes out of the high grass of the infield. The FOD was also deposited from the occasional stray mortar that just 'coincidentally' exploded around the airfield. Investigations into the shelling would be pointless as no one from the TDF or JNA would accept responsibility for shelling a UN position. Within half an hour we had begun our second run into Sarajevo. It was a mirror repeat of the inaugural load. By 4:30 in the afternoon we had made six aid runs into the city. I lifted the side racks back up into position and replaced the securing pins on our last trip. Ranger and I were exhausted and looking forward to putting our feet up. We had had our fill of being shot at for one day. The sun was now over the suburb of Butmir as we pulled into our parking spot for the night. We clambered down out of number 6 and I met him at the front of the truck. I was happy it was over and we were safe.

Shaking his hand vigorously I said, "Thanks buddy, good job."

"Ah whatever, you did the work, I slept through most of the last three trips," he replied, shrugging off the thanks.

"Whatever, if you could sleep through that bit of driving, you're more fucked in the head than me."

I smacked him on the back ushering him ahead of me toward our waiting carrier's ramp. Within a minute of shutting the aid trucks down, we climbed into our track and headed for Beaver Camp. Once in the confines of our compound the lot of us celebrated with a cold Pivo. Just one, as sentry duty and such details still required our sober attention. Enjoying the moment, I revelled in the view provided, as the sun was hanging lazily over the ridge to the west of Butmir. Its reddish glow cast against the interior wall of our room. Like pro hockey players in the dressing room after a glorious win we stood around retelling the day's events. The two bullets that slammed into the wall by the door normally would have caught everyone off guard. The interesting thing was that nobody flinched. Everyone continued on with whatever it was they were doing as though nothing had happened. A couple of butterflies would have garnered more attention. At least they would have added some beauty to this forsaken shithole. The sun went down and the fireworks struck up a new show. I killed time by cleaning my rifle and doing some short letter writing while I waited for my sentry shift at 23:00hrs. There was no point trying to sleep before it. That is, providing I could sleep.

It was common practice for snipers from all the sides in the conflict to shoot regular citizens in Sarajevo. The French Marines had organized anti-sniper posts. These posts were set up to observe snipers killing innocent people and to provide proof that these crimes were taking place. In one case when a UN vehicle was placed in a particular OP, sniping from the Bosnian Parliament buildings would cease. When a UN vehicle was removed the sniping of civilians would resume. These posts were designed to observe and record these criminal snipers. Each side would deny that this sort of activity was taking place, and that it must have been the other side committing the action. We knew it was a pile of crap. Other posts were designed to kill criminal snipers. Part of the United Nations Mandate allowed for 'the protection of civilians by the Use of Deadly Force.'

When we first got to Sarajevo, I personally witnessed a pregnant woman being shot. The scene unfolded so fast that it was unbelievable at first and none of us could react. It was across the Sava River, so not only did I witness it, I was also helpless to do anything about it. This would be commonplace for us in Sarajevo, and the list of incidents would only become longer. To this day the incidents still haunt me. Another similar occurrence happened later that day. A Vandoo section was on patrol when they were involved in rescuing a woman who had been gunned down along with two others. She was fortunate to be alive.

Sgt Jacques pulled his carrier up to the scene to create a blocking device to try and pull the innocent to safety.

Sgt. Jacques and another soldier exited the track and crawled to the aide of the first victim. He was dead. Jacques crawled to the next casualty, dead. He made it to the woman and quickly pulled her in the direction of the carrier, the whole time under 'effective enemy fire'. There were some soldiers there who appeared to be TDF providing covering fire to the UN troops. With all the effort that Jacques and the others put in, the outcome was traumatic. The subsequent political ramifications exploded. The locals were angry with us for not having removed the dead, only the living. We were also perceived as helping the TDF, and the Serbian government played it up that way. They would learn to stop us and order an inspection of the inside of our vehicles. We would of course decline, however, if they held us long enough that some of the track commanders might cave in merely to show faith. Unfortunately, it set a precedent, and opened a door to abuse by the Bosnians and Serbs alike for later UN vehicles. This was shown after our withdrawal with the execution of a government official in a UN vehicle. It was a crucial mistake by that commander, as we would not have allowed the inspection, had we been carrying a subject of that nature. There most definitely would have been a gun fight.

After the shelling our positions took the night before, this day started like any other day in Sarajevo. It was 05:00hrs, and the symphony of soldiers waking in a war zone could be heard, with razors being clinked on the edges of metal bowls and the bursting of mortars just outside the wire in the suburbs. My cot was still somewhat creaky, even after four months of intermittent use. I got up and made my way to the ablution tent. This was set up outside and was the area where we washed and shaved. After a needed shave and whore's bath I proceeded to the parking lot where my Iltis was parked with the others. Capt. Burke showed up just as I finished my pre-trip and we buckled in for the wild ride ahead that would take us to the PTT building. Post-Telephone-Telegraph is what I believed it stood for. The PTT was the home to the UN HQ in Bosnia-Herzegovina. With all the skill I had mustered in driving, 'since I was a kid on the farm,' we took off. Veering through dragon's teeth and the burned out hulk' of cars and trucks we dodged shots from indiscriminate shooters.

The following day a team of four APCs and crews went to the Holiday Inn to conduct bargaining for lodgings. Our officer staff, headed by Major Devlin, went inside, and we remained in the parking lot securing our foothold. Having a bit of fun outside, Garcia and I took a photo of ourselves standing with the Holiday Inn sign. Meanwhile, inside the meeting was not going well. The UN was prepared to pay $35 US per man per night. The building was worse for wear and would require a lot of work to make it safe for us to use. The managing staff of the Holiday Inn Sarajevo wanted us to pay $150 US per man per night and for that price they would provide food as well. An interesting concept considering one of the main reasons we were here was to provide food to a starving population. The two sides could not come to an agreement and the officers came back outside. We were 'coincidentally' pinned down by sniper fire. It was late in the day and we opted to wait for darkness to fully withdraw from the area. We returned fire when we could actually see where it was coming from, but most of the time we just sat behind cover and waited for nightfall. Dusk came and so did the urge to use the toilet. I walked up the steps of the Inn and I went inside. Walking up to the desk I asked,

"May a few of us use the bathroom facilities? We've been pinned down out there for a few hours and would like to use the washroom."

"No you may not. Your commander would not bargain in good faith. The media pays good money. You are UN scum, here to do the Serbian people injustice, American puppets. So go back outside and die," he commented with venom.

"Okay no problem, just thought I'd ask. Have a nice evening." With that I walked back outside.

"Well what did he say?" Leon asked, shuffling side-to-side, doing a humorous rendition of the green apple two-step.

"He said he would prefer if we shit on the front steps," I said smiling deviously.

"What?" He stood there in disbelief for a moment.

"He said he would prefer if we 'shit' on the front steps." I repeated unbuckling my belt as we walked. In unison, we dropped our drawers, and left a deposit for them a few feet from the front doors. Like grade school pranksters we ran down the steps laughing, jumped into our waiting carriers and sped off under the cover of darkness.

In the days ahead the captain and I would no longer be using the Iltis for getting around. The constant incoming fire was too dangerous for the soft skinned jeeps. APCs would provide the armoured protection we would need. We arrived at the PTT building and walked inside early in the morning as Capt. Burke had some meetings to attend so he would be a few hours. So I did what soldiers do best when they are on a break. I found a good place to hide. Recce platoon was lodged here at HQ so I took the time to go visit some of my buddies and shoot the breeze while I killed time. I had been there about an hour when a French soldier appeared. He was looking for me. So I obliged him and stepped out in the hall. It was here he told me that my Pl. Comd had offered my service to the French Marine commandos.

"Well isn't that just fuckin lovely. Gone an hour and he pimps me out to do shit-jobs for these guys!"

The French soldier looked at me with a raised eyebrow and said,

"No shit jobs, mon-ami, you have been invited by my commander to join us in protecting General Mackenzie."

"No shit eh?" I said in disbelief.

"Je ne parle pas Francais," I offered up my lack of French.

"No shit," he said smiling.

"Get your equipment and meet us in the lower parking level. We leave in ten minutes."

Although outwardly I looked cool and collected, I was out of my mind excited. We had been doing an exchange with the French so it seemed plausible to me. They would ride with us for a few hours and some of our guys would ride with them. This would prove to be a once in a lifetime for me. I wished I had brought my camera. I assembled with the marines and they gave me a basic rundown on their SOPs. Speed and action of violence was the cure for any would be assassin. Protect the General at any cost. After all there was a million-dollar bounty on his head. I was brimming with excitement. The French were carrying 5.56mm Bullpup assault rifles which were more compact than my C-7. The Bullpup was less likely to be yanked away in a crowd than my longer rifle.

Oh well, make the best of it, I thought.

General Lewis Mackenzie strode through the door with a couple other officers in tow. His confidence was very noticeable as he spoke with the Marine in charge, he then turned and acknowledged me. The commando had obviously pointed me out. Gen. Mackenzie walked over and shook my hand.

"Glad you could make it, son. I understand your platoon commander said you would enjoy coming out for a few hours."

"Yes sir, I wouldn't miss it for the world," I beamed.

"What's your name soldier?" he asked, looking me over with his tactician's eyes.

"Corporal Casey, sir."

"Okay, but what's your first name?"

Did he really just ask me what my first name was? He is a General. Why would he give a shit what my first name was? Answer him dumbass, I quickly ordered myself.

"Scott, Sir," I replied calmly. He turned a bit to shield his coming comment.

"Alright Scotty, these boys are highly trained Marine Commando's, so don't make them look too bad okay?" He winked.

"I'll try and go easy on them, sir."

Even though I could see he was deeply distracted, he patted my shoulder and we enjoyed a chuckle. The group of us mounted up in our respective vehicles. Gen. Mackenzie and his driver got in their VBL Panhard. I climbed into a Vab 4x4 with the rest of the commando bodyguards. This was the first time I had been inside a French APC. It was dubbed the VAB4x4 for only having four wheels. It has a big brother called the VAB6x6 for obvious reasons. The VBL was an agile and very quick recce style armoured car. It had a low silhouette, bullet proof glass and came outfitted with an electrically fired machine gun which could be fired from the protective interior. All perfect reasons for our top General in the Balkans to use the car.

We arrived in downtown Sarajevo moments later. The French Marines and I hurriedly exited the VAB and covered the General's movements from the Panhard to the front door. Our weapons moved in unison to where we were looking, scanning every possible location for would be shooters, as though in a frenzy. He went in to have a meeting with the TDF Vice-President Ejup Ganič. His dedicated Marine guards followed him inside, the others and I remained outside watching for activity. As I watched for any would be assault, I reflected upon our short conversation and the Generals demeanour in my head. He had acted as though we were equals and because of that, I respected him now more than ever. He was a good officer and he really cared about his soldiers. The city although under siege had quite a bit of daytime movement. There were no people strolling through the streets window shopping or sitting in corner cafes sipping hot coffee. They were, however, looking for water and food or lost loved ones. They would run from one building to the next trying to avoid being sniper targets. I envisioned them to be more like rodents scurrying along in search of crumbs trying to evade being seen by the cat. I felt a deep sadness for them.

It was a short meeting and General Mackenzie returned quickly. He was visibly pissed off. We covered his exit from the building and the General again mounted up. Quickly, we were off to the PTT building again. I strained to see his VBL Panhard armoured vehicle as we sped down the city streets. Bullets pinged off the steel side of our VAB. I learned later that he had warned Vice-President Ganič that if they continued to set mortars up near UN locations that he would authorise us to kill any of his TDF soldiers on sight, a very ballsy thing to say, considering we were UN peacekeepers. I was impressed. Outside of the usual pot shots at us I was glad that the trip was uneventful. Generally, that kind of conversation would have gotten us in a pickle of some sort but Gen. Mackenzie made it clear we were not to be messed with. I thanked the French Marine commander for the invite. I then wound my way back up through the maze of hallways and stairs and found Capt. Burke. As we made the descent back downstairs I thanked him profusely for the bodyguard mission. He looked at me with a quizzical look on his face.

"What bodyguard mission would that be?"

There was a bit of a silence as his question struck me off guard.

"Whatever, sir," I said to counter his jesting.

"Seriously, what bodyguard mission?" he asked stopping at the door to the back of the PTT building. The concern on his face was evident.

"Are you kidding me? You didn't send me with Gen Mackenzie?"

My face in turn showed my obvious surprise. As we stood there for a moment I tried to figure out who had sent me. I re-wound the events in my mind to the French Marine who had called for me by name. He had called me by name, had he not? The whole scene now became confusing. Interrupting my thoughts Bill spoke again with conviction.

"Scotty, I didn't send you on any mission. I thought you were hanging with Recce platoon this whole time." We stepped out the door and headed to our waiting carrier. I shook my head and shrugged. We mounted up and headed for Beaver Camp. As I watched for bad guys, I could not shake off the weirdness of the day.

The task of staying vigilant was easy enough. It was the business of determining which side the bad guys we encountered were on that was difficult. We had figured that, generally speaking, anyone wearing the standard JNA dark camouflage uniform was a Serb soldier. Anyone wearing a hodgepodge of civilian and military gear was Bosnian TDF. A soldier waving a thumb and first two fingers was definitely Serbian. A soldier waving the peace sign was Croatian. Anyone waving in general was Bosnian. Those who did not wave at all just plainly hated us. Clear so far? Now the UN wanted to rely on its ace peacekeeping force, us Canadians, for a mission in the newly created Sector Sarajevo. This is where who's who gets murky. In the ethnic melting pot, you can find Bosnian Muslims, Bosnian Serbs, Serbs from Serbia, Bosnian Croats, etc. It gets crazier still.

Let's throw a few rival street gangs in there, fighting over drug territory. It is only within reason to believe that people who were hooked on drugs before the war would still require their supply during. One simply just does not get over a heroin addiction just because there is a war going on. Let's not forget the drug bosses still want their revenue. On many occasions I witnessed gang members doing business. Although it became common place, it surprised me at first. We were doing a drop at DP-19 the Olympic stadium. I was standing watching a UNHCR fellow give directions to the unloading crew as to where to stack the aid when two teen-aged males and a guy in his early twenties rounded the corner and passed by.

"Hmmm that's odd, its forty-nine degrees," I said aloud to myself.

One of the boys was wearing a long trench coat style jacket. Something about the jacket caught my attention and I cautiously followed them at a distance. We did not go far which was good, as I did not want to get too far from the security of my guys. There it was, the thing that caught my eye, the muzzle of an AK-47. With that I adjusted my position, sinking to one knee and leaning into the concrete of the stadium. I was not sure what they were doing initially. They were definitely uneasy. So I observed them. I did not want them to be making plans to waltz in and take our loads of medical supplies. After a few minutes, two guys in their thirties showed up from the other direction. After a brief discussion the twenty-ish year old and one of the older guys shook hands. The teenager without the AK switched his backpack with the other older guy for his sports bag. Each opened and inspected the contents of the swapped bags. Nods were exchanged and the meeting was over. I knelt there in disbelief at what I had just witnessed. We were supposedly delivering humanitarian aid to the beleaguered citizens of Sarajevo, yet I had just witnessed a lucrative drug transaction. I was by no means ignorant or naive to the ways of the world but this transaction just blew my mind. The scene that had just taken place added to my growing confusion as to what we were really accomplishing. This was trivial of course in comparison to the genocide that had been committed so far in this conflict but it added to it just the same.

The Amb track clattered to a stop in front of me. My ears absorbed the high idle of the Detroit diesel as it screamed for lowering the ramp. Our Coy medic, Pierre Langevin, came out hunched over till he cleared the roof. He gave me a slug in the shoulder as he walked by.

"Lucky for you I know a good medic," I said to him threateningly.

"Oh ya, who?" he questioned, waiting for a compliment.

"He's with Alpha Company," I joked, knowing it would be just the thing to get him into a bantering rally.

"Don't get into a spot where you need medical attention, Casey," he threatened back with a smile.

"Don't worry there's no one within a thousand miles I trust with a scalpel anyways." He flicked me the bird over his shoulder. I laughed and turned to the track. Sitting in the hatch, sat the driver, Ben Sylvester. After listening to the razzing Pierre took he sat quietly, not acknowledging my presence immediately.

"Holy shit I don't believe it." I started off with incredulity.

Ben looked down at me knowing abuse was coming his way, after a brief pause, I knew he was eyeing the bait.

"What?" Ben responded with caution.

"The Queen actually let her lover leave Buckingham Palace."

His face went flushed red with anger. Ben loved the Monarchy and Queen Elizabeth herself. He was an avid supporter of the Crown. I did too, but it was fun to torment the shit out of Ben. He was easy to rile on the topic. Like now, when I spoke of the chap who broke into the Queen's chambers. I razzed him that she slipped the locks off for him. He went berserk. It was times like this that many soldiers revel in the humour of bantering. I fought desperately to suppress my laughter.

"What the heck does that mean?" The venom rolling off Ben's tongue indicated that he had swallowed the hook.

"The stables finally got shoveled out this past weekend."

I was having trouble not laughing.

He sat thinking about it for a few seconds, and his eyes were narrowing as each tick of the second hand went by.

"Are you implying that the Queen would have an inappropriate relation with a stable hand?" he stammered the words.

"Ah keep your shorts on, I'm just bustin your balls, Ben. It was actually the gardener," I said bursting out loud, knowing it was the sinker.

Ben turned his back and faced toward Butmir.

"Hey hold that." I said grabbing my camera and clicking a few black and white photos.

"You know Benny; you've got the only carrier in the battle group that has a G-PIG mounted." Nicknamed the 'G-PIG', a General Purpose Machine Gun, as it is formally called, is a 7.62mm belt fed medium machine gun from the 40s and 50s. Not surprisingly it was still in active service with the Canadian Forces.

"Yes I know and I had to fight for this. We are in an ambulance so we aren't supposed to have any armament."

"That's bullshit," I scoffed.

"They kill their own civilians, so I'm packin a gun. Fair is fair," he said.

"You got my vote, buddy."

"Thanks Scotty Dog Woods," Ben said using the nickname he playfully gave me referring to a portion of the Gagetown training area in New Brunswick.

"I still can't believe they actually brought that old blister down here. It's older than the carrier." Ben threw his hands in the air,

"That's Canada's way."

I waved good bye and walked off to my UNHCR truck.

During our aid runs I was getting a feeling that the supplies we were dispatching at the DPs were not all making it to the civilians they were intended for. Proof of illegal use of United Nations supplied goods was difficult to prove as we had to stay within our mandate. Following the aid, we delivered, to see where it actually went did not qualify in that mandate. However, if it walks like a duck and squawks like a duck, it probably is a duck. Our aid convoy was three quarters of the way unloaded when the urge to take a leak hit. I told Capt. Burke where I was going via hand signals and proceeded around the corner of the warehouse.

There at the back of the warehouse and out of the watchful eye of the UNHCR were a couple of military trucks. To my surprise they were loaded to the top of their cargo racks. In the back were two soldiers, shirts off, with side arms on their hips. They were hunched over struggling to move the goods in the back. One of them stood up, stretched, turned and saw me. The cargo was all marked UNHCR. I turned and stepped back around the corner. I stopped and cautiously snapped a photo of the two of them. I walked back inside and passed on what I had witnessed to Bill and the UNHCR delegate. Unfortunately, when we got back outside the trucks had mysteriously disappeared. I was pissed. At least I had the photo for proof. Sadly, I would have to wait till I got back to Croatia and my Foto-shop buddy. I was systematically losing my sense of humour with the whole scenario.

In the evening of July 21st I stood in the hallway and watched Sgt Stanley walk directly to his sections door. He kicked it open and said,

"We'll be doing a fighting patrol in half an hour, Orders in ten, in here. The rest of you clear out."

The guys from 2section assembled in their room. Ten minutes later Sgt Stanley stood in front of them. The room was silent.

"Orders, 2section will conduct a fighting patrol in the area of Beaver Camp." he paused, "Mission. 2section will locate and destroy enemy mortar positions and personnel around Beaver Camp." He repeated the mission statement twice. He then broke the mission into parts. How the section would get to the objective, what they would do once they got there. That was obvious. They would kill anyone involved with using a mortar near our camp.

Two days earlier I had been with General Mackenzie when he informed the leader of the TDF that this action would be carried out if they did not stop firing from around our camp. They had pushed their luck and tonight there would be two patrols going out conducting a fighting patrol to kill them. Stanley next told the section what they would do to return to the camp. All the SOPs were covered again to ensure everyone was refreshed and ready. After all the information was issued he asked for questions. There were none so he wrapped up the orders group. 2section then geared up. Each soldier grabbed three fragmentation and three smoke grenades. Most of the section was carrying C-9 medium machine guns, with most men carrying four to five extra boxes of ammo. One man was designated the signaller and he of course carried the radio. A couple of the guys were tasked to carry M-72 anti-tank rockets, should there be any armour or vehicles to destroy. The patrol formed up in line in the hallway and I took this moment to take a photo. I wished I was going. I really wanted to vent some of my near boiling rage on some scumbags. The guys had removed anything linking them to the United Nations. They did not want anything to have bright patches on it should shit go sideways. I shook hands with a couple of them and wished them happy hunting. The last fellow I shook hands with was Bobby Stone. I knew better than to think those cheeks made him innocent. He was far from it. He had good values but would not blink an eye when it came to getting dirty. "Be safe out there you long-legged streak of misery," I said to him as he strode down the hallway with the rest of his patrol buddies.

"I'll bring a present back for you," he said through a smile.

Two section moved outside and they mounted up in a waiting ML. The truck would take them to the start point. They climbed aboard, each man helping the other. The rear flap was rolled up and they drove off into the night. The patrol was being driven in a UN truck and the headlights were on. Bad move, as this affected the night vision of the patrol. They arrived at the drop point, half blind, and jumped out into the dark. Things went from hyped up to holy crap in seconds. The guys had jumped out of the ML right into the path of an enemy patrol. The tension was high. Minutes passed with not much in the way of moving or breathing going on. They chose not to engage each other. The enemy patrol moved on without issue.

Our fighting patrol moved to their primary objective and set up in all around defence. The first part of the mission was to observe. The second was to kill. With that, arcs of fire were given to each soldier. These would overlap so every stitch of ground would be covered by a blanket of fire.

After a couple hours of laying still, the patrol commander, Sgt Stanley allowed each second man to close his eyes for sleep. After another hour Bobby Stone reported to me that he was awoken by Dan Chevrier's hand on his mouth whispering and motioning for him to be silent. Twenty-five feet away was a twenty man TDF patrol packing heavy weapons, including a mortar. The patrol paused for a fifteen-minute breather but carried on. Although the enemy mortar patrol could not see the Canadian fighting patrol, they behaved like they sensed that the guys were lying in wait. The radio call had been sent silently to HQ and within second's two full sections, manned up APCs, and rushed for the gate. At the gate they waited for the order to move in and extract the fighting patrol. The TDF patrol moved on, cautiously Sgt. Stanley's patrol waited for another couple of hours before they moved. They stealthily patrolled back to our camp. Bobby reported it would almost have been better to fight, just to get the energy release.

Two days passed and while standing on the airfield tarmac I was interviewed by Christiane Amanpour from CNN. She came up to me with her cameraman and we had a short conversation about how I thought things were going.

"I think we are making a difference. At least to some degree," I stated with mild enthusiasm. "I believe the people of Sarajevo are 'selectively' starving."

She tilted her head questioningly.

I continued, "Food is plentiful, to the right people, for the right price. All sides in the conflict are guilty of aid for profit. We're just delivering for the media."

The conversation was quite short. I'm not fully sure if they even had the camera on, and to be honest I did not care. They left quite abruptly because some gunfire had erupted around the corner of the building we were standing by. I learned later that day that Miss Amanpour's cameraman had been shot in the face and subsequently died while she was doing a story.

The news must have gotten out from my interview with Miss Amanpour that I was a good read. It was barely a day after our conversation that journalists began flocking to me. Britain's Sky News, The BBC and even the odd Canadian journalist appeared to be seeking me out looking for any shred of information regarding how I thought the UN peace mission was going. The troops noticed too. It was flattering at first. It appeared that they thought I had the inside scoop somehow. Bunch of dumbasses I thought. I am just a Corporal. I could not begin to contemplate about what is really happening here on a global scale. It was laughable. They wanted to report on the big stuff but did not know the difference between a high ranking officer and a non-com. Unfortunately, all the attention could only lead me to some personal security issues. If the media thought I was somebody, then it was safe to assume that the local war parties might think the same thing. It got to a point one afternoon standing on the tarmac while waiting to go out on a convoy that I blew my fuse.

"Excuse me, Corporal Casey, might we have a word with you?" a correspondent asked.

"No. You may not have a word with me. You may take your questions and cameras and fuck off. You are going to get me killed or possibly some of my buddies killed, who are unfortunate enough to be standing close by."

"Surely one question or two wouldn't hurt." he asked, pushing the boundaries again.

I got up from the pallet I was sitting on and stepped in close to assist in making my point. "I guess they don't teach you ass-clowns much, eh? Like what it means to be sniper checked?"

"Sniper checked?" his voice cracked.

"Ya, it's when you want to get someone you don't like blown away by the enemy. Nice and clean. You don't have to get your hands dirty. All you do is salute him, and the enemy thinks he's a General or some shit like that. And BLAMMO he loses his brains all over the fucking place." I paused, my nostrils flared and I lowered my voice to a growl,

"The bad guys are always watching us, even right now. That bullshit 'Press' patch on the fancy body armour you're wearing doesn't mean shit. If you ever come near me again, I'll be saluting you and so will all my friends. Get it?" His face dropped and he chunked down a hard swallow,

"Yes sir, I get it."

"Don't fucking call me sir. I work for a fucking living. Pass it on to your pals. Now beat it," I ordered.

My eyes pierced through his scrawny angular face as though it would burn a hole through it. I was not interviewed again. When our day of aid runs and escort duties was done, we made our way back to Beaver Camp.

After dismounting from our carrier I splashed a bit of water on my face and walked out to the main gate. The gate had a control arm that could be raised and lowered manually. One man was currently standing on duty on the ground. Up on the roof was a miniature bunker. Two men were up top behind the four rows of sandbags. They were manning a .50.cal. I chuckled to myself,

"Now that's the real control arm."

The sun was dropping below the ridge between our camp and the airport.

"Hey guys, how's it going?"

"It's going Casey, how about you?"

"Ya its all good. Hey where's Garcia?" I asked.

"He's over there on the south perimeter, in a trench."

"Okay thanks, say cheese."

I clicked a photo of them before they could offer any obscene gestures. I walked along the curb staying close to the shrubs for cover as I made my way to the south wire. As the trench came into view so did Leon Garcia.

He was facing me with his rifle pointed at my chest.

"I'm from the government. I'm here to help you," I said jokingly.

"About time. I sent Dillon back fifteen minutes ago to send the new shift up," Leon commented sternly.

"Just for the record I'm visiting, I'm not on shift." I climbed down on the edge of the trench and let my legs dangle. The steel sheeting, called riveting, that lined the walls of the trench, was cool on my calves. He pulled himself up and sat opposite to me.

"See anything?" I asked.

"Nah, just the usual shit," he replied. "When did you get in?" he asked.

"About twenty minutes ago. I came right out as soon as I heard you were out here."

"Well thanks. Hear from home at all?" he asked, making small talk.

"Home? Ya right, like she gives a shit whether I make it outa here or not. I'm worth more dead."

"Well what about the kid?"

"What about her? I miss her but there's not much I can do from here." I softened my tone, "I just hope she remembers me."

"Ahh she'll remember you," he consoled me. I sat quietly a moment and noticed dusk was moving in.

I changed the subject, "You figure we're making a difference?" He sat for a second.

"I couldn't give a shit. I've got my ninety days for my medal, so they can ship me home anytime."

"What and leave all the danger pay we fought for behind?"

"Danger pay, HA! What a joke, it only brings us up to where 7-11 clerks are gettin paid." "Well maybe so but at least we're gettin it finally," I tried to be positive.

"Scotty, you know as well as I do, a couple hundred bucks a month is not enough for the shit we are facing daily."

"You mean it ain't the glory?" I scowled, sarcasm dripping off my words.

Hearing something coming, we both looked towards the quarters.

"Whatever, you know what I'm sayin."

"Ya I know, I'm just bustin your balls. It's crap for sure, at least they finally gave us the highest level," again I was trying to be positive. The relief sentries showed up. We could clearly identify them so we did not use the standard 'challenge procedure'. A challenge procedure is like a short code. If the magic number is 7, and I say 4, then you should say 3. 4+3=7. Responding incorrectly could be fatal.

"Well why don't you assholes go back to bed, I've almost finished your shift for you," Leon said exasperated.

"What the Hell's your problem?" asked Cory Wilkerson.

"You jerk-offs are only half an hour late," he said angrily.

"Well you can thank Dillon when you get in, because he didn't wake us up," Wilkerson growled back.

Even though we were whispering it was evident they all wanted to scream. "Okay guys, chill and keep it down. Come on Garcia, let's go, and good luck guys," I said, trying to smooth things over.

"Oh ya, you guys could brush up on your field craft too. You sounded like a bunch of Yanks. All you were missing was the glow sticks tied around your necks," Leon said bitching them out some more.

I gave him a light shove.

"Let's go, young fella." Garcia and I walked silently along the brush back to the quarters.

With the restraints of 'peacekeeping' placed on us, we were all close to the melting point. Although Canadians are renowned for peacekeeping, we were trained as soldiers who fight wars first. All of us had trained extensively for full throttle battlefield conditions. And even though this was a battlefield it was not ours. Unlike the years of battlefield conditioning, we had only trained for four weeks to do this half-assed warfare. The stress was high and it was taking its toll.

We all did our turn doing security for our camp and this early morning was no different. Walking from our south east perimeter trenches to our living quarters after a quiet sentry shift I was treated to a wakeup call. Instinct quickly forced me to a crouched run in the early morning mist. A well hidden sharpshooter in an apartment complex across the Sava River had opened up on me. I dodged and weaved from bushes to buildings within our compound. With each step my laboured breaths were audibly obscured as the near hit of snapping bullets creased the air. Every move I made was like a life sized personal chess match where I was manipulating my pawn like self. One hundred metres now separated me from the safety of our quarters. It was apparent that with each shot he fired, the shooter was learning quickly how to give lead time. Each shot he took got closer to me. With a running jump I threw myself down by a half dozen stacks of empty sandbags. The impact forced spit to explode from my mouth as I hit the ground so hard that I thought I broke a couple of ribs. As I struggled to get air into my burning lungs I rolled over once and pulled a full sandbag up under the fore stock of my rifle. Lifting my head, I dared to find where the shots were coming from to no avail. Dropping from a window just above me, shattering glass and splintered wood from his shots fell on and around me. In front of me the sandbags were puffing from his incoming fire. The hot steel jacketed shells burned the dark green nylon material of the sandbags. Because the sandbags layers were stacked on their side they acted much like

Kevlar. Small dirt clumps flew through the air in front of the bags. I could not help but laugh cynically through my controlled hysteria.

"So this is peacekeeping?"

I lay motionless for a minute. The shots kept coming in sporadically.

"Hey asshole, I guess you didn't notice the blue helmet?" I yelled angrily from behind the protection of the stacks.

I knew the UN colours meant almost nothing but the venting made me feel better momentarily. As I was trying to figure my next move a horrendous explosion rocked the buildings across the river. I risked looking up again.

Gray concrete dust and smoke boiled out of the side of one of the apartment buildings.

Almost instantly flames began to lick up the outside walls of the complex. Although no more shots came my way I lay there for awhile.

"Karma's a bitch, eh, fucker?" I shouted in relief and I thanked the Lord above for the miracle of providing a well aimed enemy RPG. My ribs ached their disapproval as I pulled myself up from the shallow sandbag retreat. Without letting the pain in my side control my direction I strode slowly toward our barracks. As quickly as I had been running for my life I was now strolling for the door of our quarters.

"This is fuckin crazy," I muttered.

Once inside I made my way to my bunk. A newspaper lay open on Ray's cot. It was open to a satirical cartoon of a Canadian peacekeeper dodging bullets. The caption read, "I've got to find a nice safe war somewhere!" The sharp pain of my bruised ribs stabbed me the instant I started to laugh. I lay back on my bed, closed my eyes and continued laughing till I cried from the pain.

Later that evening, Capt. Burke and I went over to the PTT building for a last minute O group with the UNHCR reps. While there I enjoyed the displays of fireworks that were non-stop in Sarajevo. If it was not the constant stream of tracer rounds lighting their way to their targets, it was the explosions from mortars and artillery. One of the more memorable nights of carnage not directed at us was on the main road in front of the PTT building. I was visiting recce platoon while waiting for Capt. Burke when I heard a light vehicle heading toward us from the northwest. The driver was on a mission. He never let off the throttle when changing gears. The vehicle was making one Hell of a racket as it got closer. When the vehicle was within three hundred metres I grabbed my camera and stuck it out the window, frantically switching it to continuous shutter. The film absorbed the light as the vehicle drove straight into the line of light anti-tank mines that were across the road. They exploded with such force that the windows of adjacent buildings shattered. The truck as I could now make out in the light of the explosion was now fully engulfed in flames. The driver's door fell open and off onto the ground. The torso of the driver fell on the jagged steel of the door. What was left of his lower body remained in the cab. Two men carrying AKs had survived the blast and jumped from the back. The first one was well on his way to breaking the one hundred metre dash when he was mowed down by a hail of machine gun fire. The second guy ran in the opposite direction. He took four or five powerful strides and on the sixth detonated a second mine that turned his body into an eye piercing flash of light and a red mist in the eerie glow of the fire.

As 22C sat observing its arcs a T-54/55 rolled up to test the Canadian will. The turret on the T-54/55 traversed and pointed in the direction of 22C. The crew commander of 22C,

Sgt. Stanley clicked his ICS, intercom, switch,

"Stone, grab the 84 and bring it up top here."

Bobby Stone dropped down into the belly of the carrier and returned with the 84mm Carl Gustav recoilless gun. He placed in on the roof of the track in plain sight of the Serbian tank. The tank moved its turret again and elevated and lowered its main gun. "Bring up the RAP rounds and prepare to engage," barked the Sgt. Once again Stone descended quickly and returned with the tank killing shells. The T-55 again moved backwards and forwards the whole time aiming at the Canadian APC.

"Bring it to bear on him, Bobby," ordered Stanley.

"LOAD," Stone yelled.

Neidermeyer opens the venturi and slides the rocket in the breach, closes the venturi and confirms it's loaded by yelling,

"READY!" Neidermeyer then hollered, "Back Blast Area, CLEAR!"

Bobby responded by yelling, "Standby," and sat waiting patiently for the order to Fire.

Seeing the less friendly side of the Canadian peacekeepers, the main battle tank roared away. The situation dissolved as quickly as it had erupted. Nevertheless, it takes quite a bit of time to come down from these nonstop adrenalin rushes.

AUGURIES OF INNOCENCE

"The world is a dangerous place, not because of those who do evil, but because of those who look on and do nothing."
~ALBERT EINSTEIN

"This ain't Cyprus. We don't conduct the same spit polished bullshit here," came the words from Quinn Moses.

"This is a real war zone, No. 1," I threw in for dramatic effect.

Truth was I was madder than Hell. WO Goddard had come up with this little time waster of a task. We did not conduct any of those static peacekeeping routines like they did in Cyprus. We did not have daily inspections and we sure as Hell did not count ammunition, except for resupply. So I could not understand why we were sweeping a parking lot in the middle of a 'real war zone.'

In times of boredom it is normal practice to keep the troops busy. Track maintenance, weapons cleaning, going over drills, and of course PT, physical training. I do not have issue with those things. I do, however, have a problem with foolish actions like sweeping a parking lot when there is a high sniper and artillery threat. This task we did under extreme duress, one blisteringly hot afternoon. Quinn and I were handed two heavy duty brooms and were shown the area to be swept. I had no issue with doing shit jobs. We all have to spend our time in the proverbial barrel. The issue here was that we were sweeping a parking lot that was not in need of sweeping and was in full view of many high-rises where shots were known to be fired at us from. Luckily we only got shot at a couple of times during the ridiculous task. It was the fastest sweeping job in the history of the Regiment. I am a firm believer that sniper fire is a big motivator.

Later that afternoon, one of the Recce platoon tracks rattled up about one hundred metres away from ours.

"Hey L-tee I'm gonna go say howdy." Burke nodded and I jumped out the man door in our APCs ramp.

"It was pretty haywire, man," said Brock Nemecheck.

I could see the adrenaline was still pumping. Brock was a BC boy too. He had a look in his eye that said he might be a little crazy. I think it was probably from too many hard hits in rugby. Regardless, he was a tough brute that you did not want to mess with. He continued his story,

"We rolled around the corner and there they were. Four douche bags standing in the middle of the road. So we pulled up to have a chat and they say we are not proceeding any further."

"What was the issue?" I asked.

"We couldn't figure that out because it escalated before we could talk it out" he continued.

"So this one dude grabs an RPG and points it right at us."

"Holy shit, that turned the heat up right away eh?" I added.

"Oh ya, I flared up, I reached down on the console and busted a frag out of my pouch. They were all standing, like in the middle of the road with no cover. So I pulled the pin and held the grenade up out of the hatch so they could see it," Brock told us.

"Then I just sat there and smiled."

"That is so you, Brock", commented Norm Allison also from Recce Platoon with a smile.

"Ya so then the leader goof looks and sees what I'm holding and I think he pee'd a little.

I said 'go ahead but a couple of you assholes are comin with us'," Dave added.

"So I said to him, pretty dumb to stand out here with no cover eh, bozo?" Brock was reliving the scene, grinning his crooked grin the whole time.

"So what happened?" I questioned further.

"Ah they backed down and left. We watched them for a bit though just to make sure they didn't try to flank us and attack," he explained.

"It was intense for a few minutes with them not moving an inch and us holding our ground too," he said, concluding his story.

"Well you guys did what you had to do. Can't show these ass wipes any sign of weakness or they'll steam roll us," I praised them.

We shot the breeze a little longer and then I got up and went back to my carrier.

After a day of running aid into the city I thought my day would be more or less over. However, a driver was needed for a short tasking so I volunteered. We had been detailed with providing security and transport for a UN radar det on a high feature in between downtown Sarajevo and the sub urban area of Dobrinja. At 2030hrs we made our way up the hill through the maze of streets to the top of the hill where the Ukrainian Armoured Command and Reconnaissance Vehicle was located. N. Company had been delegated with securing the area inhabited by the ACRV and its crew. This piece of equipment was a valuable asset to the UN. It was fitted with a radar system nicknamed Big Fred. It was being deployed to determine where artillery and mortar fire was coming from. This was necessary to assist in stopping attacks on UN positions as well as to maintain the fragile ceasefire.

I revved our APCs Detroit diesel engine up. Turning right in the driver's seat I grabbed the ramp lever and shifted the locking handle down and back, which sent the ramp lowering to the ground. The relief section from 5Pl. ran down and out into the growing darkness. They deftly took up all around defensive positions. One by one the daytime security section was replaced. The newly relieved section mounted up and once again the familiar scream of our APCs engine sounded as I raised the ramp. In seconds we were navigating the road back down the hill. Sergeant Glass and I had elected to go with only Black-out Drive lights on. These were very small lights that would provide just enough light to see. They would be much more difficult to be seen, thus, making us less of a target than we would be with standard headlights on. As a UN vehicle we were required to travel with our headlights on. Some rules have to be broken for the safety of the troops. It would be difficult for anyone to establish if we were driving white UN vehicles or camouflaged vehicles in the dark. So the choice was made.

As our M-113 clattered down the hill we came face to face with a Volkswagen Golf. Inside were three men armed with AKs. The road was too narrow for a side by side pass so we came to a stop, nose-to-nose. After a few seconds of the stalemate the driver began waving his arms about violently. The passenger in the front seat took stronger measures by sliding his assault rifle out the window. I momentarily admired his courage. It was not until the steel tracks on my 13ton APC made their first metallic clanking on the pavement just feet away from his paper-thin VW that I noticed a change in his disposition. Clank, clank, clank. The sounds, slow at first gradually picked up tempo as gravity took over. In the minimal light of black out drive the VW driver's skin had taken on a pale hue with the realization of his worsening predicament. Without wasting the time to use the clutch he jammed the transmission into reverse. Sgt. Glass keyed the intercom and asked me,

"What the Hell are you doing?"

It was as much a statement as it was a question. I turned my head and looked into the Sgt's eyes. Looking forward again my eyes narrowed and I began laughing hysterically. Stomping the accelerator to the floor, a guttural, almost psychotic scream elicited from my core. With minor corrections to the tiller bars I guided my 13ton missile toward its target. I had lost it. I was going to kill these ungrateful shitheads. We came here to ease suffering and bloodshed and they treated us with such disrespect. I had had enough. The chase lasted about 900 metres until, with precision that would have made Jim Rockford proud, the driver swung the front-end of that Golf around in the first wide spot. I never saw him touch the brakes. Once down off the hill I switched the lights on. We arrived back at Beaver Camp a half hour later.

The afternoon of the following day I walked into my bed space at Beaver Camp. The aluminium rails of my cot creaked as I sat down. I inhaled deeply. My rifle lay across my lap as I leaned forward. Hanging my head, I slid my brain bucket off and slowly let it drop to the floor. My lungs began to burn. The blue helmet, scratched and battered, landed with a metallic thud. I exhaled quietly. A bead of sweat rolled down my nose and dripped onto the floor beside my helmet. I sat there staring at the drop.

In the drop I could see a woman and two children. They ran with makeshift containers full of water. The scene played over and over in my head. I watched as the containers fell to the ground spraying the precious liquid they contained. In much the same way as their bodies lost their blood. I watched them being gunned down. It was horrifying.

Earlier in the day I had sat helplessly in the turret of the TUA watching through the scope as the scene unfolded two and a half clicks away. The little boy who was trailing behind, was the first to go down. His cries brought the woman who I assumed was his mother, running back to his side. She too, was then shot repeatedly, her lifeless body falling onto that of her dead son. Our APC was running to recharge the batteries. No one heard my screams of horror as they resounded off the inside of my metal encasement. This fact only added to my helplessness. As I sat watching, the little girl-who had been only a few steps ahead of the woman and little boy-turned and ran back. I yelled in vain for her to stop. I began frantically searching for the shooter. It was all too far away to engage with the C-6 coaxial. I was enraged at the brutality. If I found the murderer I was going to launch a 147mm rocket up his ass. The T.O.W. missile was all I had to engage him with. I had to try and save the little girl. I kept searching from where the bodies lay, as if to trace a line, and where I thought the fire would be coming from. I saw her body jump sideways. I inwardly cursed at the clarity the scope provided. The little girl fell, convulsing, the water slowly spilling from its container. My heart sank like a ship's anchor. I took my eye away from the tear drenched scope. I had failed. I wiped my face on my t-shirt. After a couple of deep breaths, I twisted the weapons controller to the left so I would not be viewing the bodies immediately. As I was scanning the buildings my faith in humanity was gradually slipping away. I could not find the cowardly killer anywhere. After what seemed an eternity a hand tapped my leg and I slowly slid down from the gunner's chair. My two-hour watch was over. I looked at Ross without saying a word and silently made my way across the tarmac to catch a ride with the first available track going back to Beaver Camp.

An hour later I sat in disbelief of the brutality and waste that was seared into my consciousness. There is nothing in Martial Law, even if it was enacted here which it was not, that could warrant such an atrocity. I tried to understand what could be gained by such an act. What kind of twisted thought process could make something so despicable seem okay? I had to get out of this place. Self preservation had to kick in. I was trying desperately to hold myself together. Every cell in my body lusted to kill the animals responsible for this twisted ugly display of inhumanity.

As an added safety measure the company filled and stacked thousands of sandbags around the base of our quarters. A work party of seven of us were tasked to fill bags the day following my turret terror. It was 09:00hrs and we had been filling bags for about two hours when half a dozen bullets snapped past us. Instinctively we hit the ground and strained our eyes to find the attacker. One of the guys did not go to ground. He just stood there rambling away. He acted oblivious to the fact that someone had just shot at us.

"Contact!" screamed an unknown voice.

More rounds began to zip past seeking out human flesh. We struggled to get a fix on where the shots were coming from.

"There are just too many windows and hiding places,"

I raised my voice so everyone in our digging crew could hear.

Leon Garcia to my left yelled angrily, "McTavish is drawing the fire!"

McTavish was to my right, still standing, and mumbling something inaudible. I clambered over sod and a shovel to get closer to him. He held his shovel in his hand shovelling air into an imaginary sandbag.

"McTavish, get down!" He continued, now waving his arms about. "Get down you fuckin idiot or so help me I'll shoot you myself!"

Garcia, two thoughts ahead of me, pointed his C-9 at him and screamed,

"You are drawing fire on us!"

McTavish's faced cleared as Garcia's screaming jarred him back to reality. He fell to the ground immediately. Now, more focused, we determined the rounds appeared to be coming from a building across the river to the south. Garcia and I had a clear shot from our positions.

"There, weapon signature!" I pointed.

"Got it, watch my tracer," he screamed. He fired three round bursts into the subject window from his C-9. I fired a few rounds into the opening as well.

"He's down!" I hollered above his last burst.

We waited to see if there was going to be any more action.

"Good shootin, buddy," I said, complementing him on his kill.

My adrenaline was coursing through my veins. I searched methodically over the high rises through the trees for more bad guys. Another battle raged somewhere off in the distance. It fell silent around us. I wondered during this lull if McTavish had actually lost his faculties or was he standing defiantly against the shooter as if to egg him on. I did not know for sure and I was very glad he did not get popped. A few moments later the silence was broken by the sound of shovels filling sandbags once again. What else were we to do, given we were not finished our task. It only took another hour and a half and we completed the sandbag job. The troops quickly scrubbed the dirt off and we headed to the airport just before noon. Aids runs downtown needed to be done. Tommy jumped up into the passenger seat and slid his rifle out the window as I had done. I shifted the tandem axle Volvo into gear and we followed the lead APC out the gates of the Sarajevo airport. A smile crossed Tommy's face as the first blast from the air conditioning hit him. I tossed a couple of M67 fragmentation grenades on the dash.

"Just in case," I said under my breath. My eyes watched the grass that had grown to the height of a wheat field across from the airport entrance. Scanning left to right, then to the windows above the field, it was clear for now. As a four vehicle aid convoy, we kept close enough together for support. However, we were spread out enough to minimise an effective ambush by would be attackers. Our trucks were laden with much needed food and medical supplies. We headed NE along one of the city's main paved tributaries. Rifle shots could be heard above the noise of the engine. Our convoy had just crossed the Sava River when a small car called a Zastava screeched around a corner and cut-off our lead APC. The 50.cal machine gun on the lead APC commander's cupola immediately swivelled to bear down on the car. The driver of the Zastava put his foot to the floor and lost our 40km/h max speed convoy in the dust. We drove for another five minutes and began to enter a choke-point on the road. Dragon's teeth and a handful of concrete blocks littered the road in a fashion that made everyone slow down. On the other side were our friends in the Zastava. They were now brandishing AK-47s and had adopted poses from a cheesy American style war movie. The fellow in the centre of the four raised his arm and signalled for us to stop. The SOP was to stop for nothing, and the new black smoke belching from the right side of the APC confirmed that we were not going to break those SOPs. One of the bad guys raised his AK and fired directly at the carrier. He did not even have time to acknowledge his mistake when the first 50.cal round tore his chest cavity open. The second round slammed into his left forearm severing it just above his watch. He fell onto the travelled portion of the roadblock. Our 50.cal gunner fired at the now scattering thieves forcing them to run for cover.

Tommy along with the C-6 gunner on the lead APC picked up the runner on the right and fired a burst from his C-7 into him as he jumped the ditch. He fell like a bag of shit and rolled back down in the gully. I would love to have been the one firing, however, I was more concerned about navigating the steel dragon's teeth. One mistake with those and we could become a sitting duck. The truck briefly bumped as I drove over corpse.

"Hey Tommy, he's a one armed bandit," I hollered through the adrenalin rush. We shrieked with laughter.

Our convoy proceeded and the rear-guard APC fired a half belt of 7.62mm rounds from his C-6 medium machine gun into the scrub to deter any foolhardier behaviour. The rest of the journey to Delta-Papa 23 went quietly. We unloaded our commodities and returned reluctantly to the airport. I say reluctantly because we had to break one of our SOPs. Never take the same route back. Even though we could take care of business it was still unnerving a lot of the time to be here.

The following morning, I was driven over to the airfield again to do some more shifts with the TUAs. The smell of the earth was fresh even though the hull down position was three weeks old now. I breathed in again. It was nice to breath in something pure instead of the usual smells of war. Just to the right of the open man door in the ramp at the back of 73A was a small folding table. On it was the green Coleman stove that each track carried. Ross stood there smiling, patiently stirring lunch. The silver foil bags of ration packs had been replaced by the bright yellow of KD. I was back with AAP. We had all chipped in from our care packages.

"Smells good, brother," I commented.

"It'll be ready in a couple minutes. So get a plate," he said happily.

The KFS, knife, fork, spoon set each grunt is issued with is designed to slide into one another and lock that way. In the handle of each is a slit. This slit was just the right size that the button on our combat pants would fit through it. It became the unofficial spot where most of us kept them.

"Hey Kenny you got a spare KFS? I left mine on my other pants back at camp," I exclaimed

"Yup, there's a set of gut wrenches in the goody box."

Each carrier crew had a goody box. These boxes had all the stuff that was left over from the ration packs. It also contained any special items the crew could acquire. Up in the turret the motor on the night sight clattered away every few minutes keeping the internal parts cool. I rummaged through the salt and pepper packs, peanut butter tubes and Tabasco sauce someone had acquired until I found a plastic spoon.

"This will do." Ross spooned out the Kraft Dinner noodles and I sat down in the dirt.

Having eaten rations for the last couple days, this meal was heavenly. The turret of the TUA whirred as Tommy traversed scanning the scene out to four kilometres. I ate, got up, washed my plate quickly and squeezed through the small door in the ramp.

"Tommy come on out of there and get some groceries into that scrawny frame of yours,"

I said.

"I left the tub of Vaseline out so you can squeeze your fat ass in there," he bantered back. "Ya I bet that's what it was for, you grubby lil' bear."

I gestured with my hand in a stroking motion. He ignored the comment and gave me a Sitrep.

"A couple T-54s changed positions on the hill to the south east. The usual shooters in Dobrinja and the ACRV crew look fine."

I did a quick MGS self test, (Missile Guidance System). Flicking up the switch cover and pressing the toggle switch I watched the green lights flash one by one into the middle, leaving the centre green light on showing that it checked out okay. I climbed up the two small steps and took his place. I adjusted the fold down seat to my height. Putting my hands on either side of the palm controller I pushed the locking buttons in to allow me to spin the turret and move the sighting system up and down. I placed my eye up to the day sight and scanned the south east hill for the tanks. I immediately found one tank but I could not see the other. The heat waves from the summer day were distorting my view. I pulled my head back and raised it up three inches till my eye found the aperture for the night sight. The night sight operated by actually picking up images though their thermal signature. The background was black and anything that was hot would appear red. It is capable of seeing through smoke and fog. Smoke is often deployed for cover of movement. Well let me tell you, there is no hiding from this baby. I scanned the hill once again. I found the first tank I had discovered with the day sight. "Bingo," I reported to myself. The second one was directly behind the first and down the hill just a bit. One of the tank crew was out on the ground. He was having a squirt. I could see the red stream pouring to the ground.

"Hey Tommy, I found your brother." Conniving, I shouted, for a response.

"Oh ya," he answered waiting for the punch line.

"Ya this Serb tanker's havin a piss and he's got a small dick like you, so I figured you must be related."

I was laughing and already searching for new targets. He yelled up through the hatch, "Well Casey, if they cut an inch off your dick, you'd have a scar on your ass!" We all laughed. My regular job as a driver kept me too segregated and it was evident now that I missed the camaraderie of a TOW det more than ever. It was good to be with the guys.

With the sun making its slow descent I walked across the tarmac of the airport. I had stopped in at Battle Group HQ and I was now walking to where the cargo planes parked for unloading. There was a Belgian C-130 Hercules currently backed in. The flurry of activity was impressive to watch. They had to get the plane unloaded so they could fly out before dark. The Herc's Loadmaster was supervising the unloading.

He was checking off each pallet of humanitarian aid as it clattered down the rollers affixed to the ramp. I nodded a hello to the multi-national force, soldiers from France, Belgium, Sweden, and Canada that were making it happen. I continued walking along the front of the terminal under the tower toward where the UNHCR trucks were parked. A shot ripped by making me jerk my head involuntarily. It looked like a brightly lit softball as it went by and the snap made my right ear sing its discomfort. I could hear someone yelling back by the Herc that they had been hit. I kept walking toward my destination. I could not help but feel lucky. I stopped and took a photo of the sunset. I had lived to see another one.

Burke and I hitched a ride in the back of 21Bravo, with Sam Sullivan behind the controls. They dropped Capt. Burke off at HQ for what he told me would be an all morning Orders Group. I dismounted as well and waved goodbye to

Sam. Sgt Glass, barely visible in the Commander's cupola, pointed toward the terminal and they drove off. Giving me an all knowing nod the Captain told me that I should disappear. I did not know how my morning was going to end. I knew at that moment I did not want to end up doing kitchen bitch or some other shit job for A. Company. So with a quick turn I strode for the tarmac.

As you stand out on the runway and directly in front of tower, HQ was to the left in the customs warehouse. To the right were attached vacant aircraft maintenance hangars. All along the perimeter fence line were the French Vab 4X4s and A. Coy Vandoo carriers dug in hull down. In the infield were the TUAs, also dug in. I strode out and visited with the guys from the TUA closest to the hangers for about half an hour. After my visit I walked back to the hangars. The door to the last hangar was slightly ajar. I strolled down there and entered. It took a minute for my eyes to adjust to the eerie darkness within the building. A few streams of dust filled light entered through bullet holes in the steel sheets above the concrete walls. I had been in the building about two minutes when a shot rang out. I fell to one knee and my rifle was immediately up in the shoulder ready to engage. I instantly shuffled to the right and out of the doorway's light. I had allowed myself to be silhouetted in its frame. It was a rookie mistake and I cursed myself inwardly. The shot came from a platform built in the southeast corner of the hangar. I could not see any movement. There was a platform built in the southwest corner as well. Each platform was surrounded by a curtain of black Hessian. There it was. Movement. The hessian moved and a figure appeared. As he climbed down and walked over to me it became clear he was a French Marine. As he approached I instantly recognised him from the mission to guard General Mackenzie. He was the marine who had instructed me where to meet.

Recognizing me, he was all smiles and he invited me up into the hidey-hole. Once on the platform, I tried to tell him about the mix up that day. He put his finger to his lips signalling me to be quiet. For the next 20 minutes I just sat and watched. I was entertained by the performance, and the show was about to shift gears. He motioned for me to lie down and look through the spotting scope. Through his partners spotting scope I observed him wave at an opposing sniper. It was chillingly amusing. Then with deadly accuracy he killed two others. I confirmed both his kills.

"Tuer," he said to me in response to my English. I had never done anything like this. This was stuff left to our snipers. I was a good shot, yes, but a sniper, I was not. Letting his French made FR-F2 sniper rifle lean on its bipod, he shimmied over and motioned for me to take the No.1 position. I waved it off. He insisted. I tried again to refuse. He made it clear he was having none of it. This was an opportunity not afforded normally so I quietly obliged, and slid in behind his rifle. I was excited to some degree I admit, and I considered it an honour for him to allow me the use of his rifle.

My stomach knotted up instantly as I slid into the shooting position. I was making a choice by lying here. One I would have to live with for the rest of my life. In broken English he had me aim from behind the hessian and fire a single shot to see where the weapon shot with me behind it. Relaxing, I took a few deep breaths took up the slack on the trigger and on the third I released partway and squeezed the trigger. What the Hell am I doing here? This is awesome. The rifle fired and bucked into my shoulder. He and I were close in zeroing. We determined that a slight correction by aiming off to the right a bit should have me in line for a good shot. I was then left to my thoughts as I scanned the buildings of Dobrinja for a target, checking windows and holes in the cinderblock. The vision of the woman and her two children exploded in my mind. I closed my eyes trying to block them out. It was no use.

I had been lying there for about twenty-five minutes when a man appeared. He was dressed in dark clothing except for his dirty grey sports t-shirt. He was sporting what looked like a hunting rifle with a big scope. I allowed my mind to wander. Could this be the same guy? The one who murdered the innocent children and their mother? I blew some air into my palm to dry up the sweat that had just formed. I tried desperately to control my breathing. I was angry. Then he did it again. He dropped to one knee and fired a shot towards a group of people running between buildings. I envisioned the unarmed woman being shot as she carried water to her home. My grip tightened in anger. He got up and ran out of sight. I lay patiently. He appeared in another window. He repeated this, darting from window to window. Then-I could just see his face at first-he quickly moved into the kneeling position again. I knew from watching that this was his pattern of attack.

My mind drifted off to when I was a young child at my rural one room schoolhouse. Some of the older boys had urged me to stick my tongue on a frozen swing set. I knew firing the shot was going to be like pulling my tongue free from the frozen metal. I was going to be leaving a little piece of myself behind. I blinked hard to snap back to the here and now. As I looked through the scope the reticule lined up on his centre of mass. Centered perfectly in the sight glass were three famous words emblazoned on his dirty grey t-shirt. 'Just Do It'. I am not sure which of my senses reacted first. Was it the jarring of the rifle snapping into my shoulder, or the sound of the report in my ears? As I mentally followed the projectile in its flight I watched it explode in the murderer's chest. He hung there motionless, his face showing disbelief and pain. His blood immediately oozed onto his shirt, darkening it as it drizzled down his abdomen. Then he fell forward and over himself. Click, was the next sound I heard, as I released the trigger in perfect follow through. I could smell the powder from the shot. It burned softly in my nose. My right ear was ringing lightly.

"Tuer." The whispered word, smashed my left ear like a sledge hammer hitting a stone. The word resounded in my head for what seemed like an eternity. It reverberated inside my skull as though encased in a sealed mountainous valley. 'Kill' my mind translated needlessly. To this point, members of our crew including me, had returned fire. However, it struck me now that I had deliberately searched for this guy and killed him. It was personal. The feeling was one of numbness combined with elation. Even if I could have spoken French I was glad we were not speaking on the platform. I would not have known what to say. The French sniper put his hand on my shoulder and with black staring eyes, smiled. I turned my head over the butt of the rifle to see him and I was instantly looking at my own reflection. Looking back over the stock of the FR-F2, with my now hollow black eye I looked through the scope for another half hour. I was secretly glad I had not seen any more "bad guys." I felt that retribution had been attained in regards to the water carriers.

I tapped my watch and thumbed that I had to get going. I got to one knee and we three shook hands. I looked one more time at the building through the hessian and I climbed down. As I exited the hangar I stopped and sat back against the cool concrete wall. I shielded my eyes from the brilliant sunlight. My mind began reeling at the internal ramifications of the last hour. I am a peacekeeper. What the Hell was that all about? They were doing it under order as peacekeepers, so I was justified in killing him, I told myself. I was wrestling with the emotions of my personal transformation. There was no going back. What was done was done. On one hand I was sick to my stomach for killing someone, on the other and perhaps the scary part, I was really okay with it. I put my head in my hands and tried to rub the sin off.

"He got what he deserved," I muttered.

"What was that?" A pair of desert boots shuffled into view and I looked up to see Dan Vecchio from Recce Platoon standing in front of me.

"I just popped a shit-rat," I said with a sudden uneasiness, born from divulging my actions.

"Oh, are you okay?" Dan asked with genuine concern.

"I guess I am. He was shooting at unarmed civilians crossing a gap between buildings." I explained hurriedly, just wanting the conversation to end.

As I stood an incoming mortar barrage began exploding only 50 metres away, silencing our discussion and forcing us to evade the stinging shards of shrapnel and dirt clods. Dan and I walk-ran towards HQ. All the soldiers and airmen at the unloading station leaned against the piles of aid, seemingly staring at me. Could they see inside me at what I had just done? Did they think I was a monster? As Dan and I neared the HQ, I could see Capt. Burke sitting with a Vandoo officer, patiently waiting for me.

"What the Hell, did you go for a run or something?" he asked looking at me with a raised eyebrow.

"No sir, why?"

"You're soaked." he said, looking me up and down and pointing.

I had not even noticed. It was forty degrees plus outside. I never noticed the heat inside the hangar. It was probably well over fifty Celsius inside.

"Went for a run eh," he joked aloud.

"Ya that must be it." I replied looking away avoiding eye contact.

"Keep yourself occupied?" he asked believing that I had found a good hiding spot.

"Ya somewhat," was all I offered looking farther away.

I did not want him to see my black hollow eyes. I don't know what drew me to that hangar. I do know that something irrevocably changed inside me that day.

Later that day I was sitting in our platoon quarters at Camp Beaver. I had been fidgeting with my gear in an attempt to stay busy and avoid the reality of the day. I had just laid my flak jacket on my cot when Tim Gorman walked in.

"Hey Casey, what's going on here today?" Tim asked in his jovial way.

"Not much Timbo, what's shakin with you buddy?"

"Not much, just gettin in from a patrol. Did you hear what just happened to Calvin Bartley?" His demeanour was changing slightly and his eyebrows rose to show his concern.

"Aaah no I didn't. Don't tell me it's something shitty," I said, knowing by Tim's voice that something was not right. It was not normal for Tim to be this serious.

"No, he's alive thank God. Holy fuck man, he got his leg blown off though." Tim's voice was shaky as he began to tell the story. He was visibly upset by the new tale.

"What the Hell happened?" I pried sternly for more information.

"His section was doing a perimeter check and Calvin stepped over a half downed fence.

When his foot touched down on the other side, Ker-fucking-boom!"

"Holy shit," my jaw sat hanging open momentarily.

"PMA-3?" I inquired about the hockey puck shaped mine.

"They think it was," Tim continued,

"He just stepped down and the next thing anyone knew he flew eight feet in the air and landed like a ton of shit. It was a shit show, Scotty."

"How much of his leg is gone?" I asked.

"Not sure, but at this point it's below the knee."

"At this point?" I quizzed again.

"Ya, at this point it's below the knee, but they may have to amputate further depending on the damage."

"Fuuuck." I sat there contemplating the whole situation.

"It could have been worse," Tim added.

I cut in sternly,

"Ya it could've been worse; he could've blown up his whole section." I said gruffly and almost void of feelings other than anger. Tim looked at me with questioning eyes obviously stunned by my blunt comments.

"Fucking idiot knows better than to step over obstacles like that. They taught us that shit as far back as battle school. And we just did refresher training before we deployed. What the fuck was he thinking? I'll tell you what he was thinking, he wasn't, period!"

"Well that's kind of heartless," Tim said disappointed.

"Hey it sucks he lost his leg, I won't deny that, but come on Tim, when was the last time you pulled an FNG move like that?"

Tim shook his head reluctantly not wanting to answer. After a brief pause knowing I would not let up he caved in.

"Not since battle school."

I really was sad for Calvin's loss, but I was mad as well. Unfortunately, the 'mad' had the floor for the time being.

"His section let him down too. They should have stopped him before he started to climb over that fence. We all know better, Tim."

Tim shrugged in submission and looked out the hessian covered window. He knew I was right. The shitty thing is I did not want to be right. What was driving my straight forward tirade was I did not want anyone else to make the same mistake. Even though I was not there I wanted to take the last couple hours back so Cal could have his leg again. It just sucked all the way around. Not only did Calvin lose his leg but this would also definitely put a dent in company morale. That would be an unwanted distraction. I was hoping it would not be the beginning of a run of casualties. We had gone four months with minor stuff and that was remarkable in itself. The room fell uncomfortably silent. Tim turned and walked out, leaving me with my thoughts. He had to deal with this in his own way as well. I sat there thinking, hoping, that I had not sounded like a completely heartless ass. My conversation with Tim hounded me for days. I knew better than anyone that I could be an asshole but holy cow that may have been over the top. I cursed myself. Contemplating that, I leaned back on my flak vest and looked up at the cracked white wash on the ceiling. Tomorrow would be a new day. The struggle with my outburst ended when Sam walked in.

The flak vests we had been issued had finally broken in nicely. I had not even noticed it until then when I saw Sam's vest. Mind you it was still uncomfortable, bulky, and what most of us considered as quite a useless piece of shit. These jackets although lighter than the flak jackets the US forces used in Vietnam were the same in that they were not bullet-proof vests either. They were not police style body armour, that we were quite certain of.

"Well how do I look," he asked laughing his usual quiet laugh.

"You look like a slacker who should buy a poor disenfranchised soldier a beer," I said jokingly. I could already feel my energy changing to a lighter mood.

"Oh that's funny, I thought I looked like someone who had just been shot in the throat," he said, his face flushed now from smiling.

"Ya whatever, you sure it's not hemorrhoids?" I poked.

"No really Casey, I just got shot in the neck. Look."

With that he pulled the neck flap of his flak jacket down.

My eyes widened. There on his neck was a red spot the size of a golf ball. Before my eyes it was rapidly turning colours. Looking at the darkening bruise I said,

"You're not shittin me are you?" I stepped in closer to examine the near wound.

"No I ain't jokin. I was walking across the parking lot and the next thing I know I'm looking close up at the pavement. Like it knocked me right the fuck over?"

He was still giggling. It was obvious even though the shot did not pierce the skin that he was in mild shock. More like stupefied that he had been shot and lived to talk about it. I could not believe the day's events so far either. When would it end?

"You wanna see the medic?" I asked.

"No I'm good; I'll keep my eye on it. If my neck gets any worse, I'll get you to call Starlight."

"Ok, sounds good, buddy." I replied satisfied he would ask. I looked at my flak jacket sceptically.

"No fuckin way this hunk of shit took a straight on shot," I whispered to myself.

The days went on and a few more guys got shot. The rounds had to be at the end of trajectory shots with almost no kinetic energy left in them. The jackets were still cumbersome pieces of shit. We all concurred that we had one spectacular Angel looking out for November Company. The day ended with the staccato of machine gun fire erupting from across the Sava. Tomorrow would be a new day.

KILL OR BE KILLED

"We used to wonder where war lived, what it was that made it so vile. And now we realize that we know where it lives…inside ourselves."
~ALBERT CAMUS

Aid convoys were going out at an overwhelming pace, and today was no exception to the rule. The thoughts of being overworked and underpaid all came to a grinding halt when I encountered the children's hospital. I have rarely been as sickened as I was today. There are always innocent civilian deaths in war. It is a cost of war. WWI is a perfect example of that with more than one million civilians lost. On this particular day I was driving my number 6 truck for an aid delivery. We had just crossed the Sava River when on the right hand side of the road I noticed a building in amongst some others. Sounds normal except for the fact that the building in question was razed to the ground by fire, yet the surrounding ones did not even have any fire damage. I scrutinized the building's contents and I was horrified when I recognized the metal racks as beds. On those beds were the charred remains of children, dozens of them. I looked away. Blown by the wind, the water from my eyes immediately created dusty streaks across my face. By this point I had become so internally cold that I hoped they were tears.

It was now mid July and we drove out to Delta Papa-23 which was located on the eastern edge of the city. There was a large warehouse for distributing our cargo. The delivery at DP-23 was going well. We were lending a hand to the men unloading the trucks. Suddenly the air was full of white dust as one of the swampers fumbled a bag of flour and it exploded on the side racks of Donny's truck. I broke into hysterical laughter when I saw that it had covered Dean Thiessen who was standing on the ground with his hands in his pockets. He extended his left arm and flipped me the bird. Everyone else joined in the laughter. It did not take more than a few seconds and I was wearing a handful of flour. Then it was on, a full-fledged flour fight. We were all laughing and covered in flour dust. The UNHCR representative shook his head knowing that saying anything would just make it a bad day for him. The horseplay ended and we dusted off. The trucks were unloaded and we mounted up for the trip back to the airport. We made the turns out of the DP and lined up in order, APC then the trucks followed again by an APC.

The convoy had been travelling for about ten minutes when shots from the left side of the road pierced the air. A couple rounds creased the sheet metal of the cab of my truck. I could see the wood racks on the truck in front of me splintering as rounds connected with it. We kept driving and no more shots came in. We wound through the streets and finally made it out to the main road that would lead us back to the airport. Just ahead on the left was the destroyed building with the burnt child corpses in their beds. I looked to the right as we went by. Another minute and the lead APC and truck crossed over the Sava River. As we drove on the bridge Tommy said,

"Good God, that is harsh."

"What's harsh, Tommy?" I asked, not knowing where he was looking.

"That," he said, pointing down toward the river.

My foot came up off the throttle as I leaned over the centre console to get a better look. I wished I had not.

"Oh my God, that's fucking raw," I agreed.

There on a sandbar were four mangy looking dogs. Two of them were tug-o-warring over a severed arm. The other two were feasting on the remains of a second man. One of the two feral mutts feasting was only partially visible, as it was tearing away at its human meal, buried halfway up inside the abdomen of the body. The image burned in my memory.

The following day was horrific for some of my buddies. I was very fortunate that I was not involved in the devastating event that took place as a consequence of a moment of kindness.

A small throng of young children had formed under the windows of Recce Platoon at the PTT building. They were drawn in by the troops throwing candies down. To the kids, this was fantastic. Many had not had sweets for a year or better. The guys were enjoying the moment of actually bringing joy to these disenfranchised children. A handful of candies would hit the ground and the scramble was on. Giggles and cheers would erupt as each child got a candy from the melee. There was real joy at this very moment.

The explosion ripped into the ground disembowelling one kid as he was thrown twenty feet by the force. The blast dismembered two others. The rest had shrapnel wounds in varying degrees to their bodies. It was a despicable attack. The guys had the gruesome task of putting the kids into body bags. For many in Recce Platoon and their visitors from other platoons it would be a day that would haunt their minds for years.

The ICS crackled in my ears. I was in the hatch today of our rear guard track.

"Casey, watch the right side here, the lead track just took fire from the house on the right." I clicked the switch, "Roger."

I picked up the C-6 and set it on the right side and watched in the direction I was assigned. I fumbled a bit with the bipod but finally got it into a half decent position. I laid the belt of ammo out so it would not jam or snag. Just as the track ahead of us had received fire so did we. The metallic pings of incoming fire ricocheted off the side of our carrier. Shots cracked by inside our ludicrous arm swing method of determining effective fire. This shooter was definitely trying to kill us. I clicked the safety off and strained, looking into the sun for my target. The ICS clicked,

"Hundred metres out and in the upper left window, Casey!"

I angled my weapon up and to the left by lowering myself in the hatch. Even before I could see him I squeezed the trigger. I fired some controlled bursts toward the window.

The tracers were verifying that I was hitting right on target.

"That's it Casey, rock and roll, continuous rate go on!"

I squeezed the trigger and held it unleashing a barrage of fire while I spun in the hatch to stay on target. Ray was firing his C-7 into the building as well.

The brass casings were ejecting all over the upper deck and the links were falling into the open hatch. A couple of Sven's casings tinked off of my headset and one went down my collar.

"Ah fuck that's hot!" I yelled and kept firing.

The barrel was starting to smoke as the cleaning oil on it burned off. Sven's spent casing burned all the way down to my belt where it dropped out to the floor below. Months of having our hands tied behind our backs came surging out through my arms and went straight out of the smoking barrel. The shots that hit the building were kicking out puffs of red dust from the cinder blocks hidden under the white wash paint.

"Cease fire," came across the intercom. Capt. Burke was smiling as he turned in the cupola. Sven smacked me on the back. He screamed above the wind and the engine.

"That was awesome. You dropped him like nothin, Casey!"

My adrenaline was coursing through my body like crazy. It felt good to kill.

Three weeks went by with Alpha Company, Vandoo providing airport security. November Company had spent that time running the city's gauntlets delivering aid. The combination of boredom and tales of our often harrowing dashes into the city had prompted A. Coy to plead for the chance to escort a convoy. The HQ staff finally cracked and some of A. Coy's troops were selected. We of course were not privy to who or how they were selected. So at 05:30 the following morning the new convoy security APCs and their crews were on hand and appeared ready. There were three aid trucks in the first convoy. The lead A. Coy carrier clattered out the gates of the airport for the first time since we had arrived. At fifty metre intervals were me and my truck with Quinn Moses riding shotgun. Ray Gondol and Tommy in the 2nd truck, and the 3rd truck manned by Danny Weston driving with Bill Ringly in the jump seat, all followed by the rearguard Alpha Company track. We were headed to DP-19, the Olympic stadium, the worst part of the city, if there could be a worst. We had not even gone half a klick when the first shots creased the air. We never slowed down and we were soon out of range. A right hand turn, and the convoy was headed south down the main drag and past the familiar Rainbow Hotel, named for its myriad of pastel colours. Next to it on the right side of the road was the newspaper building. More indiscriminate shots came from there. So far it was a pretty standard run. Except for the fact Alpha Company was not returning fire. We whistled past the UN HQ PTT building. Two more intersections and we hung a left. Directly across from the Bosnian Parliament we turned right and headed east toward the Energoinvest building. The twin towers with their mostly shattered blue glass windows were on the right. We were not completely around the corner when my windshield shattered just above my head. The metallic sounds of bullets piercing the thin skin of our truck distracted me momentarily from watching the road and

I slammed into a curb. The carrier in front of me made a sharp left, a corner that was impossible for us to make.

"Where the fuck is he going", Moses screamed in anger.

I grabbed a fist full of gearshift and now with no APC to provide cover I aimed for the hole between two dragon's teeth and a ruptured Energoinvest gas railcar. Hurtling under a low over pass, made Moses and I both duck, and we manoeuvred through a few more dragon's teeth and a couple of burned out vehicles. I looked in the mirror and the two other aid trucks were right with us. Liquid poured out of the sides from where shells had torn into containers of supplies. Steering was becoming difficult as air was escaping from a bullet hole in one of the tires. Neither Quinn nor I, nor any of the other November Company drivers even saw where the bad guys were. We made it to the stadium without further incident. We did however wait till our N. Coy Recce Pl. escort showed up. They escorted us back to the airport and Alpha Company never left the airfield again till the day we extracted from Sarajevo. That was a defining day for many of us Royals, trust no one but The Men in Black.

I had fired my first TOW missile in the winter of '87 at the range in Manitoba. Here I was now, in the Olympic city of Sarajevo, with the trigger cover up and an armed missile in the tube.

I had been scanning the local hillsides within the 4km range for any tank movement or large groups of infantry when I heard what sounded like a 50cal. firing to the south end of the runway. With my palms I pushed the release mechanisms that allowed the turret to traverse and the sights to be moved up and down. I then spun the turret 90 degrees to the right and scanned the buildings in the suburb of Butmir. As I criss-crossed the ground in front of me I spotted what definitely appeared to be a 12.7mm Soviet heavy machine gun. I clicked the ICS,

"Tommy, move back up out of the hull-down so I can get a positive ID on this gun." I said. A hull-down position is when an armoured vehicle is dug in to afford less of its silhouette from being visible, thereby providing less of a target to shoot at. All our TUAs were provided hull-down positions as they were placed out on the open areas of the airfield. With tanks this close I mentally applauded Gen. Mackenzie and Col. Jones again for having the balls to bring the TUAs.

Tommy put it in reverse and backed up slow so not to raise any suspicion should any unfriendly people be watching. As he backed up I could clearly make out a T-54/55 with a gunner just rockin the 12.7 machine-gun.

"That's good there, Tommy," I then clicked the ICS to the radio side and called our section commander,

"…73 this is 73Alpha…CONTACT...Over…."

"….73 send...Over…." the radio crackled in quick response.

"…73Alpha...Contact...one T-55 at south west side of runway, range approximately

800metres, target appears to be engaging One platoon, can we get confirmation...Over…."

"…73 Roger...wait one...Over."

I sat impatiently observing the enemy gunner. I knew in my heart that if it progressed I was going to blast him without call sign Zero's okay.

"…73Alpha...73 Over…."

"…73Alpha go…." I said impatiently.

"…73...if that T-55 depresses its secondary armament more than 2mils, kill him, Over."

My ICS headphones crackled with the response. Finally, I said to myself.

"…73A Roger…Over."

With that Sgt. Franklin began to give fire orders to me and to the two other TUAs. If I fired this missile and killed this tank we had to kill every piece of armour, we could see or they would kill us for sure. I guided my cross hairs onto the 'sweet spot', where the turret meets the hull. I pulled the lever of the left launcher down, it clunked into place and I yelled,

"ARMED!"

With my right thumb I lifted the trigger cover. It felt as though every eye was on me, just like I was firing my first missile all over again. I kept the tank in the crosshairs and waited. I waited for what felt like an eternity. After about ten minutes of firing over the Vandoo positions the commander of the T-55 turned his head and I could see him plain as day. He was looking at our TUA. It was then that he panicked. His face went blank and his hands began to fidget. I am quite certain that he shit his pants when he saw me aiming directly at his tank. Quick firing calculations were undoubtedly running through his head. It was clear he was dead if he moved his turret even slightly in this direction. It was a deadly serious predicament. I wanted him to know that I was definitely locked on. I raised my hand out of the top of the turret and gave a little wave. Sheepishly, he waved back. I moved the turret up and down which made it look like I was nodding. I could not help but smile. The commander ceased firing and backed away from the airfield.

After a day and a night, my stint with AAP was over. I was making my way across the runway from 73A's hull-down position to the main terminal when a familiar putrid stench wafted in on the breeze. It was so strong that I deduced it must be coming from something close by. I did not want to look for whatever it was. Unfortunately, I was on a direct path through the grass. Twenty steps led me to it. There, lying in a contorted semi-fetal position was the corpse of a JNA regular. His rifle lay right where it fell. My eyes made their way up his lifeless form as I kept walking. A torrent of flies flew out of the black hole in the side of his head. The image left me with no doubt as to the manner of his demise. In an automatic reaction my body lowered as I walked. I suddenly felt so exposed. The person who shot him could very well still be active. I quickened my pace and strode to the aircraft hangars. As I made my way along the front of the building a door opened. It was the same door I had entered and exited from over a week earlier. The soldier I was looking at now was not a French Commando, but rather the tall and lanky Canadian from Recce platoon, Dan Vecchio. He was about six foot four with a solid frame. He had a quiet demeanour that only added to the respect that his tasking commanded. In his hand was Canada's sniper rifle, the C-3, 308.cal Parker Hale. I smiled but the gesture was not returned. I looked into his hollow black eyes and my eyes temporarily re-visited their own darkness. The image I saw was dark and full of angst. We turned and walked silently together, each knowing what the other was thinking and feeling. The 800 metre walk to the Customs building ended and we entered HQ. As we parted ways he turned and quietly said, "Thanks."

It's an interesting study in human behaviour this whole combat thing. Some guys are cool as ice, some are wound tight, and some are just plain scared shitless. Emotional shutdown was my mechanism for stability, or as I call it, "Flicking the switch." Fear does not discriminate where rank is concerned either. Two of our sergeants were terrified to the point that one of them would not take his position at the 50cal. in the commander's cupola. That Sergeant had one of his men 'man the gun' while he curled up on the floorboards of the carrier. That action soon became his nickname for the remainder of the tour, 'Floorboard.' I had a major outburst with the other sergeant and my attack on his cowardice was so abusive that Sam Sullivan had to restrain me, and he pleaded with me to stop. Unaffected by his plea's, my onslaught continued till I had said the obvious, that he was a useless fucking coward and that he should give up his rank. Being further restrained by Sam, I looked at the sergeant with disgust, I turned and walked away. He could not argue, as he stood surrounded, by his own section all of whom were nodding silently at my tirade. In my opinion he should have been relieved of his command, along with a few others who would not stand their posts. Let me be clear, I was scared but I was also a volunteer infantry soldier. Combat was the job we signed on for, like it or lump it. Scared or not we had a job to do in the Balkans. Thankfully this chapter was coming to a close and we would be heading back to Croatia and The Krajina. We had spent a month sluggin it out in this bitterly disputed city. Now that we were leaving, a multitude of feelings crept in. Driving along I was sad to think that there were so many people suffering. I was angry that the United Nations had held us captive from really making a difference and I was confused by the mixed messages of the warring factions in relation to our being there. I had tainted views towards the media, with exception of the BBC and CBC, for their twisted manipulations of the truth. And lastly there was the lack of trust and the bitterness to our French-Canadian counterparts, not just for our regimental rivalry, but more for bailing on us under fire. The difficulty with the last issue was that we still had three months remaining in the tour under their command. To actually be leaving Sarajevo seemed surreal.

The long road move back to The Krajina was uneventful. It was still unbearably hot. The quarters were still cramped and the REMEs continued to do a stellar job of getting our fleet of relics back to Sector West. The biggest event in the 300 kilometre journey was entering Sector South and getting a close up look at a Soviet made BMD that was in the Ukrainian arsenal. The BMD was the Soviet Airborne air droppable compact battle tank. That being said it is understandable that in comparison to being under fire every day in Sarajevo the trip back seemed mundane. The next three months in comparison to the Siege of Sarajevo would provide us with a relatively safe environment.

DEAFENING SILENCE

"A people free to choose will always choose peace."
-RONALD REAGAN

With the road move from Sarajevo concluded the Battle Group had to pick up where it left off. Our platoon houses had been pre selected and still had to have minor construction repairs done to them before we could inhabit them. The conditions were lack lustre to say the least. In fact, our accommodations in Croatia were disgusting at best, before we moved in anyways. When they were not moldy modular tents they were buildings that had been used by combatants. The plumbing was out of service so they would do their 'business' in the toilet till it plugged, then move to the bathtub. They would then poop their way from the farthest corner to the door. When the room was full the Croatian or Serbian soldiers would close the door and stuff rags under it to curb the unpleasant odour. From here they would move to the next room, repeating the procedure. This would continue till the house was no longer habitable or the frontline had moved too far for the dwelling place to be convenient. Enter the Canadian UN contingent again. With shovels and disinfectant, we would clean the houses up and move in. One of these buildings was used in this toilet-like manner by pigeons as well as by people. It was duly named Pigeon Palace and it was located in the village of Bijela. We shovelled the floor and swept the dried bird droppings and human feces out. The air was a solid haze of powdered poop. There is speculation that many of us now have respiratory problems as a result of having carried out these practices. Pigeon Palace was the place where a few of us witnessed something that most people never see, baby pigeons. They were a homely bunch of chicks. Some had fallen from their nests in the broken ceilings and now lie dead on the floor. Their gray bodies were sparsely covered in yellow feathers and their beaks had a lump halfway down their length. None of us wanted to kill any innocent creatures. They had been born in an unfortunate place and time. We did our best to remove the live chicks so that they may have had a chance of survival, although we knew that once we had our scent on them the mother would probably leave them to die.

The following afternoon I was sitting on the concrete steps located at the front of Pigeon Palace when a couple of the guys came walking up. I did not pay them much mind till I saw that they were walking really slowly and one of them had a string of 550 parachute cord tied to his wrist. The other end dangled to the ground. The end of the cord on the ground appeared to be moving. That's when I spoke.

"What the Hell have you two freaks got tied to that string?" They were both laughing as they watched his pincers grapple at the air. Tim Roberts replied,

"It's Elvis. He's our new Platoon mascot. He's a really bizarre looking bug is what he is."

"And how do you know he's a he?" I asked.

"Who knows for sure but it's still pretty cool."

It was the weirdest bug I'd ever seen. It was a beetle the size of two thumbs with crab like pincers that came out of the side of its square head and was just one of the reasons we all shook out our boots and other gear regularly. The experience Barry Appleton had had was another reason. He had been sleeping quietly when all of a sudden he woke screaming. He was clawing at his head and screaming for the soldiers surrounding him to kill him. To the troops, it appeared that he had lost his mind. Not unusual for many of us. So after watching him being mentally tortured, one of the guys finally obliged and knocked him out cold. A medic was called, who found a beetle the size of a man's thumb in Barry's ear.

I continued to sit on the steps mindlessly watching the activities of the local Hrvatska Policija. They would pull up in their beat up blue and white Zastava squad car and climb out, stand and look around nervously before entering the Police station. They would shuttle a large duffle bag in from time to time. A search in the near future would confirm my suspicions that there was a secret inside the walls of law enforcement. Floorboard shuffled out onto the steps as

I observed the policemen and informed me that I was entitled to a seventy-two-hour pass in Graz, Austria or Budapest, Hungary. I informed him of the peculiar activity across the street. He did not seem particularly enthusiastic about my concerns about the suspicious activity. Knowing I was wasting my time to go on about the police I chose Graz, Austria. I stood up turned away from the sergeant, and within twenty-four hours I was on my way for a well deserved break. In the seven months I served in the Balkans amounted to over five thousand hours on duty. I was lucky enough to enjoy my seventy-two-hour whirlwind R&R leave in Graz, Austria. My wife had flown in just for the special occasion and, right on cue, I showed up and ruined her holiday. The first thing I did was take a really hot half hour shower. She was somewhat unhappy with that but I didn't give a shit. She had no idea what it was like to go without a shower for more than a day. We fought some and I drank some and then some. The rest of the details are frankly, fuzzy.

The short vacation was good but it was all quite surreal and within a few hours I was back in The Krajina. It was as though the seventy-two hours never really happened. I threw my overnight bag on the corner of my bunk and quickly changed into my combat gear. It had felt weird to be in civilian clothing anyway. Within a half hour of being back in country I was in my Iltis and heading for the temporary Coy HQ in Pacrac. Patrolling and checkpoints had continued in my absence. I walked into the Coy HQ just in time to listen to the chatter as the radio came to life with a checkpoint contact.

"...2 this is Charlie Papa 4... Sitrep...Over...." Crackled the call on the November Company

HQ radio.

"...Charlie Papa 4 this is 2 send...Over...," replied Glenn Draper, the Company

Communicator.

"...Charlie Papa 4 Sitrep...we have three men in custody...Men have Ontario driver's licences...We are currently searching vehicle...Request Watchdog and Civilian Watchdog to this location...Over...."

"...2...Roger...Out..."

Meanwhile, on the ground at Check Point 4, Cpl Sheldon and Pte. Baran searched the vehicle driven by the three supposedly Canadian residents. Cpl Jesmond kept his C-9 machine gun levelled on them. M/Cpl Jag was asking questions,

"So if you are Croatian why do you have Ontario drivers' licences?" The question was met by silence.

"If you are Canadian why are you here in Croatia?"

Again no response from any of them.

"Master Corporal Jag."

"What?"

"You're gonna want to see this," replied Sheldon.

"Well, well, well, what could three good ol' boys from Ontario have use for AK-74s and brand new HV uniforms?"

"The three of you better lie down on your fuckin bellies real fast and spread your arms and legs out. If any of you gets to flinching about, Corporal Jesmond here is going to empty the entire belt into your lyin ass', you got it?"

"Now hit the dirt." With that the three got down on their bellies and spread their arms and legs as instructed by Jesmond who was eager to get them secure.

"Sheldon, get on the horn and tell call sign 2 we need Watchdog here ASAP. Tell them what we have and that we are holding position."

"Already done, Sunray."

Turns out after further interrogation, the three were mercenaries for the HV. After a brief conversation with Capt. Blundell our Company second in command, I returned to Bijela by way of Daruvar.

The following morning, I loaded up with Capt. Burke and we headed out for the location assigned for Coy HQ. The cleanup of the Pacrac community hall was in full swing when we arrived. The work party was made up of grunts from each platoon. I had been tasked to help with the project. We had converged at the soon to be N. Coy HQ. at 07:00. Work commenced at 07:15 following a quick briefing by the CQ as to what had to be done.

Tommy, Ray, Will and I were tasked with hauling all wood debris and anything else that could be burned. Will started a fire and we pulled out some doors that had been half destroyed and threw them on the flames. Tommy and Ray began tearing down an old set of shelves that were mostly rotten and would not support any weight. We worked at this project for a few hours. Brush had to be cleared for visibility should we be attacked. We kept throwing all the fuel we could find onto the burn pile, so the fire was growing. The temperature was in the upper 40s. That fact combined with the roaring fire meant we were dehydrating and burning out quickly.

"I don't know about you guys but I need a break," said Tommy.

"Amen brother," I concurred.

We sat beside my jeep which was parked in the shade of the hall.

"Man is it ever hot," I commented.

"Ya it seems like its hotter than when we were in the show," added Will.

The Company clerk came by and I snagged him by the shirt sleeve.

"Hey Gerry, grab a picture of us here, would ya?"

"Sure no prob."

We leaned against the jeep. Click.

"Thanks buddy."

I put my camera away and off he went.

"Sure glad we aren't with 8 Platoon," I said directly.

"Why not?" Ray asked.

"They are moving into the old Pacrac hospital and from what the L-tee tells me it's a real mess."

"How can it be any worse than this shithole?" Dave questioned.

"Well just imagine," I responded.

"I'm headin over there with Burke tomorrow, so I'll let you know how bad when I get back to Pigeon Palace."

The clean up was completed just after 2pm and we shuttled back to our respective platoon AOs.

The next morning Captain Burke and I mounted up and left Bijela by 06:00 hours. I could tell something new was up by Bill's demeanour.

"Where we off to, sir?"

"We have to go to HQ for a briefing. Then we are going to go do a people transfer," he replied.

"A people transfer. That oughta be rich," I quipped.

"Yes it's the first of many transfers to take place," he informed me.

"Who's running this show today?"

"Captains Haley and Fletch." Haley was tall and lanky and had been my Pl. Comd. for a year in AAP back in Germany. He was a stand up guy. Fletch on the other hand was an annoying little weasel that most of the troops disliked.

"Right on, and what's our job, over watch?" I asked unassumingly.

"You nailed 'er. We will be the back-up. If all goes well, then we follow one of the transferred groups to ensure they aren't engaged by bad people."

"That would be a bad thing. If shit goes sideways, we'll have another complete uprising." He agreed by saying, "It would be square one all over again except we'd be deeper in the middle of it."

We travelled the many roads we needed to get to where the arranged transfers would take place. After approximately an hour and a half of driving we followed a skinny little gravel road into what appeared to be the middle of nowhere. The trail came to a clearing at the top of a hill. On either side of the hill was an Iltis. Standing beside the jeeps were Captains Haley and Fletch and their drivers.

"This is where it happens," said Bill.

"I'll be over with Bralorne and Jensen," I told him.

"Sounds good but stay spread out. You know the drill," he said with concern.

"Roger that L- tee."

I met up with the guys and had a short bullshit session.

I made a suggestion,

"Be a good idea if we cover the transfer as best we can."

"Agreed," said Donny Bralorne.

"Where do you want us?"

"Well I would suggest that we should stay on the same side of the road. That way we are together versus one of us being cut-off. Agreed?"

They both nodded in agreement.

"Two of us down here so we can hear the civilians or whatever they are. The other up on that high feature with a clear shot at anyone instigating." I paused, "Any suggestions?"

"Sounds good enough to me Scotty," replied Donny.

Jensen nodded again.

"Steve, you are a better shot than Bralorne and I, so why don't you set up on the high feature?"

"Okay sure, use my discretion on targets?" He asked.

"Hey buddy I'm just wingin it too. I have no idea what to expect here. I'm no sergeant.

This is the first one of these transfers for all of us," I continued,

"Whatever happens don't shoot Blues and pray like Hell the officers have done their homework. Do you guys have anything to add, because this is a team gig?"

"No it all sounds good to me, Scotty."

"Yup it's all good bro," they responded together.

"See you when it's done then," I said to Jensen and he turned and headed for the knoll.

"Not if I see you first," he said to me with a wide smile.

Donny Bralorne and I found a natural hollow in the ground that would provide us with cover should we need it. From this vantage we could view the road clearly. We watched as the officers turned and walked away from each other down the road on their respective sides of the hill. Capt. Burke stood at the top of the hill and waited patiently. After about twenty minutes Capt. Haley reappeared and he was carrying a broom stick with a UN flag attached to it. Behind him were an old man and three old women. They stopped just short of the crest beside his Iltis. Another five minutes passed and Capt. Fletch appeared on his side of the hill with a UN flag hoisted as well. Following him were five women and three children. They stopped at his Iltis. Both officers were carrying white flags tied to radio antennas. They waved at each other and commenced walking toward one another.

"This is going well," I said quietly.

"Sure is, eh," Donny replied, in almost a whisper. The two groups met at the summit. They looked at each other for a moment. Then one lady reached out her hand. A gunshot echoed across the valley to the south side of the ridge.

"Are you fucking kidding me?" Donny whispered angrily.

Everyone froze. The lady had her hand extended, too afraid to withdraw it. We were high on the intensity of the moment. While the three of us sentries rapidly searched for the impending attack the second lady extended her hand without showing fear. The two ladies' hands met and

they pulled each other in close and gave a hug of peace. I did not have time to take an emotional register of the scene that was playing out. We were too busy to get wrapped up in feelings and the like. We had to remain vigilant.

"This is history, Scotty," Donny said to me.

"It sure is," I agreed.

We scanned the bush all around for any signs of someone who might want to disrupt this event. The civilians walked past each other and continued on their journeys. We waited a few minutes before we reeled in. Once back in a group we formed all around defence and Capt. Haley spoke first,

"That went well."

"It sure did, Tom. I was not sure if my group of ladies was going to go through with it.

They were scared shitless," Capt. Fletch responded.

"And that's how history is made gentlemen, good job all the way around," Captain Burke added confidently looking at all of us.

Later that afternoon Burke and I drove into Pacrac to HQ to pass on the info about the transfer. I took a drive over to the Pacrac hospital to visit with the guys there. When we arrived the boys of 8 Platoon were in full swing cleaning up the hospital, a task I was fortunate enough to be absent from. The absence was based purely on the fact I was not in their platoon. They had been cleaning for most of the day. The hospital was in absolute disarray. Part of the hospital had been used by one force or another after the war started. In their usual form Croats or Serbs had trashed everything. And as usual some rooms were full of human feces. Other rooms were full of used medical supplies. In a couple of rooms there were vials of stored blood. Why would an aid station with bleeding soldiers not use stored blood? There was blood on the floors and walls. In amongst the debris that the troops were cleaning up with shovels, with brooms, and also with their bare hands were syringes and used needles. Some of the soldiers of 8pl were poked by those needles. The fact that this happened is sickening. The proper equipment to tackle most jobs was non-existent. This was no exception. No masks, no gloves, no eye protection. It was believed later on that the apparently unused blood was actually blood taken from Aids infected patients of the hospital. The hospital was abandoned by our troops. Even after the clean-up, it was determined to be unsafe for us to occupy. I am sure the Croats laughed at us for that.

Warm summer breezes and children kicking a ball on the soccer pitch. That is what the month of August should normally inspire in a person's imagination. I had just finished picking at my supper and was leaning back on my chair watching Sky News from Britain when the journalist produced the day's top story. I slowly let the chair lean forward so the weight was once again on all four legs. My jaw hung open slightly as I stared at the images on the t.v. The photos I was currently viewing were akin to something I had only seen in WW2 documentaries of the Holocaust. On the soccer pitch, gone were the images of innocent children kicking soccer balls with young spirited glee, where the only referees to be seen were parents watching over their youngsters. Today, in their place, were hundreds of emaciated men of Bosnia. No parents to watch over them but rather men in uniform brandishing automatic weapons. Separating the guards from the prisoners were no white lines of chalk. Instead there were tangled coils of concertina wire where the lines for the sports field should have been. The sound was turned down on the t.v. but that did not mean I could not understand what the story was all about. My shoulders sagged as the camera angles changed to ensure that the world was indeed witnessing a repeat of an ugly chapter in European history. With my mind reeling I sat in utter disbelief at the footage. Even with everything I had seen to this point in relation to the slaughtering of civilians and just death in general this not so new barbaric display made me sick to the core of my being. Without bothering to clean my melmac plate and KFS I got up and quietly left the mess hall destined for the sanctuary of my room.

Closing the makeshift curtains that poorly draped my windows I sat sullenly in the semidarkness. At this low moment I believed there would never be peace in Yugoslavia. Our mission even given its varying degrees of success was in my view a futile waste of time, resources and most importantly the people's minds who had been trying to help preserve lives here. I now believed that the Canadian peacekeeping mission was a failure and because of that, I too, was a failure. My thoughts were beyond rational at this time. For whatever reason, I was taking this recent development personally. Over the course of the last few weeks we had been hearing stories of these types of camps. There was however no conclusive evidence to substantiate the stories. UN observer teams had tried to inspect but had been denied access to many of the critical areas. I knew from my own experiences that people had been executed, but when executions are conducted, without witness and the evidence only found afterwards, it is difficult to lay blame because the criminals have moved on. Some of the stories defied logic and defied the essence of humanity. Like the alleged atrocity in the village of Koritnik where Serb militiamen were said to have pushed over 50 Muslim, men, women, and children into a concrete basement and then tossed in hand grenades till the screaming stopped. Or the story of the Vuk Karadčič elementary school where reports came through civilian channels of Serbs bleeding out 400plus Muslims for wounded Serbian blood transfusions. Serbs had borne the brunt of the reports because they had the most to gain. All for the Greater Serbia. Serbs were not alone as Croatian militias were accused of their own brand of butchery as well. It was believed that the Croats had upwards of forty camps where over 5500 Serbs had been killed.

We, as peacekeepers, the ground representatives for the United Nations, were viewed poorly by all sides for our failure to intervene to stop the killing. The reality was that the UN did not want to get involved on a major offensive in the Former Yugoslavia. Neither did NATO. This was based on the fact that there was no clear frontline and the terrain would be brutal to fight in. Those two tough facts combined with the knowledge that the enemy and civilians would be indistinguishable, and the reality was that any military mission would be a catastrophe for outside powers. In essence it would reflect the same light as Vietnam or Lebanon and inevitably end in failure. So there we sat in the quagmire that was Yugoslavia, praying that if and when we made it out of here we could be viewed as heroes.

It had been two months since I had been to Camp Polom. In other words, I had not been there since my CBC interview when we embarked for Sarajevo. I was shocked when I drove through the gates. The camp had been transformed into a small town. Everything had been painted white. The grass appeared to have been mowed recently. There were even flowers planted. I drove straight for the AMU. I had a couple of buddies I had met earlier in the tour I wanted to visit. It was not a special trip. I had dropped the L-tee off so he could phone home. And they were both just really good guys. I enjoyed harassing them about being pretty cool for Base WOGs, and they were very interested in how I had managed to read and write, seeing as I was a Grunt. It took a minute of driving around the camp to get to the AMU office. I pulled the jeep into the parking spot marked 'AMU Officer Parking-Only'. I stepped out and walked up the steps and kicked the door open.

"Is it just a rumour or is this the busiest puppy mill in all The Krajina," I hollered obnoxiously even though the office was only twenty by twenty.

"Holy shit, those Vandoos will let any riff raff onto this secure base," M/Cpl Larry Taylor shouted back.

"Who says I came in the front gate?"

"Of course, what was I thinking, you're a grunt, and nobody told you that the front gate was the way in."

"Well at least I've been outside the wire, Larry."

"How's things keepin, Scotty? By the looks of you, The Show was a tough go."

I looked at myself in the reflection of the window.

"The Show? You've heard the name? Piece-a-piss. And what the fuck do you mean by, by the looks of you?" I replied with a jokingly egotistical flare.

"Ya right, that's not what the Vandoos have been saying around here."

"Well that's what separates them boys from The Men in Black," I said with a hint of pride.

"Where you hangin your helmet now?" Larry asked.

"To the south east of here, in Bijela."

"Hmmm, never been there."

"Gee I'm surprised. I thought all you WOGs would have been out collecting war souvenirs," I said jeering at him.

"Fuck you, grunt," he shot back with a nasty grin.

"Thank you for the compliment. Now kneel in honour REMF."

I quickly ducked the barrage of pencils, pens and paper clips as he hurled a plastic desk organiser at me.

"Have to try something other than shrapnel, Larry. The Scroats can't kill us with that shit either." We laughed hysterically at our bantering.

Hey where's the big guy?" I was referring to the AMU Warrant officer Ed Drummond.

"He's gone home."

"Uh huh right and I'm gettin promoted to sergeant later today," I joked.

Larry's voice lowered,

"No really he RTU'd three weeks ago. It was sad. He just cracked one day."

"No shit. That's horrible."

"It's the shits alright. Eddy was a good guy."

The conversation struck me hard. Ed was a good man and this place had destroyed him mentally. It was not right. At that moment the door flew open and a snotty looking

Navy Sub-lieutenant stood in the doorway.

"Whose filthy Iltis is parked in my spot?"

I stared at him. Larry started to explain but he was cut off by the scrawny officer.

"Isn't it customary to salute an officer, Corporal?" he commanded, looking at me with disdain. My hand squeezed the receiver group of my rifle tightly.

"Yes it is," I said flatly without lifting my arm.

"Catch you later, Larry."

"Excuse me Corporal, who are you with?" "I expect you to answer me Corporal!" the 'fish out of water' commanded.

My eyes dimmed and sinister thoughts began to boil in my brain. I walked straight toward him. He must have read my mind because his shoulders rolled forward, cowering like an abused puppy. I kicked the door open and walked out without responding. Ed was a good man with a heart of gold. This screwed up war had destroyed the mind of a good friend, and with that knowledge I had one more scrape in my own mental armour. The days ahead would show I was not the only one hanging by a thread.

"Hey Hansley just killed a shitter," shouted Brock as he entered Pigeon Palace through the front door.

"He did what?" somebody asked.

"Ya you wouldn't believe it, guys. He just opened up on the platoon porta-pottie," Brock was laughing as he told the story. I joked along

"A little excessive force for not putting a new roll on, don't ya think?"

"No doubt," Ray agreed.

"So I hope it was empty," I said.

"Oh ya, it was empty, and thank God it was, 'cause he shot the Hell right out of 'er."

Brock said shaking his head.

"What, he shot a magazine into it?" I asked.

"Ah no, he fired half a belt from his C-9," Brock said still shaking his head.

"Half a belt? Holy shit. That's fuckin crazy," Ray said.

"No kidding, sure a good thing no one was in there."

"So did somebody call the meatheads or are they going to deal with it?" I asked, hoping it would stay in house.

"No they called the MPs."

"Oh shitty, he'll be up the creek with this one," I replied.

I stood in the town square in Bijela. It was a quiet evening. In the centre of the square was a concrete and stone fence built in the shape of an octagon. The fence stood two feet high on one side and gradually rose to four feet on the other. In the centre of the four-foot section and against the wall was a now blackened bronze bust. He had a bullet hole in his forehead and one in his right cheek. The Ustaše symbol was emblazoned graffiti style on his chest. I wondered how Tito the President who had held Yugoslavia together for so long would feel about the disrespect that had come to his effigy if he were still alive today.

"You wouldn't be here if he was alive," I muttered to myself.

"Thanks for kickin the bucket. I could be lyin at the quarry gettin a tan and drinkin pops ya, jerk."

I turned and walked back to Pigeon Palace. Smoke wafted around the corner. As I rounded the corner someone yelled,

"Fire in the hole!"

I immediately dropped to one knee to avoid whatever explosive was about to detonate. I did not move quickly enough.

Shrapnel came whizzing at me. There was no way to avoid it; I caught the brunt of the explosion. My face stung from the impact. My arms and legs were pelted with shrapnel from the device and I fell over behind the corner. It was searing hot and my skin relayed it was not happy. My hands went to my face and they came back warm and wet, blood and lots of it. I was obviously in shock because I did not feel any pain. I was not screaming like someone who had just been fragged. Then it hit me. I could hear laughter coming from around the corner. Not only were they hysterical, but they were oblivious to me.

"Did you see that?"

"Ya that was fuckin awesome." The comments were followed by more laughter.

"I'm gonna go get another can."

"Hey get peas this time, there was only one can of beans left." I looked down at the blood on my hands.

"Baked beans," I said to myself. I got mad, but that emotion turned instantly to laughter. I was not wounded. I regained my composure, turned the corner and walked right past Jason Baker. He was the one who had thrown the can on the fire. His face was filled with shock the instant he saw me. He did not utter a word. I smiled as I walked by and patted my rifle,

"Gonna go clean this, be needing it soon, you wait here." The look on his face was all I needed. I walked down the hall to my room and laughed my ass off. I needed a shower anyway.

"What the Hell is it with guys killin the shitters?" I asked.

"Hell if I know, they must be gettin frustrated or something. There sure aren't any 'live' targets anymore," Ray responded.

"You are talkin about Hansley right?"

"No," I said sharply. "You haven't heard? Garcia shot the crapper right over there-I pointed-last night."

"Get the fuck outa here," Ray said stupefied.

"Ya he was pissed to the eyeballs. Good news is he only fired five shots," I added.

"Oh well only five shots that's bugger all," Ray said laughingly. "Well it's not so funny for

Garcia. Glass called the meatheads."

"Are you kidding?" Ray looked at me with a disgusted look.

"No I'm not kidding he called 'em straight away. So much for looking out for your own,"

I said.

"No doubt he could have given him shit jobs for a month instead of having him charged," Ray suggested.

"Yup but he wants to prop himself up like he's the man. Even though he's as big a coward as Winsome when the shit starts flyin," I said with venom.

"Let's not forget 'Ol' Hanson, too," added Ray.

"Ya it just isn't fair a guy gets a little haywire and they charge him. But if he's a coward they promote him."

"Promote him? What the Hell are you talkin about?" Ron's eyebrows flexed with anger.

"Oh you haven't heard the biggest piss off news out of this war? Hanson, after getting his Sarajevo coward petition together, has been promoted to sergeant."

Ray just stood there looking at me. His eyes said it all. "Ya I said the same thing Ray, only louder."

Yes, things were better here in The Krajina, or at least superficially they were. It would be difficult to ease years of hatred over the course of 270 days. To believe that the war was over because of our presence was not possible for me. I am sure it was not possible for the people of the Former Yugoslavia either. Life for me, although I was away from the safety of my home, was good. I did not have an entire ethnic group wanting to kill me based on my ethnicity. Or did I?

Tommy and I were patrolling the streets of Omanovac when a poster on the door of a storefront caught my eye. I climbed the stairs so I could get a good look at it. It was a nice black and white portrait of a gentleman in a suit. He looked like a politician I thought as I started up the stairs. I stopped and read it.

UNPROFOR
Go home

My blood pressure must have gone through the roof because Tommy stopped at the bottom of the steps.

"What's wrong, Scotty?"

I could not speak. I was visibly shaking with rage.

"Can you believe this asshole?" I finally manage to blurt out.

Tommy came up and read it. He stood there quietly.

"I don't have a clue what the Hell we are doing here Tommy. We help feed the starving, we provide medical aid to the suffering, security to those who are caught in the open all the while getting shot at ourselves. And then we're subjected to this kind of garbage."

John was nodding his head.

"I'll tell you if this son of a bitch was here I'd slot him right now on these steps and I wouldn't lose a night's sleep." I was so mad; tears were rolling down my face.

"Come on Scotty we gotta go." Tommy put his hand on my shoulder and tugged.

I was driving between Sirač and Badeljavina mid August on my way to pick up Capt. Burke. The road had seven-foot corn rows that seemed to encase the road. I had been enjoying the trip. It was much quieter in Sector West since our return from the chaos that was Sarajevo. I actually found it enjoyable some days. I was cruising along a straight section of the road when I caught sight of something dark in amongst the corn. It was too late to react as I saw a man, with a hunting rifle, step with one fluid motion onto the road, raise the weapon and fire. At that exact moment my jeep hit a pothole and my body jostled to the left snapping my head quickly along with it. The windshield exploded in front of me as the snapping of the bullet smashed my right eardrum. He reloaded and fired. I went from serene to psychotic in the blink of an eye. I slammed on the brakes. He fired again and as quickly as he had stepped out of the corn, he had faded back into it. I slammed the shifter into neutral, grabbed my C-7 and as I bailed out I sprayed a 30 round mag in the general direction of his tracks through the corn. I knew better than to give chase though. He could have been trying to draw me in deeper and into an ambush. I quickly grabbed the mic of my jeep's 524 radio set and with the adrenaline coursing in my words, called Coy HQ.

"…2 this is Zulu 21 Whiskey Contact…Over…"

"…Zulu 21 Whiskey this is 2…Send…Over…"

"…Zulu 21 Whiskey…Contact…This call sign has been engaged by lone rifleman…I'm currently on the road between Sirač and Badeljavina…He is in a corn field on the north side of the road approximately three clicks from Sirač…. Request you send a carrier out to clear the area…Over…"

"…2 Roger…22Charlie is already on route…Send ammo casualty report…"

"21 Whiskey…reference one…Okay, one magazine…Over…"

"…2 Roger that…RV our location soonest…Over…"

"…Zulu 21 Whiskey…Roger… Over…"

"2…Out…"

When I got to HQ in Pacrac I was met by a crowd of well wishers. They had really just come out to hear about the action and check out the damage. A few of them took turns sitting in the driver's seat and looked out the window through the spider webbing cracks. Some of the unit cowards stood by chuckling. I could not wait to get out of this place, not just because of the bad guys but because of guys like Glass, Winsome, and Hanson.

Three weeks after we returned to Croatia from Bosnia I sat on the back porch of Pigeon Palace, our new home in Bijela. Settling in should have been a breeze, but it was strangely quiet. I found it difficult to sleep. It was so quiet that it was akin to sleeping in a moving car so often that you could not sleep in it if it was parked. With that here I sat out back with the only sedative we had at our disposal, Pivo. "What the fuck are you lookin at?" I blurted angrily.

The cleaning lady dropped her head and started up the steps.

"You assholes are so lucky we're in the middle of this shit and not on the fuckin war path."

She looked toward me with vacant eyes.

"Ne razumijem?" I asked

She shook her head. Of course she did not understand.

"Well me neither." I threw my bottle at the carriers parked thirty feet away. It smashed on the trimvane of the left one, scattering shards of brown glass over the ground. By 19:00hrs I was so drunk I could barely stand, let alone walk. Somehow I managed to stagger to my bunk. I woke the following day at 0915hrs. The camp was empty. There was a note on my helmet.

'Bet your head hurts dumbass. I'm in the kitchen. RG'.

I got dressed and went to the room that held our mess hall. Ray Gondole sat at a table drinking coffee.

"Well if it isn't Sleeping Beauty."

"Am I in shit?"

"Na, it's all good. I told Winsome you got in at zero-four."

"He bought that shit?" I asked.

"Did you wake up on your own?"

"Ya."

"Well then I guess he bought it. And now you owe me one." Ray chuckled and sipped his coffee.

"You're a good friend, brother."

"Ya whatever."

He passed off the sentimental stuff regularly. Ray was always subdued that way. I knew however that he appreciated our friendship.

The boys from 5Pl. were having a beautiful feast at WC-11. The pork was roasted to perfection and the trimmings had been acquired by some of the crew while they were in at HQ in Pacrac. A pig roast was the icing on the WC-11 cake.

"Where the Hell did you crazy mother fuckers find a pig?" I asked in astonishment. "We came track slidin around this corner about four clicks from here and there was this sow standing in the middle of the road. Axle tried to avoid her but she turned and we just clipped her," said one of the guys.

"She was squealing like Hell," said another.

The excitement grew as they relived the event.

"Ya, then Tony grabs his C-6 and jacks a half a dozen rounds into her smarty," added Garcia excitedly.

"We gutted her right there. What we don't eat we'll give to the ol' timers that come through here every day." Axle was brimming with that.

"Ya that's his idea. Figures it's a good way to keep the peace with the locals."

"I said we would just pin it on the Newfie," Tony joked.

"Youse kin shove da blame up your harse, bye," Axle quickly shot back.

"Well after we torched the bridge it's probably a good idea to keep our noses clean eh?!" I said flatly. We all had a good laugh at the memory of the bridge a blazing away. The ride back to Bijela was a long and groggy one. The feast had made me food drunk. All I needed now was a beer and I would sleep like a baby. When I got in I went straight back to my room and was halfway through a when WO. Goddard strode in. He informed me,

"The skipper needs to go to the Argentineans HQ to set up a citizen transfer for tomorrow." I just looked at him with a blank expression.

"Listen Scotty, I know you've been runnin for forty-eight already but I don't have anyone else to go."

"No worries Warrant, lots of time to sleep when I'm dead."

The heat was almost unbearable in my room. There was only one east facing window and I quickly threw it open. I could feel the heated pressure release as I cracked the windows seal. It would take some time for it to cool down. I dropped my skid-lid on the floor. My flak jacket was next to slide off my sweat drenched torso. It fell to the floor standing as if it was still on my frame. I laid my rifle flat on my poncho liner. I sat down on the chair I had acquired from a house across the village square. I lifted my barrack box lid open with my bayonet in one fluid motion as I pulled it from its scabbard. With my other hand I deftly scooped out a Heineken. I had become wiser as the tour progressed. Before heading out in the morning I would fill my barrack box with ice and some beer. By the time I got back the ice would be melted and the beer would still be cold. It was not a fridge but it did the trick.

As I cleaned my rifle I tipped a brew back. After cleaning my weapon, I had another beer and did some felt pen painting on my wall. My art work consisted of the Canadian and UN flags with the words 'In the Service of Peace' underneath. I went through three large blue felt pens and another couple of beers. The mural covered a four by eight-foot sheet of plywood in size. I stood back and cracked another beer as I admired my work. I looked at the colours and then at the written words. Mixed emotions were churning through my chest. There was a minor feeling of personal accomplishment in addition to: feelings of being unlikeable. The effects of no food or sleep combined with the beer began to show. In my drunkenness, I had slipped my blue pen out of the lines. I stepped back and to my left, facing away from the drawing and toward the wall that housed the door. What happened next shocked me.

In another violent outburst I slammed my fist through the wall. I retracted my arm and punched the wall in a two fisted flurry. I kept smashing the wall until both my fists were cut and bleeding and the Yugoslav version of drywall was destroyed.

I sat on my cot with my eyes engulfed in an internal sea of red. I was seething with rage. I popped another top off of a Pivo this time chugging it down so quickly that it was spilling out the corners of my mouth. It drooled down my face and onto my combat shirt. I am not sure why I started to cry, but tears began streaming down my face. My head fell forward and I stared at the floor, tears dripping into a pool on the wooden floor between my boots. Looking at my hands slowly turning them over to see the knuckles, my insides felt like they were ripping apart. Seeing the injuries made me angry with myself. I closed my eyes in frustration. Instantly the vision of the little kids with the water bottles being slaughtered pounded into my head. The dogs fighting over the arm in the river bed. The hole in the side of the soldiers' head. The eyes of the dead were staring at me asking me, "Why?"

"AAAGGHHH!"!! I screamed at the top of my lungs. I threw my quarter full beer bottle at the wall. It smashed into a thousand pieces. My head rolled back and I looked at the ceiling. Just then the door opened. Sgt. Winsome peered in.

"Everything okay?" he asked timidly.

"Ya it's fuckin groovy, Sergeant."

"Okay," he said quietly as he closed the door. The slower pace back in Croatia was taking its toll on many of the troops. Some of the guys were fighting with Croats and Serbs just to get the rush of battle going again. Fist fights were happening with the locals as well. Lying back, I stared at the ceiling. I desperately needed sleep. But I did not want to close my eyes. I lay there awake till morning when I got up and went back out on patrol. Driving from Pigeon Palace in Bijela to any of our checkpoints or other platoon locations became such a chore that I began timing myself. I drove my Iltis as fast as the governor would allow on a regular basis. The adrenalin rush of the previous five months had been replaced by a flat line day to day existence. After the hair raising start of being thrown into battle at the beginning of the tour to the Hell that was Sarajevo, this sixth month was as boring as ever. With that boredom came a dangerous complacency, hence, the breakneck driving that I was partaking in to get a rush. I was not alone in this sort of practice. It more or less just crept up on us. On one of my Mach 1 trips out to WC-11 I got my wake up call. I had just gone by the Pakra monastery when, under the shade of the canopy of trees that covered the road, my eyes did not adjust quickly enough to the change in light. I am sure what could have been the only surviving cow in all of Croatia stood in the middle of my path. In my bid to ensure she stayed alive and my jeep did too I swerved hard right to the more open side of the road to avoid the bovine blocker. My Iltis slammed hard into the ditch. The forward skid plate screeched a horrible tune as it passed over some basketball sized rocks. As my poor little jeep went farther up and off the road the more leaves were stripped from the trees. The mirrors folded in and so did I with my body straining against the seatbelt. My C-7 rattled in the crook of the mirror in retaliation for the sudden change of course. I steered the jeep turned projectile back toward the road. The friction caused by the defoliation slowed me down enough that I did not rollover when I manoeuvred down onto the trail again. Getting back on packed ground I got out and did a quick once over to look for damage. Down the trail in the direction I had just come from stood the cow chewing away at her cud seemingly unaffected by the near collision. The Iltis was much the same. The new scars would go unnoticed as they blended in with the old ones quite nicely. I pulled the remnants of the forest off the protruding parts and resumed my trip at a somewhat slower pace. I arrived at WC-11 a half hour later. I carried a crate of 5.56mm ammo into the bunker. Sven and Leon unloaded the other supplies and took them to the tent. We sat and shot the breeze for about half an hour when the distinctive sound of an M-113 superseded its arrival. A moment later and it came sliding around the corner in a hail of dust and small rocks. The ramp dropped once it was parked and everyone dismounted. During the small talk that followed Axle brought up the fact that someone hit the rhubarb at a high rate of velocity back this side of the monastery. According to him,

"The lucky bastard flew off de road and nare touched a blade of grass fer tirty tree feet, bye. E's lucky e's not dead cuz e flew between two Jesus big trees e did." I looked off toward the bridge from the back window of the bunker and confirmed my earlier decision to be less haywire with my driving just because I was not getting shot at enough.

"Hey Scotty, what's happenin, buddy?"

I heard the cheerful question as Ranger kicked open the door to my room.

"Ah nothin much," I replied solemnly.

He immediately sensed my downhearted mood.

"Don't sound like you're a very happy little boy," he chirped still trying to be upbeat.

"Just got some shit on my mind that's eatin me up a bit," was my response.

"Trouble at home?" Ranger questioned already knowing the answer.

I lowered my head. There was more to it than just marital issues. My wife was very capable of hiding her infidelity but I still had my suspicions. The shitty part was some of the guys knew but never told me. At this moment, however, she was the least of my concern.

"Ranger that shit will never go away as long as I'm married to her." "Well then what's got you so down?" my friend again inquired.

"This stays between you and me, okay?" I said with a straight face.

"Okay, just us."

His solemn demeanour confirmed that this would go no further. He pushed my poncho liner to one side of my bunk and sat down.

"When we were down in The Show I um well," I stammered not knowing how to get the words out.

"You what?" Ranger pried gently.

"I killed a guy with a French sniper team." I blurted out. Until now I had not spoken a word of the killing to anyone.

"You did what?" His question hung in the air. I took an uneasy breath and I began explaining.

"Well I went into one of the hangars and there was a French sniper team in there."

He sat silently listening without looking me in the eye. I recounted the story to him in explicit detail. When I was done he looked at me and said,

"You took all this time to tell me there were a couple of French dudes in a hangar?" He said blinking his eyes at me.

"Did you hear what I said?" I questioned him, somewhat annoyed.

"Ya I heard you. You shot some Scroat because he was a fucking dirt bag. Sounds pretty simple to me," he replied as a matter of fact. Before I could say anything he added,

"Anyone of us would have done the same thing. You did the world a favour."

With that he patted my shoulder and stood up.

"Gotta go, we're heading to Whiskey Charlie One-One, and I don't want to miss my ride." I knew he did not want to deal with the emotional side of the issue.

"Thanks Ranger," I paused and sighed, "For listening I mean."

"You'd do the same for me," he replied as he stepped out the doorway. I felt a little better getting it off my chest. It felt good to know that he thought it was justifiable too.

I leaned back on my cot and flicked the switch.

PIN THE TAIL ON THE DONKEYS

"Cynicism is humor in ill health."
~H.G. WELLS

A few days passed with nothing much in the way of excitement. We patrolled the streets and just kept a watchful eye. Checkpoints were still operating as usual and this practice ensured illegal weapons were not making their way back into the UNPAs. Villagers were walking about the streets in relatively the same fashion as before the war. To them, I could see, the energy in the air was different, like they felt safe for the first time in several years. Fools, I thought. My attention shifted from an overview of the scene to one of more individual scrutiny. As the townsfolk walked by I scanned each carefully, looking for any clothing that was out of place or eye contact that signalled avoidance. Somewhere in this village were bad guys. It was just a matter of figuring out which ones they were. With each minute that passed I waited for the AKs to come out and for someone to open up on us. Whether the day had brought new hope to the people of Sirač or not I was still wary. I walked methodically down the cobblestone and dirt of the street till I met up with Capt. Burke. We continued walking to the Iltis and climbed in. In a cloud of dust, we drove in the direction of the sports field.

This was a special day for the people of Sirač, as well as for the surrounding area. A sporting event had been in the organizational phase for the last two weeks. Now here on the reclaimed Sirač sports field where we had lived for three months was an impending soccer match. Capt. Burke and I stopped to watch for a few minutes. We were not as enthusiastic as the locals. Well I was not anyway. Even though it was a clear sign that things here appeared to be stabilizing I was unsteady. The opposing teams lined up and the first whistle blew to start the match. We stood watching the event from a distance. I could not help but look past the game into the surrounding brush. Capt. Burke and I watched for approximately fifteen minutes and he decided all would be okay. We mounted up and carried on to Pakrac. The soccer match went off without a hitch. This peace was what we had come here for. However, I still had difficulty believing that life for Croatia was returning to normal. With the shot that had been taken at me just days earlier I was justifiably sceptical.

249

The last days of August rolled in and things in Sector West had quieted down for the most part. In my opinion, that just meant the bad guys had just hidden their weapons and aggression for the time being. It was downright boring.

"Hey Moses, let's go for a walk and check this town out. I want to get some good black and white shots."

He nodded his head at me. I slung my camera around my neck and we walked out of the HQ's courtyard. Pacrac was deserted. We walked down the streets like tourists, tourists with guns. It was amusing to think of it that way. I chuckled as I said it over and over in my head.

"Check this out, Casey."

I rounded the corner so I could see what he was looking at. It was a corner building that had been burned out during a battle. My Canon camera clicked away.

"You know what that says, No 1?"

"Nope," he replied. I was referring to the big metal sign on the peak of the building.

"Buduchnost," I enunciated. "Translated it means, The Future, quite the premonition eh?"

"Ya no kidding. I wonder if they thought of it that way?" Quinn asked.

"Do you think any of these assholes think much at all?" I quipped.

"They shit on the floor of the houses they live in. Rocket scientists they are not," I added.

We walked another block, rounded the corner to the right and walked halfway down. There on the left was a stone house with a gaping hole in the side of it. The hole was a perfect circle and the size of the front end of a transit bus. We just stood there looking at it, our jaws hanging somewhat open. Randy spoke first,

"Now I'd like to see the kid's ass that broke that window."

"No shit, I know my dad would've tanned mine," I joked along.

"Here, No 1, I have to have a picture of me standing in front of this one," I said passing my camera to Quinn. He took the photo and then we continued walking. After another half hour and few more photo ops Randy and I headed back to HQ. It still amazed me how much damage had been done to this country. As we closed in on HQ we noticed that there was a German Marder painted white. UN markings were emblazoned on the sides.

"Germans?" Quinn got the word out before me.

"I guess. I didn't think they were up for this," I speculated.

As we got closer I stated the obvious.

"Pretty good tans for Germans."

Quinn nodded. There were already a couple of our guys chatting with the Marder crew.

They were standing on top looking at the German made hardware.

"Who are these guys?" I asked.

"Argentineans,"

Les Roberts chirped from his position atop the Marder. We had a little meet and greet. We showed them our C-6 that Moses was packing and we checked out the inside of the Marder.

"Pretty sad eh, Quinn?"

"What's that," he asked.

"It's pretty sad, little Argentina has the APCs that Trudeau refused to buy for Canada," I exclaimed shaking my head.

"What was the deal?" Moses inquired.

"The Germans offered ten Marders at a significantly reduced cost for every Leopard tank Canada purchased. Trudeau said no and bought the antiquated M-113s from the Yanks instead." I relayed the story with contempt.

"Good call Mr. Prime Minister. Not," Quinn commented sarcastically.

August turned to September and it was still quite warm. The locals were celebrating weddings and such. Only now there was very little of the wild-west stuff we encountered when we had first arrived. No one was shooting AKs into the air with wild abandon as regularly. It still happened but it was not very often and was well away from our watchful eyes.

The following day in an impromptu semi-rushed ceremony we assembled in three ranks and waited patiently for Capt. Bradley to issue to us our UNPROFOR medals. I stood sharply to attention along with the other guys from 5Pl. The lot of us were griping and not impressed with the fact that here we stood in a combat zone dressed to the hilt in S-3s. That is right, full dress uniform. We were pissed off from the onset of the mission that we were even forced to bring them. As I stood there I wondered who would get shot first. It probably would not happen. But none of us could rule it out. Crazier shit had happened to us.

"Wouldn't this be the way to go, in S-3's on a parade square in country with no ammo in our rifles," I whispered to Dan Botarro who was standing to my left.

"Ya just great, Hanson would probably get promoted to WO for 'being in combat'," whispered Dan.

"Don't get me started," I said growling under my breath.

Capt. Bradley made his way down the line and pinned the gong on my chest. There was no feeling of pride. I was already wondering what the Hell we were accomplishing here.

He shook my hand and commented.

"Good job, Corporal Casey. Almost didn't get to do this."

"Yes Sir, could have missed the whole thing if I'd been a better driver," I laughed it off. I knew he was referring to the shot through my windshield only two weeks earlier. He laughed with me and moved on.

There was a short over-all congratulations speech for a job well done and then we were dismissed. I could not get back into my combat gear quickly enough. Capt. Burke and I drove back to Bijela.

With the issue of our medals and the feelings many of us had surrounding them it would not be long before inner thoughts would find their way to becoming outer thoughts. It seemed at the time that I was virtually incapable of restraining myself. That in itself was very much out of character for me. My state of mind had been changing for months at a pace that was barely registering.

Insubordination has never been something the military has taken lightly. To avoid being insubordinate a soldier sometimes has to bite his tongue. Sometimes you have to bite it hard to avoid saying how you feel. I was having a hard time keeping my comments to myself by this time. I had not really realised I was saying whatever I felt. Good, bad, or otherwise. It appeared as though I just did not give a shit anymore. There are moments when lack of respect brings out insubordinate comments. This fact combined with stress and other factors were taking hold of many of us. I was not immune to it at this point. Ray Gondole and I forged a strong friendship while serving in The Balkans War. We felt the same about the war, the people, and some of our NCOs. Sgt. Winsome was one who, through his cowardice, had lost our respect. Ray and I had gotten in from a late night patrol and had finally hit the sack at 0430hrs. Bright and early at 05:00hrs Sgt. Winsome, who had enjoyed his usual nine-hour wrestle with his pillow, kicked open the door,

"Good morning ladies, rise and shine!" Ray and I both rolled over and in perfect unison growled,

"FUCK OFF!"

Sgt. Winsome retreated quickly, knowing full well he could not withstand a beating from one of us, let alone from two of us exhausted grunts. Had he pushed it, I know for a fact that he would have been the victim of a tragic farming accident. We had no respect for him or his rank. Ray and I managed to get another couple of hours of rack time. I was not overly happy about my lack of regard for these individuals. By mid morning I was up and raced off to Pacrac and then out to WC-11. From there it was back to HQ in Pacrac then back to Bijela by way of Daruvar. It was smoking hot outside and the temperature had left me burnt out by the time I parked behind Pigeon Palace. It felt good to get out of the sun. My room although not air conditioned was remarkably cool. I threw my gear in an organized pile on my bunk. Sand and grit from the day's drive bit into my neck every time I turned my head. I sat on the foot of my bed and as I stripped and cleaned my rifle I mentally tallied how many kilometres I had driven. "280 clicks," I said mumbling to myself. I lightly oiled and reassembled my rifle. I grabbed my towel and shaving kit. I walked back down the hall and out the back stairs. The Croatian lady we hired to do laundry and other jobs nodded and kept singing her little song. I am sure she hoped I was not angry today. So I smiled to reassure her and kept going. There in a tree, behind a Hessian shower curtain, suspended upside down was a 20l water can and from it hung a short piece of garden hose with an L-shaped flashlight taped to the other end. The lens had small holes drilled into it to allow water to pour out like a shower head. It was not home but it was heavenly in this shithole. I stripped off the remainder of my clothes and slipped my feet into a pair of flip-flops. Unfortunately, someone had beat me to it and had gotten the warm water. "Shit that's cold," I blurted out, my body jolting in response to the frigid water. It had just been refilled and was now ice cold.

"Them's the breaks, Corporal Casey," came the comment from the other side of the hessian curtain.

It was Garcia.

"Ya I don't know why I'm shocked; I've only had two warm showers since I got here."

I soaped up, shaved and felt like a new man when it was over. I refilled the water can and re-hung it. I was thankful the day was over. I could sit in my room and have a beer.

Maybe I could work on the wall mural I had been painting for the last month. It was 22:30 when Ray Gondole came in. I was stretched out on my cot listening to Nirvana's, 'Come as you are' on my Sony Walkman. I looked at him and before he could get it out I cut him off.

"Not a chance, I'm not goin anywhere. I haven't stopped for two fuckin weeks." My voice was escalating with every word. "When I'm not drivin the L-tee around or runnin shit all over Hell's half acre I'm doin sentry on the 2-4 shift. They can go pound salt!" My voice was beyond elevated.

"Everyone in the whole fuckin company has had two R&R's but me, besides I haven't had a relaxing beer in a couple weeks and I've chugged a half dozen in the last hour."

Ray, as usual, stood there quietly tolerating my onslaught.

"I'm shit-faced so I can't go." He just stood there looking at me with a stupid ass half grin on his face.

"Oh for Christ sake Ray, what do they want now?"

"I was wondering if you wanted to go down to the kitchen and watch the news. They are showing some stuff about the forest fires back home." I sat there staring at him. My face was beginning to turn red with frustrated embarrassment.

"Well don't I look like quite the asshole," I said, realising no one had called on me.

"Mmm hmm, you're right. You are an asshole." Ray commented matter of factly in his usual calm manner.

We laughed. I got up and started for the end of my cot.

"Are you coming?" he asked.

"You bet. Just gotta throw my shirt on."

With the changing peace climate, day trips to town were being offered as short R&R breaks.

"Alright lads, some of you have managed to get an evening off in Daruvar," called out WO. Goddard.

His comments were met by cheers.

"You'll be transported by ML. Departure time is 17:00hrs. You will be picked up at the Daruvar train station at 20:00hrs. Are there any questions?"

"Who's going, Warrant?" came from somewhere in the platoon.

"Not you Axle," Goddard shot out with a smile.

Each name called was answered by the reply of Sir.

"Dempster."

"Sir."

"Jensen."

"Sir."

After ten names were called I was beginning to wonder if my name would be called. I was looking forward to a night off and then it came.

"Casey."

"Sir."

"Garcia."

"Sir."

"Alright, the dress is combat uniform, UN headdress, any other questions before I dismiss you?" WO. Goddard asked, knowing we would do just about anything for a night pass.

"What about weapons, Warrant?" Jensen asked from the back of our group.

"What about them, Cpl Jensen?" Goddard asked exasperated by the question.

"Are we taking personal weapons?"

"No. No weapons. We are going to show the people of Daruvar that we believe in what we have done."

"Who's next on the list after Garcia, Warrant?" Jensen was pushing for some reason I could not quite figure out. He seemed jumpier than the rest of us.

"Gilbert," the name came out of the WO's mouth with an exhale of frustration.

"He can have my spot then, I'm not going." Jensen commented calmly now.

"You're sure?" he asked.

"Definitely, Warrant."

"Ok Gilbert, you're up."

Jensen gave up his spot for the very reason I would have given mine up except I had my contraband handgun which was tucked comfortably at the small of my back in my combat pants waistband. There was not a hope in Hell I was going anywhere in this country without a weapon. We were all getting short and I did not want to risk getting in a shit show without a weapon this close to going home. Later that day we mounted up and went downtown. It went without a hitch. We enjoyed a couple of beers and some dinner at the only operational hotel. No one appeared openly hostile. I still watched everyone with a vigilant uneasiness. It was amazing how Daruvar had changed. Not all but most of the rubble was cleaned up. People walked the streets with almost a free and easy kick in their step. As we drove deeper into the town I could see what appeared to be some sort of festival. It was in full swing and the locals were rejoicing. The most notable aspect of the party goers were the women. Don't misinterpret, it was the fact that there were women here at all. For six months, other than the odd interpreter and the couple cleaners, we employed in Bijela, there had simply been no women. I was stunned when a woman came up to me with twin five-year-old boys in tow. She smiled and told the boys I was Canadian. She then said something I did not understand until the boys extended their hands. I shook them both and they turned away shyly saying,

"Hvala."

"Nema na emu,"

I offered back. After telling each of them they were welcome I gave each a candy from my pocket. I continued walking to the photo shop. Life had returned to Daruvar. It did not change the reason why I was here though. This was still a war zone. I still wore a flak jacket and beneath it was the concealed CZ in my belt. I looked at each person I encountered as a threat. I watched the shadows for what I could not openly see. Life had not returned to normal for me.

I was still dead. And dead I would remain, until I returned home. The reality that the people that lived here were not completely trusting in the peace was still evident.

FRESH MEAT

"Just because everything is different doesn't mean anything has changed."
~IRENE PETER

It was the middle of September and the PPCLI arrived today. It was a subtle surprise. We knew they would be replacing us; we just did not know when. This lack of information was for the security of the civilians just as much as it was for us. If the warring factions knew there was going to be a change-over they could exploit the distraction with an uprising. They could also exploit the new guys with their lack of understanding of the tactical climate. The hand over went off without a hitch. We had some of the FNGs from the Patricia's join us in a raid on the local police station. There was Intel that the Scroats had been gathering heavy weapons and explosives and hiding them in the police station. That's how ballsy or stupid these jerk-offs were. They had them in the police station right next door. When we first arrived this was normal behaviour; however, it was now completely unacceptable.

The new system of peace and legitimate policing did not allow for them to have machine guns and grenades anymore. A breaching section, outfitted with a battering ram for knocking the doors off their hinges, from 5pl with some additives from the newly arrived Patricia's, stormed the Policija building directly across the road from Pigeon Palace. It was the shortest patrol distance netting a catch during our tour. Watching from my vantage point in Pigeon Palace ten men secured the exterior of the Police station. Six of the ten stormed in the front door with weapons at the ready. They quickly subdued the police officers and went to the task of removing the cache of weapons. The police officers were treated respectfully. This was done because we also had to work closely with them. They also lived directly across the street. We did not need to start a feud in our own camp. The guys walked two hundred metres return and netted a half a dozen AKs, an RPG, grenades, a 12.7mm heavy machine gun and a good cache of ammunition. The raid showed the replacements that danger could settle right under their noses. It also showed them that they should listen to all int and check out the leads that it presented. Another lesson attained from this raid was that no indigenous people could be completely trusted.

Standing in the Pl HQ room of Pigeon Palace, I listened with horror as the radio call came in.

"...2...this is 62...Over."

"...62...send...Over...."

"...2...this is 62...62Alpha has just exploded...they just disappeared...they must have hit a mine...I think…they're all dead...Over."

So close to going home and the instability of the region was stabbing at us again. Without looking away from the radio I whispered aloud,

"We may not get out of here alive, kids."

On the 15th of the Sept. Sgt. Jeremy Willis' armoured personnel carrier struck a TMA-3 anti-tank mine. Although the guys calling it in had thought them dead, they all survived the ordeal with little or no injury. The November Company Angel continued to watch over us.

The next day a Combat Engineer, Sgt. Cornelius Mike Ralph was killed on the same road while clearing the road for mines. Another anti-tank mine had been laid by one of the opposing factions to destroy the other. His death rattled the entire Battle Group. Sgt. Ralph left behind his wife, and two daughters.

The talk of getting on a plane and going home, was the flavour of most conversations in the last few days. Many of the guys had already left for home and there were only a few of us left. The change over with the Patricia's had gone smoothly. Now it was their turn to 'keep the peace.' It would not be long and the remainder of us would be boarding a plane and flying home.

Sept 28th had arrived like any other day. I would find out by noon that it was my day to ship out. I had been waiting with a degree of disbelief that I would make it to this day. Chalks had been assigned for departure out of Croatia. No dates were assigned to correspond with the chalks however. I knew I would be leaving; I just did not know when. All my gear was packed early in the morning after I got the word. Now as I stood in the parking lot waiting for the bus ride to Zagreb I could not help but feel lost. Living in this place for 210 days had somehow made it my home. I had become accustomed to the environment. As crazy as it sounds, I was comfortable in this insane adrenalin-pumping way of life. I walked through the halls of Pigeon Palace a couple times. Standing in the doorway of the now vacant room Ray and I had bunked in, I reflected on the memories held within its walls and the solitude and sanctuary that it often provided from the crazy world outside. The spilled beer and the sleepless nights. I was going to miss this shithole. Leaving the room, I stumbled around, lost. Bumping around in a daze waiting for some direction, I went back outside and sat on my pile of gear. All the goodbyes had been said so there was nothing to do but wait for transport.

The buses arrived in a hail of dust. Before the dust had completely settled I boarded and found a seat at the back. Looking out the window I was overwhelmed with mixed emotions. Glad to be leaving, wishing I could stay and wondering what would happen to the Patricia's. Sitting in the halfway comfortable charter bus seat I looked out the window at a world that I was leaving behind. I was excited and dejected at the same time. An odd feeling of emptiness was creeping in. The flight home was to be an emotional one.

My buddy Robertson and I stood together and looked at the ugliest 747 we had ever seen. It was painted a flat orange red. It was dreadfully ugly but we loved it. We all stood out on the runway in a gaggle as it taxied up to us. There was not the typical covered gangway for us to board. We climbed a large flight of stairs to the doorway to true freedom. The freedom to leave this troubled country behind. Robertson and I grabbed a couple seats towards the back and settled in.

We did not say much at first, choosing to observe the rest of the lads getting seated. With what must have been one of the quickest refuel and resupply ever, we taxied out to our designated runway. The jet's turbine engines began to whine signalling that we were going to really be leaving. This was not some carefully planned prank or a horrible nightmare I allowed myself to believe.

We were airborne for about fifteen minutes when the most bizarre thing happened. The stress of the last seven months came out as Robertson and I began joking about being so happy we could cry. We laughed hard about how we were hardened grunts and they did not cry. Well it didn't take long before the two tough grunts who were laughing, turned into full blown balling their eyes out, and laughing at the same time, grunts. We had said we would not believe it was over till we were on the bird and out of Yugoslav airspace. Then and only then did we relax, somewhat. The flight was euphoric. I stared out the window at the pure virginity of the puffy white clouds that hung in the air below us. They were beautiful because they covered up the ugliness below. My mind wandered back to Sarajevo, then to Bijela and Pigeon Palace. The PPCLI were now doing what we had done for many months. I hoped they would not botch up what we had accomplished. The clouds broke and the patchwork quilt of European farms began to appear. We were getting closer to the peaceful world we had left months earlier. I wondered what it would be like. Had it changed in any way? Would my baby girl remember me? That was the first thought I had had of her in weeks. I suddenly felt guilty for not thinking of her more. Silly, I thought, I would have the rest of my life to cherish her. Looking out the window at the beautiful scene made me feel anxious about getting off the plane. For weeks I had looked forward to this day and now that it was here I was terrified at how I would behave.

My thoughts were put on hold as the captain announced that we would be landing in twenty minutes. The landing at CFB Lahr, Germany was completed by a boisterous cheer with all on board ignoring the seat belts signs and giving the pilots a standing ovation. We exited the plane and walked along the runway. The scene was surreal in that there were no white UN trucks or APCs racing around. The tower was intact and so were the hangars. I looked down at the tarmac and noticed it was smooth with only the odd crack in the asphalt. Gone were the scars of shrapnel and bullet marks. We were on a sterile Canadian Forces Base. Everything was clean and bright. There was a small band playing by the Air Movements Unit building. The soldiers from the R22^{e}R shuffled off to one side and we shuffled off to another. With lack lustre quickness we marched to waiting buses and boarded for the sixty-five kilometre journey to CFB Baden. The ride was quiet and everyone looked out the windows, lost in their personal thoughts. This was the end of seven months of unrivalled stress and the beginning of life after war.

TICKERTAPE PARADE

"In peace, sons bury their fathers; in war, fathers bury their sons."
~HERODOTUS

The coach slowed and stopped at the front entrance to CFB Baden. After a quick walk through by the MPs, we were allowed to enter the Base. The trees lining the road were a welcome sight and seemed to be waving us in happily. The bus driver made a right turn and we entered 3 RCR's home. It felt strange to be there even though it had been our home for three years.

We arrived to business as usual on the Marg. There was no band or fanfare. Troops were standing about and some who had been conducting training stopped and gave us a quick glance and then continued on. In their defence their lack of interest in our arrival was purely innocent. Our departure from the Balkans was shrouded in secrecy to protect us and our replacements from escalations in violence in the Krajina. That security level would have been recognised on base in Germany as well. After unloading the buses, we formed up in three ranks. Major Devlin stood before us and commended us for a job well done. With passion he relayed that he was proud to have had the honour to serve with us. The Major spoke to us from the heart as he did each time he addressed the men. I know it to be fact that every one of us was proud to have been commanded by such a decent man. This speech was to be the extent of the Hero's Welcome. Family members stood by waiting for our leader to dismiss us. He did so promptly knowing that we all wanted to see our families. I walked straight to my wife and baby girl. My daughter broke free of her mom's restraint and toddled to me on wobbly legs. I squatted down and she teetered into my waiting arms. I held her tightly and felt her warm breath on my neck.

"Daddy," she whispered.

The last time I had seen my child she had not yet learned to speak. Emotion was trying to infiltrate the moment and I felt my eyes well up, but I could not form a tear. I stood and gave my wife a hug, we smiled at one another and walked to our car. I spent the rest of the day explaining how our trip went. I skirted her naive questions about the war, trivializing it as a holiday. I stood gazing almost blankly at my surroundings. Standing at my bookcase, I ran my hand over one of the wooden shelves. It was clean. The smell of Lilacs permeated the air. I spied the air freshener neatly placed on one of the end tables next to our pillow adorned couch. While dinner was being prepared I went and stood in our spare room where my rucksack and kitbag sat waiting for me to clean up. I opened the kitbag. I stared into it, transfixed by the combat gear exposed like cloth entrails. Within seconds, my wife's question came from the kitchen.

"What the Hell is that smell?"

"Ah, nothing. Just had to get my shaving kit out for tomorrow," I stammered, zipping the bag closed. In the evening we went to bed and I lay awake for the duration of the night, lying motionless so as not to disturb her. The night was eerily quiet.

I watched and waited for the sun to rise from my window, on this, my second day at home from the Balkans. After seeing it crest the horizon I quietly got on with my day. My wife slept soundly, oblivious to my rustling about as I got dressed. I peeked in on my baby girl and watched as she lay so peacefully. The little bundle we had brought into the world was beautiful. As I gazed upon her, she stirred a little so I softly closed the door. Quickly and quietly I exited the apartment, closing the door behind me. Once at street level I strolled north for about a kilometre. Birds were chirping and the sun felt good. Ahead of me between two large earthen dikes lay the famous Rhine River. When I reached the eastern bank of the Rhine I turned and followed the trail south along the top of the dike. Across the expanse of rolling water lay France. It was what most would say was a perfect morning. Something was not right though and I could not quite put my finger on it.

"That's it," I exclaimed to myself.

My empty left hand twitched involuntarily.

"Can't put my finger on it."

The realisation that I was not carrying a weapon hit me. I suddenly felt naked and for the first time in months, absolutely vulnerable. My mind had a mini panic attack. I did not have my rifle. My eyes darted across the grassy areas around me, then quickly to the horizon, followed immediately by scanning the length of the dike.

"Clear." I spoke aloud.

My heart felt as though it had done a back flip and landed in a pile of broken glass.

'This is crazy,' I thought. I looked at the water and at the swans swimming along gracefully. Magnificently, they paddled against the river's current. I had seen nothing like this idyllic image for months. I lowered my head and looked at the stones at my feet. How in the Hell was I going to be able to look at the world with any kind of innocence again? My idea of the world was skewed by the harsh reality of war. I pondered how the world could be made any different by the efforts of our peacekeeping mission? Only forty-seven years ago this place, Germany, was the centre of the world's living Hell. Somehow the Rhine lost its beauty. The swans turned to ravens. The wind seemed to usher in iron grey clouds as I walked home.

My little girl was awake and mobile when I opened the door. As I stood in the doorway watching her, I understood that she would become my reason for living. I had not been home for forty-eight hours and my wife and I were already at odds. Truth told I realised at that moment that I hated her. I would learn in time that the feeling was mutual. I was raised in an abusive split family who lived by the code of denial. Although I was not abusive, this code was how I lived my marital life also. I focused on my little girl; she was the innocence that gave me hope. I stayed on my matrimonial course by coexisting and immersing myself into my day to day duties as a soldier.

Within days of returning to Germany one of our sergeants, Jarrod Riker, was killed by a drunk driver. It made me crazy to think that he had survived the brutality of war only to come home and be killed by someone's poor life choice. I was angry and wanted desperately to lash out with unbridled vengeance. If this would have happened down there, in Yugoslavia, I knew retribution would have been swift. We were no longer there and our days here in Europe would be numbered.

In 1993 as a result of budgetary cuts, the Canadian Forces was scaling back operations in Europe and our base, CFB Baden, was scheduled to close. With that closure, our home for five years, the 3rd battalion was dispersed between the 1st and 2nd battalions still in Canada.

I had only been at CFB Petawawa, Ontario for a few months when Tommy was struck and killed by an impaired driver. He had turned ghostly white pointing out my leg wound back in Croatia. Now his memory crackled in and out of my mind like an 8mm film ghost. The guys who had served with Tommy throughout the battalion felt the pain and sorrow of his loss. He and I had been very close friends and I was devastated once again. Unnoticed, even to me, I began a slow withdrawal from everyone.

The senseless deaths, doldrums of normal life and the barrage of intrusive memories, were exacerbated by a generalized, perhaps unwarranted, but vinegary disgust for human beings. My heart had all but shut down to my love of life. Consequently, I began to spiral out of control.

One night while still in Germany I consumed a 40-ounce bottle of rye whiskey. Bawling my eyes out, I was experiencing the typical combination of sadness and rage of someone who was feeling helpless. The atrocities I had witnessed were haunting me daily. My helplessness to save those civilians who were being decimated by the thousands had eaten a hole in my soul. Inwardly, I was screaming for my sanity. I wanted the daymares, as I called them, because they were not typical nightmares-they were actually during the day in my conscious mind-to stop. I wanted it all to end.

Swigging back another mouthful of courage I slid the magazine into the handgrip of my 9mm handgun, chambered a round, and stuck the muzzle in my mouth. Trembling I took up the slack on the already feather light trigger. The oily metallic taste of the handgun's frame overpowered the whiskey. Tears trickled down my flushed cheeks, pausing before dropping from my chin to my t-shirt. Even in my inebriated state I could feel the eyes of someone staring at me. Then there was movement. Out of the corner of my eye I noticed two little hands crinkling the fabric of the arms of the couch. I realized that my two-year-old daughter was standing there watching me.

"Daddy crying," she muttered innocently, her big blue eyes locking with mine. So lost and so drunk, I had forgotten that she was in my care.

I sold the gun the next day.

Divide and conquer are tactics used in business and on the battlefield. These tactics are not something you would expect to find being used against your own troops in peacetime. Sadly, that is exactly what we Balkan War vets experienced when we posted into our new battalions in Canada. We were broken up and placed into different platoons. That was expected and completely acceptable. It is intelligent structuring to place seasoned soldiers among the less experienced ones. However, in our case, the splitting up was not done for that reason and things would only get worse for The Men in Black.

November Company had endeavoured to go into a war zone dressed as peacekeepers with the traditional blue helmets or blue berets. We were required to have empty magazines on our weapons-a visual deterrent it was called. An order we all disobeyed. Our unit commanders had the wisdom to overrule the United Nations minimalist 'light peacekeeping force' policy and brought our heavy weapons and ammunition. We had taken Chapter 6 UN Mission rules and bastardized them into what we all jokingly referred to as 'Chapter 6 • Lew's Rule.' Dubbed for Gen. Lewis Mackenzie's authorization to adjust the rules and fire at the bad guys. But, we still stood the line in a war zone in bright white vehicles. Driving with our headlights on 90% of the time. We may as well have had flashing carnival lights to indicate our positions. UNHQ was located in Sarajevo. Hundreds of kilometres from where we were primarily located in The Krajina. Even with all of those imposed ludicrous conditions, we had survived combat. My hope was that we should have been revered for that fact alone. Instead we were treated like contaminated waste and were viewed with disdain.

This was not the army I had enlisted in. I believed that soldiers with combat experience should not be shunned. My expectation was that they should be embraced and used to bolster the confidence of inexperienced soldiers. Instead of embracing that opportunity to weave our new combat Veterans into the social fabric of our regiment, they chose to create an environment of cynicism and mistrust, by way of baneful disregard. Failure to reintegrate our soldiers effectively within our ranks was just the beginning of a greater failure to reintegrate soldiers into civilian life in the future. After November Company was dissected and scattered between the remaining two battalions, I personally felt it was for less than respectful reasons and motives. The men of November Company tried repeatedly to explain the lessons we learned to the up and coming soldiers who were to be deployed. Knowing what to do under effective enemy artillery fire is taught as a fundamental part of basic infantry training. The training manuals all state that the soldier must, when the first incoming mortar or artillery round explodes, run as fast as he can, out of the kill zone for approximately one kilometre. This immediate action drill was practised regularly so it became second nature. All immediate action drills were practised in the same manner, so they became instinct. Many of us had found in reality, however, that this drill actually put us in harm's way. What needed to happen instead was for us to have the discipline to hold in place long enough to figure out what kind of pattern was being fired. If a soldier was to follow the standard WW2 drill, he might actually end up running directly into the next round. Trying to get this new, experienced-based message across to the officers and senior NCOs of our battalions after we got posted back to Canada was an insurmountable problem. They had rigidly inculcated the same drill in the same way for decades, and therefore our concept was met with condemnation. The value of our ground level practical experience was denied. All of which furthered my disillusionment.

"You Bosnia guys think you know everything about combat."

An all too common response to our efforts to share the lessons we had learned. This inflexibility to accommodate the facts of our new reality-based warfare experience, combined with the Medical Inspection Room unofficial policy of abuse was unwelcome and demoralizing. Going to the MIR seemed equivalent to receiving a conviction punishable by torture. While that statement may sound severe, and made in jest, such a fate would have been preferable to the humiliation that many non-combat experienced Senior NCOs put you through should you require a visit to the MIR. The stigma attached to a soldier visiting the MIR was in itself, crippling. I generally have no issue with military verbal abuse when it is used as a motivator. Believe it or not there IS a time and place for it in the Army. However, during regular training and the inevitable trip to the doctor, it has no place. So strong was the negativity towards going to the MIR that soldiers with critical issues refused to seek medical attention. Ray Gondole has a broken neck from a training incident in Germany. He finally went to the doctor in 2009 and that is how he found out that the discomfort all these years was from that. Over fifteen years after he received the injury. Due to the humiliation incurred upon others, when the tour in the Former Yugoslavia concluded, very few, if any soldiers from November Company had any injuries to speak of. They were all given a clean bill of health. What could be farther from the truth? Physical injuries ranged anywhere from shrapnel wounds, lumbar vertebrae issues, knee injuries, gastro-intestinal problems, and so on. Mental casualties like those with PTSD were just as easily neglected. Some for so long that the only way they felt they could end their pain was by suicide. This decades old trend of soldiers suppressing injuries is still disturbingly common today. So too is the suicide rate. These were not just men, they were Canadians who sacrificed for others, and they were our Brothers. While we were in the Balkans we had more than witnessed the ugly truth of humanity, we had been embroiled in its depravity, and in that, who we were as men had been altered forever. Those 210 days in the Balkans had laid the groundwork for what can only be seen as a betrayal of all that is good.

One September evening in 1999 I received a phone call. Suddenly, all the mental pain I had been dealing with and trying to subdue came crashing in like a runaway freight train, again.

"Hey Casey, its Jerry," said the voice on the other end of the line.

"Holy shit man, I haven't heard from you in ages. How's it going," I asked excitedly.

"Ya I'm doin okay, you know, holdin down the fort."

After some more catch up chat Al dropped the bomb.

"Have you heard about Ranger?"

"No," I said.

The air on the line was stock still. It hung lifeless between us like the very beginning of congealing blood. I heard Jerry inhale.

"Shit, I was hoping you had."

He exhaled unevenly and once again he took in another laboured breath. It was evident he did not want to be doing this.

"Well it doesn't sound good so spit it out, soldier."

I hated bad news and just wanted to get it over with so we could reminisce about better times and have a laugh or two.

"Ranger's dead. They found him hanging in the Petawawa training area," he said through his grimace.

I stood silently. My grasp on the phone weakened as I slumped against the kitchen wall, paralyzed. My head hit the wall with a thud.

"Casey, you there?"

"Yup I'm here, I can't believe it. I phoned him just a couple days ago."

"Sorry to give you the news, Scotty."

I could hear the sounds of his throat thickening, of his voice choking up. I maintained a steady voice as the rock of strength I felt I had to be.

"No prob, thanks Jerry, I'll call you in a couple of days."

"Okay Scotty, take it easy bro," his sobbing now evident in his voice.

"I will, and Jer," I paused for a second, "thanks for letting me know, brother."

The phone line clicked and he too was gone.

As I sank to the floor my head bowed forward, unnoticed on the wall a thick trace of sweat had temporarily stained the paint where I had been leaning. Tears began to well up in my eyes, and it was not long before they cascaded down my face. The rock cracked as the memories flooded in. I could not believe he was dead. The image of Ranger's face appeared and I could picture him saying, "Looks like there's gonna be a gum fight." I half smiled and cried even harder at the loss of my friend. Then my thoughts went to the voice recording I had left for him only days earlier. How I had jokingly said,

"Hey Ranger, haven't heard from you in a few weeks, guess you must be dead. Now stop that shit and call me, asshole."

Slowly, I picked myself from the floor and as I did so the sweat stained wall caught my tear flooded stare. The stain presented itself as an inverted exclamation mark. I felt instantly weakened as though the blood from my body had been instantly drained. It's resemblance to the silhouette of a man hanging stabbed me violently in the chest. A thousand flashes of memory pulsed in my mind like sheet lightning. The image of his face appeared sitting in the jump seat of the UN aid truck, a big wad of chew in his bottom lip, grinning away. Standing outside the army barracks surrounded by buddies, beers in hand. Then to his body hanging limp, cold, broken, alone. My knees buckled and I crashed to the floor bursting out in a rage induced, blood curdling scream that shook the kitchen window glass in its panes.

"Whyyyyyyyyyy!?!"

I clambered on my knees and ripped the liquor cabinet door open pulling it free of its hinges. I grabbed a bottle of whiskey and stormed out the mudroom door.

By noon I was lying in the barnyard, covered in dirt and horse shit. Oblivious to my inner turmoil, our horses were stepping around me sniffing curiously.

"Which one of you fucking nags is going to stumble and end this shit?"

The words spewed out as a mixture of personal venom and spit in my slovenly drunken state. The loss of one of my best friend's years after the war was more than I could bear. We joined together. We went through Hell together. And now, he was dead. It crushed me. The message I had left kept playing over and over in my tortured mind. I spent the day as a blithering drunken mess in the pasture. Linda, distraught with compassion for me, stood at the kitchen window periodically to monitor my whereabouts. Knowing better to leave me alone with my demons. What I had put her through on that day. On countless days before and after. Even though I was in her presence on a regular basis and showed deep love for her, my disassociation from the world left her feeling alone more often than not. As the spouse of a Veteran she tried her best to be understanding and to provide comfort to a man who could not accept the worthiness of life and love. I could not believe in the goodness of the world for the most part, no matter how hard she tried. As it was for the Men in Black, she had no one to reach out to either. Like the mark of the branding iron just pulled from a fire, what she had to endure with me, has been burned on both our souls alike. We parted ways two years before this went to print.

The next few months found me an emotional wreck. I understood the clutches of suicide all too well. I had been on that edge. Why had he not called me for help? Why was it that I did not call him more often? Even though I could rationalize that I could not control his situation, I still have not forgiven myself. More guys have died since we got back than died in combat, mostly by their own hands. The society we had pledged to protect was about to let us die, or worse, they were willing to let us suffer.

The rate of suicide amongst former military personnel is 46% higher for males and 32% higher for females, as compared to the civilian population. Released Canadian Armed Forces males in the 16 to 24 age group show the greatest deviations, with suicide rates more than double the national average. As soldiers we had been stringently pre-tested for service. Being held to a higher standard than any other occupation. With the suicide rate being grossly higher than the national average, it certainly sets a benchmark. Another non recorded number is that of the Catholic Denomination French Canadians of our battle group. Because suicide is considered evil, it is not often admitted by many Franco-families as the cause of death. Since Ranger's death, nearly a dozen members of November Company have taken their lives.

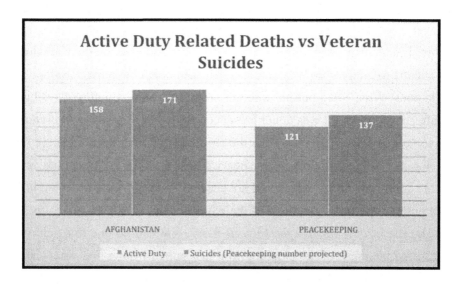

PERFIDY

*"The feeling of not belonging, of not being entirely worthy, of being sometimes hostage to your
own sensibilities. Those things speak to me very personally."*
~ANTHONY MINGHELLA

The global community has built a belief system that what we do as soldiers
is for the greater good. It would be safe to say that Canadians are no less a part
of that belief system and buy into that contract without much thought. With the
legacy of peacekeeping missions Canada has been a party to, and their successes,
it is easy to understand how average hometown boys can get swept away on the
thoughts of how they can make a difference. Farther away now this ideal has not
changed with our troops being deployed to Afghanistan or the new peacekeeping
missions that have been endorsed-and unless the United Nations can present itself
as something other than the toothless tiger it is, modern peacekeeping should be
scaled down to humanitarian relief efforts. Unfortunately, what is not mentioned
with respect to this ideal is that not everyone in the global community has the
same set of standards that we share. The difference in belief systems is easily
recognisable in peacekeeping missions like Somalia, Rwanda, and the Balkans
War. All carried elements of genocide, some more appalling than the others.
In those cases, not enough thought was put into equipment/weaponry, mission
severity, effective ROEs, withdrawal contingencies and the extreme probability
of casualties. I must emphasize that events such as rape, torture, genocide, and
warfare are almost universally recognised as traumatic events. It goes without
saying that the consequence of war is thousands of wounded men.

A soldier with shrapnel, gunshot wounds or missing limbs is easily
identifiable. Without marginalizing the significance of physical wounds in any
way, the wounded mind is particularly devastating-and made all the more so
due to the fact that it is invisible. In 1980 the American Psychiatric Association
officially recognised the invisible wound, giving it the clinical term Post
Traumatic Stress Disorder. PTSD from combat trauma is a beast all of its own.
Moral injury is the precursor to PTSD. When a soldier witnesses or perpetrates
actions that are viewed to be unethical by society, he develops issues with safety,
trust, esteem, and self worth. All of which may affect his life negatively. PTSD

271

is created by the betrayal of the fundamental core values we learn as we grow. We learn to be kind to one another, to share and be honest. Core values, both individual and societal can be compromised during times of war to a degree that upon homecoming, a soldier has extreme difficulties behaving as he had predeployment. As part of training, and in war, a soldier learns to kill other human beings, to share only with those he trusts, and to lie to save his skin. Betrayed core values may be precipitated by a range of points from something as straight forward as the previously mentioned promotion of M/Cpl Hanson to Sergeant even in light of his refusal to stand the line and go to Sarajevo; to something psychologically more complex such as homecoming to a unit that intentionally and systematically broke down camaraderie; to something politically frustrating as the United Nations complete lack of understanding of what was really going on and their inability to lead the world effectively through it; to the moral travesty of our government reducing benefits for Veterans; and ultimately to the almost inconceivable experience of witnessing the horrific crimes against humanity, genocide. These betrayals are exacerbated upon homecoming when the combat Veteran is disregarded by his government and seemingly forgotten by his fellow citizens. If our Vets do not become woven back into the social fabric of our nation and they find themselves slipping through the cracks of support, the world Veterans live in becomes a bleak and dark one. As you will read on the following page; in extreme cases a seemingly sinister side can develop in the Veteran.

The Cecil Hotel bar in Vancouver B.C. was all but empty. Poorly seated on a ratty stool at the end of the bar sat a rough figure. In front of him, a dirty half glass of draft beer, standing watch over its drunkard, who appeared to be passed out. At a table behind the drunk sat two unkempt men in their mid twenties, whose nasty life choices had already made them older and weathered. On his return from the bar's toilet, one of them had spied a fifty-dollar bill sitting unprotected under the passed out rogue's glass. The bartender turned away momentarily unaware the two were plotting to remove the bank note. Such behaviour was typical in this section of Canada's major west coast city. There was no disputing Vancouver was beautiful, but like any metropolis, it harboured an ugly lining of degenerates, spoilers, and thugs.

The larger of the two miscreants got up and headed straight to their drunken victim. His walk was more a slither, and his eyes were glazed like a second see-through eyelid. When he reached the drunk on the stool, he took one look over his own shoulder to check on the bartender's whereabouts. With the bartender tending his beer glasses, the perpetrator reached for the bill. His predatory soiled finger and thumb had barely pinched the note when a hand pierced the air with the speed of a lightning bolt. The prey at the table sprang to life contacting the thief's throat with a knife-like chop that sent the former predator flailing to the floor. With two steps the prey was up and now delivering a swift strike to the thief's temple. With deadly precision the blow landed on target and the body of the perpetrator fell limp on the dirty hardwood. Like a rat, the second man was now up and scurrying for the door. He let out a shrill scream when the trap of the drunk's forearm clamped around his neck. The scream he emitted was cut short as his head was forced forward and down over the drunk's iron tibia successfully cutting off the blood flow in the rodent's carotid artery. His hands scratched about helplessly trying to break free, which only helped to speed up the ending. Within seconds his brain succumbed to the blood loss and he too fell to the floor, rendered unconscious. The figure who had only moments ago been passed out at the bar walked back to his spot, tipped back the last of his beer, and quietly handed the barkeeper the fifty-dollar bill. The bartender quickly made change.

"Keep it," I said gruffly.

Three untreated years of suffering with post traumatic stress disorder had left me living among the homeless and seeking vengeance against those who stood for evil.

During the week I lived as a truck driver working a steady job. On the weekends I sought out the rush of battle, the high that no drug can produce. I lived with the dredges of Vancouver's society in the Lower Eastside. Drunks, derelicts, drug addicts, and prostitutes were my sheep. Those who exploited them became my wolves. I walked the alleys looking for the fight.

I was fighting every chance I got and living with the -let's see what'll happen- attitude. A buddy had agreed to go out for beers with me one night in downtown Langley BC. It was not too long after arriving at the bar that we found ourselves in the parking lot surrounded by four male patrons and two of the bouncers. I fought like a caged animal, however the tables turned and I suffered a terrible beating. I was laughing the whole time, begging for them to kill me. My buddy and I limped away and he vowed never to go out with me again.

For the most part I stayed to myself, choosing to avoid people in normal day to day activities. Only when confronted would I act. I had no problem with verbally or physically assaulting people in grocery stores, ice arenas, on the road, and so on. The reality of my world was that if someone were just a plain ol' normal human being who did something typically rude like butt in line, or whatever the case may be, they were getting sorted out. After all the stuff I had been through watching the human race destroy itself over such trivial things as ethnicity I sure as Hell was not going to stand by and be shit on over which block of cheese I had taken off the shelf without consulting my neighbor consumer.

When I was not working, alcohol played a significant role in self-medicating. Days and nights blurred together as my nightmares, hyper-vigilance, sleep deprivation and the endless search for battle kept me from required rest. Essentially, I had created an environment similar to that in which I had lived in Yugoslavia. The alcohol had numbed the visions and the psychological pains that came with what I cannot un-see, the horrors of the Balkans.

My individual story and its violent trajectory are not stereotypical to each Veteran. Although I can flick the switch and shut off emotions, I could not and still cannot, switch the hyper-vigilance or intrusive memories off. I am constantly on guard with everyone receiving a threat assessment by my betrayed mind. This phenomenon is very common amongst combat Veterans from the days of the Trojan Wars and the great warrior Achilles right through to present day Canadian soldiers returning from Afghanistan. In the battle of Troy, Achilles is a prime example of a warrior who has felt betrayal by his commander, Agememnon, who dishonours Achilles by underhandedly taking his plunder away from him. He also exemplifies survivor's guilt with the death of his "brother" Patroclus at the hands of Hector. Achilles believed that had he been there he may have prevented the death. Combat Vets often find themselves enslaved with learning who they have become. As ancient as the Greek philosopher Plato himself, the quest to know thyself has transcended centuries. Veterans of today will find the ritual of knowing thyself no less daunting.

As General George S. Patton Jr. so thoughtfully wrote,

> *"So as through a glass and darkly*
> *The age long strife I see*
> *Where I fought in many guises*
> *Many names-but always [it was]me."*

Those coming home will have various types of symptoms, and although Vets will feel rage, they will seldom act upon it. Depression, anxiety, disassociation, despair, survivor's guilt, helplessness, and doubt are just some of what Veterans experience. The first two, depression and anxiety are often the immediate diagnosis given to combat Vets. They are the two most prevalent and easily recognisable symptoms. These two symptoms also negate a PTSD diagnosis and the awarding of benefits detailed under the failed New Veterans Charter. The signs of PTSD are more likely to be found in clusters and not just single symptoms. The symptoms are often masked by the Vet who is either in denial or is outright oblivious. The outcome of PTSD can be very serious with ramifications including alcoholism, drug addiction, sex addiction, child/spousal abuse, breakdown of the family and marriages, dealings with the law, and in severe cases death.

My over-use of alcohol, suppressed emotion, self loathing, all combined with explosive anger and risk taking behaviours, have cost me two marriages. To this day I will be the guy, who says,

"Let's see what'll happen...."

"What'll happen" could be something as simple as throwing an all too familiar can of beans into a campfire, all the way up to jumping off a cliff into the icy abyss of untested waters below. Through lived PTSD experiences, I am gradually coming to know what Anthony Minghella may have meant when he wrote, "The feeling of not belonging, of not being entirely worthy, of being sometimes hostage to your own sensibilities." It is as though I am constantly punishing myself. Those of us with PTSD do not to subscribe to the "victim" term, but it is as though PTSD not only removes the jump or don't jump choice, it removes the boundary between punisher and victim.

PTSD is very real and many of our Veterans and currently serving soldiers alike are gripped by it every day. The media perception would have everyone believe that every soldier has PTSD. Not every Veteran or soldier has PTSD, it would be safe to say however, that they have been affected by their war in some way.

It can be said almost universally, that the medical world has acknowledged that those more prone to developing PTSD have at some point in their youth been the victim of abuse. I am not suggesting that PTSD could be avoided if mommy gave you more hugs or that parents should not discipline their children. Studies have revealed that soldiers with PTSD have, more often than not, been subjected to abuse as a child. Whether it was physical, emotional, sexual, or neglect. Child abuse of any kind betrays the core values instilled by society in the home thus providing the moral injury precursor to PTSD, my childhood not withstanding. In no way am I attempting to vilify my parents. As I stated earlier they were subjects of their generation. A rough hand taken too far, living with alcohol abuse, violence, and denial are all perfect examples of the moral injury precursor. The lesson in this is, as parents we set our children up for possible difficulties later in life based on our decisions.

What many do not realise is that PTSD from combat trauma actually changes chemicals in the brain. A soldier heading into combat experiences phases much like a caterpillar. He trains every day and prepares for his next stage. He then cocoons himself in a war zone. Like a pupae encased in a cocoon. He can move around freely inside, but he simply cannot just go home. Then while he is in that cocoon or war zone a change occurs and he emerges as a moth. A chemical metamorphosis has taken place. Moths cannot ever be caterpillars again.

SACRED OBLIGATION

"Betrayal is common for men with no conscience."
~TOBA BETA

Recently the Canadian Army has been turned into a new age fighting force. An up gunned military, reminiscent of the Mulroney-Conservative proposed, but failed, White Paper in 1987. The Mulroney government who sent The Men in Black to the Balkans had tried unsuccessfully to bring our military into the 20th century. Back to back events such as the fall of the Berlin Wall and the highly unlikely probability of Soviet attack unfortunately saw that the White Paper was crumpled up and tossed in the waste basket.

The current Harper government has built our Canadian Armed Forces to a standard where the equipment has almost caught up to our soldiers' abilities. Today, Canadian soldiers have some of the highest quality equipment on the modern battlefield. It is interesting in contrast-and somewhat painful to look back at-the gear November Company used. The equipment and weapons the government considered appropriate for us to use in the Balkans were nothing short of inferior.

The US military used weapons and vehicles in the 60s and early 70s that were cutting edge for the Vietnam War. Jump ahead twenty years to 1992, the Balkans War, and the Canadian Forces used that same equipment. Thirty years had passed since Vietnam War technology, with minimal to no upgrades for Canada into the 2000's. In the 1980s the CAF had a camouflage smock that was only to be worn in garrison. It was not worn on the battlefield and was also not to be viewed by the general public for fear our soldiers would appear too aggressive.

In 2002 Canada entered the war in Afghanistan. It was not until then that the weapons and equipment transition really started to take shape. From 1992 fast forward another 22 years to 2014 and our troops are now outfitted properly to take on any task from peacekeeping, to protecting our sovereignty or any level of special-forces operations. It could be said that hard lessons learned through peacekeeping in the Balkans War and the commitment in Afghanistan has prompted the Harper government to make the necessary decisions to provide our soldiers with the tools to perform their duties. It could be said that the hardships and suffering of Former Yugoslavia Vets are what have paved the way for Canada's modern army.

Since Harper has taken office our military has all the trimmings. The CAF looks equally, if not more aggressive, than our American counterparts. Bravo.

The Prime Minister takes full advantage of our military's new image by arranging action photo ops with CAF troops. For example, t.v. ads show our special forces JTF-2 members in a combined entry maneuver from Zodiak inflatable boats alongside, and a swift rappel descent from a Griffen helicopter onto the deck of HMCS St. John's. After the ship is secure the JTF-2 members stride over and shake hands with the PM, cameras rolling the entire time. Our 'new' CAF is the Prime Minister's arm candy.

But an examination of PM Harper's conduct while in office shows a disconnect between his like for the 'idea' of the Canadian military and his distancing himself from the human beings who comprise it.

Our military is dressed to the nines in all the glitter. Yet our Veterans are hidden at home suffering from neglect. The disconnect goes beyond Prime Minister Harper down through the Conservative ranks and can be viewed as contempt for Veterans. A perfect example is the publicized account of Conservative MP Rob Anders who was actually shown to be sleeping through a Veteran's hearing. It only escalated when he verbally attacked the Veterans who called him on his lack of concern.

It would be irresponsible of me not to mention Veterans Advocate Sean Bruyea. Bruyea's file at Veterans Affairs Canada grew to over 14,000 pages and his confidential medical file was viewed by 850 people and scrutinized over 4000 times. To illustrate the magnitude of his file my personal VAC file, which is quite extensive, is close to the same number of pages as this book. Nowhere near 14,000 pages. There is a leaked VAC document which states they were ordered, "to take the gloves off when dealing with Bruyea."

Bruyea, was later quoted in the Ottawa Citizen as having said,

"To be accused of being the enemy, that shocked me."

Although MP Peter MacKay has warned the Veterans Ombudsman not to be an advocate for Veterans, various Ombudsmen have reiterated the same thing for over a decade now. That one doctor handing out self help videos and handfuls of pills to thousands of soldiers is a far cry from real care.

The Canadian government has completely missed the mark on responsibility to its soldiers when they return home. The troops have state of the art tools of their trade. No question there. In comparison, the tools they have upon homecoming may as well be sticks and stones.

When Canadians think of the word Charter they identify with the Charter of Rights and Freedoms. This Charter is the law which gives guarantees to the Fundamental, Democratic, Mobility, Legal, and Equality rights of all Canadians. I find it interesting that the government chose the word Charter appropriate for the replacement of the former Pensions Act. The New Veterans Charter, the Charter that actually takes away that which was guaranteed.

Charter: /'tʃaːte/ Noun

1. a formal document from the sovereign or state incorporating a city, bank, college, etc, and specifying its purposes and rights
2. (often initial capital letter) a document defining the formal organization of a corporate body; constitution:

The Charter of the United Nations.

3. a law, policy, or decision containing a loophole which allows a specified group to engage more easily in an activity considered undesirable.

The New Veterans Charter, was authored to avoid the financial ramifications of caring for Veterans who could conceivably require benefits for sixty years plus. A statute first takes the form of a written bill. To become a federal statute, a bill must pass three readings in the House of Commons and must also be passed by the Senate in Ottawa. Each of the political parties, Liberal, Conservative, New Democratic Party, and even the Party Quebecois signed off on the New Veterans Charter. Including Senators Mike Duffy, Pamela Wallin, and Patrick Brazeau. All three are known for their shameful parts in the fraudulent expense claims scandal.

---

*Just before going to print: *Former Senator, Mike Duffy, was found innocent of all charges filed against him by the RCMP.*

Regular CAF pensions are calculated at 2% per year-of your best 5 years-up to a maximum of 35 years and you must serve a minimum of 20 years to get a pension. If you serve 25 years, you will receive a pension of 50% of your best 5.

A Member of Parliament, who serves a mere 6 years in Ottawa without being under the stress of combat, subsequently receives a substantial lifetime pension. Under the Parliament of Canada Act, a senator who is 65 or older and incapacitated by a proven medical condition can resign and receive a disability allowance equal to 70 per cent of his or her salary — a comfortable $94,649 a year. To the best of my knowledge a Member of Parliament has never been denied their pension once eligible. This would include Mike Duffy, Pamela Wallin, and Patrick Brazeau.

Taxpayers contributed approximately $29.4 million to the parliamentary pension; Canadians paid nearly $6.25 for every $1 paid by federal politicians.

The Disability Award for Veterans is a one-time, tax-free cash award. The current maximum is $301,275.26 based on the extent of the disability. Eligible Veterans receive a maximum lump sum payout now up to $301,275.26 and only if the Veteran qualifies for those benefits (100% disability, complete loss of function of lower limbs; confined to wheelchair) or 5% disability for (mild hearing loss) $14,929. Very few actually qualify for the maximum.

"We shouldn't have to fight on Canadian soil," exclaimed Dave Desjardins, from his wheelchair, after battling VAC for his benefits.

53% of Veterans who qualify for benefits are, nevertheless, denied.

In 2008, sixteen years post Balkans, I submitted my first claim with Veterans Affairs Canada. Since then I have submitted seven additional claims, ranging from, laryngeal paralysis, tinnitus (hearing loss), shoulder impingement, patellofemoral osteoarthritis (runner's knees) and lumbar disc disease, and of course PTSD.

Each knee, shoulder, hand, eye, or ear must be submitted as a separate claim (if a soldier loses both legs in the same blast he must file separately for each leg) so you can imagine the added mental trauma of that. Of my eight claim submissions all but two were initially denied, and four actually went as far as the

VAC Review Board hearing. The VAC Review Board listens to appeals which have been denied three times in prior submissions. This final Review Board is the end of the line. If the Board denies your claim, you may not resubmit. In all four Review Board cases, my claims were unanimously awarded in my favour. Keep in mind with each submission there is a process of seeing a local doctor, possibly multiple times, using the Canada Post mail system to send the documents which are then reviewed in Charlottetown, Prince Edward Island. Each submitted claim takes an average of sixteen weeks to review once it has been received in Charlottetown. Then the decision will be mailed back to you. How happy you would be when after all that your claim came back, more often than not, denied.

When claims are read by VAC they are not read by someone who understands the claimed condition. They are read by individuals who look for specific wording. If your claim does not use the correct wording it is denied. In much the same way as income tax works, the government does not give you a list of criteria you must meet to receive a favourable return. You either know it or you do not. It is much easier to deny a claim if the submission does not have the required information. My question is this, "How do you establish the correct information on a claim if you are not privileged to know the criteria? It appears that VAC sets the Veteran up to fail. With the mentality to be the tough guy most Vets have difficulty filing a claim in the first place for fear of being perceived as weak. It is easy to understand that submitting Vets will often give up upon the "first denial." Through that set up to fail appearance Vets have touted a slogan about the claim system, "Delay, Deny, and hope we will Die." It is cost effective for our government to have Vets give up and or possibly die than to receive benefits.

Another area of confusion for Vets is the combination Pension/ Lump Sum Award scenario. If a Veteran submits a claim prior to 2006 his claim falls under the Pension Act. If he submits a subsequent claim after 2006, the new claim falls under the NVC. Essentially he could be receiving a monthly pension for one claimed knee condition for the rest of his life, but only receive a Lump Sum Award for the other knee.

Depending on the Veteran's disability he is awarded a percentage in much the same way as insurance claims for personal injuries are paid out. Assume the Veteran is awarded the maximum $301,275.26. If the Vet requires $2,092 per month for disability maintenance, the sum will be depleted in 12 years. Under the old Pension act that $2,092 per month would have been maintained for the life of the Veteran with a 60% continuance paid to the spouse in the event of the Veteran's death. That continuance no longer exists.

In June 2011, Sackville-Eastern Shore, NS MP Peter Stoffer, Introduced Bill C-215, An Act to amend the Canadian Forces Superannuation Act and the Royal Canadian Mounted Police Superannuation Act (deletion of deduction from annuity), to Parliament for debate,

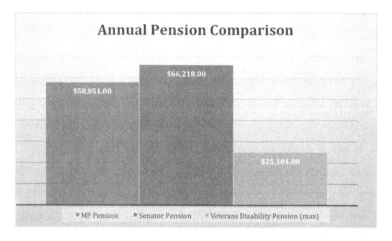

Annual Pension Comparison

$66,218.00

$58,051.00

$25,104.00

▪ MP Pension   ▪ Senator Pension   ▪ Veterans Disability Pension (max)

"Mr. Speaker, we are trying for the fifth time in the House of Commons to correct a historical wrong.

In 1966, the superannuation plan of members of the armed forces, the RCMP and that of all federal and provincial public servants were blended.

What happens is that when members of the RCMP and military receive either a Canada disability pension or the Canada pension, it is deducted dollar for dollar from their superannuation plan, which leaves many of our heroes in Canada in financial dire straits when they retire or when they become disabled. This is simply wrong. Thousands upon thousands of veterans and their families, RCMP members and their families

282

have asked that this injustice be corrected".

MP Peter Stoffer tabled Private members Bill C~215 to defeat the claw back that many Veterans face after their regular "meager" CAF pension ends.

To ease the financial burden, retired members of the CAF have their contributions split between CPP and their military pension. At retirement but before age 65, eligible retired service members receive their complete pension with a bridge benefit that eases the transition into retirement. When the Veteran reaches 65, however, the bridge benefit ceases and the amount is reduced by the amount they had received. MP Peter Stoffer was defeated in the House of Commons at the committee level. The RCMP now falls under the New Veterans Charter.

At no time has an MP had their pension money clawed back.

The Conservatives have tried to appear as the champions of the Canadian soldier.

Interesting in light of the Crown Counsel's statement in The Supreme Court of British Columbia Scott v. Canada (Attorney General),2013 BCSC 1651(CanLII)-2013-09-06 that, "The Canadian government has no "sacred obligation" to care for wounded or broken veterans." During proceedings the Crown offered this comment, "At no time in Canada's history has any alleged 'social contract' or 'social covenant' having the attributes pleaded by the plaintiffs been given effect in any statute, regulation or as a constitutional principle written or unwritten." The champions of the Canadian soldier went on by declaring that during the Great War, Prime Minister Robert Borden when speaking of Canadian soldiers was making political statements that were not to be interpreted as a 'social contract.' I also find it interesting that the Crown can, 100 years after the fact, interpret what may or may not have been inflected in PM Borden's speech.

From 1883 with the Infantry School Corps and Canada's volunteer involvement in the Boer War of 1899 to the present day War in Afghanistan, when our nation has called, our soldiers have answered without reservation. For our service members to offer their lives to uphold our country's rights and freedoms like no other single entity in Canada's history is in my opinion something very sacred. It is through this volunteer sacrifice of our young men and women that our government should reciprocally accept without reservation the sacred obligation to its soldiers and Veterans. If for no other reason than that it is so obviously deserving of veneration. A sacred obligation from our government to our soldiers; those who become what others do not want to be, go where others fear to go, and do what others cannot. If Canada does not believe in the sacred obligation, why does the government put such emphasis on Remembrance Day? Why do they remember the sacrifice on November 11th?

To deny that sacred obligation, is to deny the sacrifice was worthy of our freedom and world peace.

PRO PATRIA

"A man's country is not a certain area of land, of mountains, rivers, and woods, but it is a principle and patriotism is loyalty to that principle."
~GEORGE WILLIAM CURTIS

I have always been a steward of the Canadian Veteran, helping brother Vets find resolution to their hardships. With the advent of the internet and coffee shop wifi; as of 2010 I immersed myself within Military Minds, a not-for-profit organisation that raises awareness of PTSD and the stigma that surrounds it. The groups tag line is "Break the Silence, you're not alone." As you read earlier our soldiers are often chided for going to the MIR for help. In many cases now soldiers coming forward with PTSD issues, find themselves in a career ending position. Because of that, many make the choice to remain in the shadows. That only creates for more negative statistics, with suicides now surpassing the combat death toll. Military Minds not only deals with Canadian Vets on a 24-hour basis, but also assists Vets internationally, with help reaching as far away as Australia. The outreach of the group has crossed international borders and also the generations of war, with our services being enjoyed by Vietnam Vets right through to today's modern warriors. Military Minds offers a safe forum environment for Vets to address their issues and to also enjoy community when no other community exists. Our staff has had the fortune to help thousands of combat Vets who are dealing with their demons, with the online forum and one on one conversations seeing the benefit of hundreds pulled back from the edge of suicide.

At Military Minds we recognise that we are not doctors and we will offer a path to wellness by connecting the Vet with services. For me personally, the work I do is cathartic and gives me an avenue to provide those with something the Men in Black did not have, community. I may not be able to stop every suicide, but I am doing my best to thwart as many as possible by weaving our Vets into the social fabric of our post military community.

In 2009, November Company had a reunion. It was a two-part show. First, we would get together as a unit again and secondly we would be presented with the very first Governor Generals Unit Commendation for our actions in Sarajevo.

Nearly two decades later we were finally being recognised, albeit on the surface, for our mission. The reunion was overwhelming. Alfonso Badillo went to great lengths and spent many hours organizing the event. With assistance from the 3rd Battalion, The Royal Canadian Regiment he finished it on schedule. It is the opinion of all who participated, that the reunion was a phenomenal success. It was as though The Men in Black had never been apart. There were handshakes and bear hugs. There was shoulder slapping and rhetoric. There were even a few tears toasted away with beers for those who were no longer with us. The only thing that anyone could find wrong was that a weekend was not long enough. It felt good to belong again. The time and the distance apart had been just that.

On a side note it was great to see Maj. Gen. Lewis Mackenzie(ret'd) again. He and I had a moment to shake hands and reminisce a bit. He has spent much of his time since his retirement on the race track and supporting the soldiers of Canada. The Men in Black are living proof that the warrior spirit lives.

Since those dark days in the Balkans and the war at home, life has been a struggle but it has turned around. Many have asked if I would do it all over again.

In the defense of Canada and the good of all humanity, wouldn't you?

ABBREVIATIONS AND ACRONYMS

12.7mm – fully automatic, Soviet model, heavy machine gun

50. Cal - single shot or fully automatic heavy machine gun

84mm Carl Gustav/ Carl G - medium anti-tank rocket

AO - Area of Operation

APC - Armoured Personnel Carrier

BDG - Bridge Demolition Guard

BG - Battle Group

Bn - Battalion

C-6 - fully automatic belt fed medium machine gun

C-7 - standard rifle 30 round magazine

C-9 - Fully automatic belt fed light machine gun

Capt. - Captain

CO - Commanding Officer

Col. - Colonel

Coy - Company

CP - Command Post

Cpl- Corporal

CQ - Company Quarter Master

CSM - Company Sergeant Major

DAG-Departure Assistance Group

FNGs - Fuckin New Guys

FR-F2 - French sniper rifle

Gen. - General

HQ - Headquarters

HV - Hrvatske 'Croatian' Civil Defense Forces

Int. - Intelligence Section

JNA - Yugoslav National Army

LT. - Lieutenant

M/Cpl - Master Corporal

M-67 - Fragmentation Grenade

M-72 - light anti-tank rocket

Maj. - Major

MIR - Medical Inspection Room

ML/MLVW - Medium Logistical Vehicle Wheeled

MP - Military Police

MRE - Meal Ready to Eat

NCO - Non Commissioned Officer

OC -Officer Commanding

OP - Observation Post

Pl. - Platoon

PMA-3 - Yugoslav anti-personnel mine

PPCLI - Princess Patricia's Canadian Light Infantry

Prom-7 - Yugoslav anti personnel mine

Pte - Private

PTSD - Post Traumatic Stress Disorder

RCR - Royal Canadian Regiment

REME - Royal Electrical Mechanical Engineers

REMF - Rear Echelon Mother Fucker

Royal 22e Regiment - R22ᵉR

RPG - Rocket Propelled Grenade

sect. - Section

Sgt - Sergeant

SKOP Kit -Support Kit Overhead Protection

SOP - Standard Operating Procedures

T.O.W. - Tube Launched-Optically Tracked-Wire command link.

TDF - Territorial Defense Force

TMA-3 -Yugoslav anti-tank mine

TOW missile - 147mm heavy anti-tank missile

TUA - TOW Under Armour

UN - United Nations

UNPROFOR - United Nations Protection Force in Yugoslavia

VA - Veterans Affairs

WO - Warrant Officer

WOG - With Out Guts

ACKNOWLEDGEMENTS

There is no way to convey the love of brotherhood, so I will say this; to the boys of November Company 3RCR, thank you, for your comradeship, your laughter and tears, and for giving me the family that is more than blood. My home is your home. Pro Patria.

Major General Lewis MacKenzie, for writing my introduction, but most importantly, for putting your hand on my shoulder and being my friend, regardless of rank. Keep that grocery getter firing on all cylinders.

Thank you to Erik Shaw and the team at Tactical 16 for taking the chance with a Canadian story.

I'd like to express my thanks to Gail N. McKay who heard my voice in my writing and kept me grounded to it. For your tireless work editing, apologising for all the red ink you sent me, and helping me put this all together.

To my crew at Military Minds Inc., love you bunch of freaks.

And to my family and friends, I contemplated for some time what to write here, but there are no words to express the appreciation for standing by me when I couldn't stand myself.

CREDITS AND CONTRIBUTORS

Publishing: Tactical 16, LLC
CEO, Tactical 16: Erik Shaw
President, Tactical 16: Jeremy Farnes

ABOUT THE AUTHOR
Scott J. Casey

Scott Casey is a ten-year veteran of the Canadian Armed Forces. He is a veteran's advocate and performs speaking engagements about PTSD. He has worked for the past six years with, and is now the President of, Military Minds Inc., a global, not-for-profit organization which assists veterans, first responders and their families dealing with homecoming and PTSD.

When he isn't advocating, Scott is a heavy equipment operator and also writes for two monthly magazine publications, Pro Trucker Magazine and Iron Mike Magazine. He lives near Kamloops, B.C. where he enjoys fishing, riding his motorcycle, and shooting sports.

ABOUT THE PUBLISHER
Tactical 16, LLC

Tactical 16 is a Veteran owned and operated publishing company based in the beautiful mountain city of Colorado Springs, Colorado. What started as an idea among like-minded people has grown into reality.

Tactical 16 believes strongly in the healing power of writing, and provides opportunities for Veterans, Police, Firefighters, and EMTs to share their stories; striving to provide accessible and affordable publishing solutions that get the works of true American Heroes out to the world. We strive to make the writing and publication process as enjoyable and stress-free as possible.

As part of the process of healing and helping true American Heroes, we are honored to hear stories from all Veterans, Police Officers, Firefighters, EMTs and their spouses. Regardless of whether it's carrying a badge, fighting in a war zone or family at home keeping everything going, we know many have a story to tell.

At Tactical 16, we truly stand behind our mission to be "The Premier Publishing Resource for Guardians of Freedom."

We are a proud supporter of Our Country and its People, without which we would not be able to make Tactical 16 a reality.

How did Tactical 16 get its name? There are two parts to the name, "Tactical" and "16". Each has a different meaning. Tactical refers to the Armed Forces, Police, Fire, and Rescue communities or any group who loves, believes in, and supports Our Country. The "16" is the number of acres of the World Trade Center complex that was destroyed on that harrowing day of September 11, 2001. That day will be forever ingrained in the memories of many generations of Americans. But that day is also a reminder of the resolve of this Country's People and the courage, dedication, honor, and integrity of our Armed Forces, Police, Fire, and Rescue communities. Without Americans willing to risk their lives to defend and protect Our Country, we would not have the opportunities we have before us today.

Military Minds Inc. is the largest and leading global organization raising awareness of the stigma of, and providing peer support for, Post Traumatic Stress Disorder.

We provide support to those living with PTSD, and encourage those suffering in silence to come forward. When they do, we endeavor to put them in touch with resources in their country and area.

All of our administrators are strictly volunteers and any funds donated to MMI go directly to assisting veterans and their families. The admins at Military Minds Inc. Provide 24-7, 365 day a year peer support for our global veterans community.

Our Mission:

To increase acceptance and services for those service members and Veterans living with Post Traumatic Stress Disorder by debunking stigma, and working to enhance available resources.

www.militarymindsinc.com